THE AMAZING FRIENDSHIP OF ARGIE CORNFIELD AND CYRUS BUCKMAN

James Ernest Hammond Jr

ISBN: 1514729636
ISBN 13: 9781514729632
Library of Congress Control Number: 2015910414
CreateSpace Independent Publishing Platform
North Charleston, South Carolina

To
Michael L.
"Jake"

CHAPTER ONE

I t was along the mountain's ridge he was chasing the badest of the Kiowa chief's, Many Moons, when he remembered his first encounter and how he had been bested. Dangerously against the cliff's narrow edge he and his Paint Stud, Cid, nearly tumbled the canyon wall several times. He'd been on this Indian's tail for six months and could never hem him up, but now he had him. There was no escape from this mountaintop except through him or over the side.

Lt Col Cyrus Buckman was one of the most feared and decorated officers alive: feared by the Comanche, the Apache, the Cree and now the Kiowa; decorated by the President of the United States. He'd been shot twice, stabbed once and taken countless arrows but never faltered or shirked a day's duty.

By the time he and his trusted Paint rounded the mountain's top he realized he had been lured into a trap. Along the crest of the ridge were at least 50 braves huddled in a half circle with Many Moons in the middle. Some were on horse and some were afoot. Cid reared high and let out a loud neigh. His nostrils dripped with each blast of hot air that came against the freezing mountain air. Col Buckman looked back and forth, circling. Should he retreat? Should he make his way back down the treacherous pass? No. This was it.

"Many Moons!" he yelled.

"I am Many Moons."

"I've come to take you."

"You are the bluecoat--Buckman," Many Moons said calmly. "The one who has killed many Kiowa . . . and now the one who will die!"

Many Moons motioned to the others, circled his horse once, then twice then lunged toward Col Buckman. Cid had been here so many times that he did not hesitate, he shot towards Many Moons like a bullet from a Govt .45-70. They dove at each other with knives in hand, their chests colliding in mid-air. Col Buckman felt Many Moons' knife puncture his shoulder but his was in Many Moons' belly. They hit the ground like rabid dogs in a fiery battle, neither cowing from their wounds nor screaming out in pain. All there was . . .

"Cyrus!" his Grandmother yelled from the porch front. "Cyrus J! It's pert near supper and I want you washed from head to toe. You come by the barn gate, now! And mind your feet."

"Yes'am," he whispered.

He lay on the ground in front of the barn covered in mud and pieces of straw. He looked up at the sky; his trusted Paint just feet from him, but with a slight list to one side. Grandpa Cyrus had made him for his third birthday and had done nothing since but futile repairs. His back right leg was now a piece of fence pipe; his mane, once long and gold, came from a pony at a Kansas fair and had slowly disappeared from years of rough engagements. His eyes, that were once pieces of coal plowed from a field they farmed in Iowa, disappeared in a fight with the Comanche. His body was whittled from a birch tree that had been hit by lightning when they were somewhere in Nebraska. You see, they were both from all over.

With the wind's gust the braves that had surrounded him turned back to the sunflowers that hung over the paddock fence, staring at him with the inescapable sadness he'd known for years. He'd never lived in one place for more than two years in his entire ten of existence. He lived with his Grandpa and Grandma. His parents were killed in an auto accident before his first birthday. All he knew of them came from the stillness in photographs that were carefully stowed away in a cedar box hidden in the attic. He asked his Grandma Mattie about them on occasion and the answers would come in broken sentences so slowly that it seemed she was remembering what was tucked away. Nothing was ever said or reminisced when his Grandfather was present.

Grandpa was a lumbering man who stood six foot five inches and could lay a belt over Cyrus' backside that would near take off his britches. His grandmother would yell in pale fear, "Don't hit his kidneys, don't hit his kidneys!" He strapped him so badly one time that Cyrus couldn't sit for days and had difficulty with his chores; but he never shirked them. Never.

His Grandma Mattie was small and frail and didn't seem a likely mate for his Grandfather, as Cyrus truly felt his Grandfather had a severe disdain for the both of them.

"No wonder you ain't got no friends—spendin' all your time with *ghosts* and *Imagines*, who on earth would care to be with ya? You get that from your Gran'ma's side." his Grandfather would grumble.

Grandma trailed behind many times during chores to see they were done correctly, only once mentioning that she grained Dud, the plow horse he missed. Although Cyrus had never seen his grandfather strike his Grandmother, there were moments she cowed like a beaten porch dog at his commands and heeded them without rebuke.

She wore a pink apron that had a sash along the top sown with farm animals that looked as though they were jumping over clouds, with large pockets in front as bales of hay and where she kept cloth napkins that she would twist around and around her fingers until they turned blue. There were times she and Cyrus would "porch sit" and talk until supper. There were also times in those porch sits that Cyrus would ask about his father: what he did, who he was, was he a good man? Although he wanted to know of his mother, it was his father he imagined the important one, living somewhere in the Capitol and working for the government. It wasn't that he believed his leaving so much a falling out with his Grandpa, which was extremely plausible, it was his leaving in general that was the salient part of his confusion; the puzzle piece he couldn't find a place and it made him different. This was when he ordered his world, his private world of imagines and such.

CHAPTER TWO

It was early morning five o'clock when Grandpa was stirring downstairs and Cyrus knew it by the bangs and clangs his grandma didn't make, almost as though he was making coffee in a suit of armor. Grandpa Cyrus was a mountain of a man to most and the Beanstalk Giant to Cyrus. If you looked at him in the equestrian sense, he bettered twenty hands and carried a hefty three hundred pounds that intimidated most of the farming world. He was an intemperate man who viewed life one way: his, and he carried himself that very way. He hadn't always been so rigid until the death of his only child and young Cyrus' father. Though it was rarely spoken about, his Grandma had explained how Grandpa changed the night of the accident. His Grandfather was at times inconsolable and his zest for life seemed to have faded with the breath of his son. Young Cyrus' curiosity never lingered about the how . . . just the why.

In this house, the one Cyrus favored most against the many he had lived, his bedroom window was shaded by a mammoth pecan (pronounced pea-can) tree that made his room the coolest in the house, which said little given the overall heat. He slept atop the window box for the breeze, and it served him well in the evening swelter and in the days his Grandma had been baking for a church bizarre or a funeral; his room being directly above the kitchen and the stove pipe feet from his bed, would serve well for a bedroom in Alaska or Nepal just not in Tuscaloosa.

The dreaded day was nearing its dawn and there was little more he could concentrate on: The day of infamy. The day that came at the close of every summer: The first day of school. It wasn't learning he was abject to; in fact it had nothing to do with the precepts of school at all with the exception of being there. It was what he had to contend with between the students and himself. There was only one school in his nine years of existence he attended that wasn't so painful—Warren G Harding Elementary in Deadwood South Dakota. He actually got to stay there for two years which made for a record in friendships, what he could count on one hand with fingers left over.

It was difficult to concentrate on chores most mornings, and mistakes were critical if noticed by his Grandpa. His Grandmother faded these problems on occasion, following behind him and adjusting grain and hay dosages, closing barn doors and gates and catching anything else that could put him into the soup. It was on these small issues his grandfather was unforgiving. His punishment was immediate, inexorable and without parity.

Cyrus was a smidgen under four foot, pudgy and weaker than a one legged-horse, his Grandpa would say, and ripe for the pickin' at recess. It had always been that way, except in Deadwood. Every year this montage grew larger and the kids more ruthless. Nothing changed except for the view and more acceptable ways to find refuge. Many recesses were spent in darkened crannies he had scoped out in the first days and usually before school started. Any place he could hide for an hour.

His chores were due before school and a moment after breakfast. It was this time he had to himself, when his world of quiet sorrows were shelved and his private one came alive, when throwing hay from the loft left its mundane purpose and took on its own story. Between fighting Indians, fending for his partner's life in heated battles and the strapping from his Grandpa, he learned to meld these worlds successfully: defeating his dreaded attackers, saving the world from evil arrow chucker's and feeding the plow horse all at the same time.

But it was this day that chilled him to the marrow of his tiny bones. The day that never stopped coming—the first day of a new school. If he were just 20 pounds heavier, two inches taller and not so shy life would not be this veritable hell.

"Cyrus J!", his Grandfather hollered from the kitchen. "Rise and stinkin' shine. A new day, a new nickel you'll owe somebody."

Grandma had been up for hours, but for reasons unknown she let Grandpa rummage the kitchen on his own. In young Cyrus' thought, she found his Grandpa just as intolerable but necessary so she'd let him have his way until he was entrapped: he couldn't get the stove lit, he couldn't find the coffee, the frying pan was missing. In actuality, everything was in its place and the stove easier to light than gas soaked hay, but the inaudible need each had for the other stayed within them for fear and fear alone and seemed something only Cyrus could see. She needed her husband just as much as she loved her grandson, but it was painful. It had been so ever since the accident and Grandpa Cyrus could not seem to forgive it, or anyone in his world for that fact.

"I want you to hitch Dud to the listin' plow and tie him off at the back gate. Don't grain him 'til this afternoon after school," his grandfather said to Cyrus, who was midway down the stairs and hitching his overalls.

"Yes sir, but he don't eat so well after . . . " he began, but knew it pointless.

His grandmother set his plate to him: "Cyrus J, I have the highest hopes for your day. I know it will be a school you'll come to like."

"I reckon it will, Grandma, but today ain't school day. It ain't til next Monday; at least that's what I heard."

"Heard? Heard what from who?" His Grandpa grumbled. "You don't have any friends 'cause you don't look for any. And there ain't no one 'round here you talk to but *ghosts* and *imagines*."

"Ain't *ghosts* and *imagines*, Grandpa . . . they're spirits and they make themselves known to me. I seen 'em."

He drew a puff off his pipe and stared at the ceiling like God was speaking to him, "You need to stop this crap about imagines and Indians and things before you end up tied to a Pin Oak droolin' and howlin' at the moon."

Cyrus knew never to comment on his Grandpa's wisdom, as lacking as it was, because it came to little more than a 'pot stir' if ever he contested or questioned a thing. He glanced sideways at his Grandma, but she, just as Cyrus knew, would never make any kind of an acknowledgment past a glance. An eye roll, a smile, even a nod could provoke a backhand faster than a snake's strike.

It was near sunrise while Cyrus stood at the barn gate, staring at the horizon and the sun that was trying to come. The sunflowers that surrounded the corn glowed with an iridescence of gold and purple that shone through their pedals and spoke to him in a whisper that everything would be okay. Maybe his Grandfather was right; he was little more than a crazy man who would ultimately be tied to a Pin Oak while he drooled and howled at the moon. But although things were difficult, and at times sad and lonely, there came calm in the middle of these storms that made life, as he knew it, understandable to a measure. He couldn't quite put his finger to it, but it was something he had known; something that made him feel safe.

Armed with his hay fork and Grandpa in the field with Dud, plow and bottle in tow, the barn took on its fantasia; its world according to Cyrus. He fed the goats a wedge of hay and a gunbolt of grain and made sure the water was right. Now, the battle between he and Many Moons that had been so rudely interrupted by supper would resume.

He stood in the barn foyer with hay fork in hand that slowly turned to a sword drawn from its scabbard; his tattered overalls into a coronel's uniform.

"Many Moons!" he hollered. "I am here and we will battle 'til the death!"

Cyrus ran through the barn nip and tuck, hiding behind stall gates, hay mounds and riggin' girts.

"You can have all your braves front me, but it's just gunna be you and me in the end."

As quiet and surreptitious as the wind through the barn stood a man at the farthest end. Cyrus hunkered down next to the hay bin he was forbidden to be, squinting at the man in the doorway and wondering, "Who the . . .". He was huge. Huge to a nine-year-old's rendition; dressed in leather leggin's, a half coat about his chest and a cap of sorts that donned a feather that flapped in the breeze. At his side he held a shiny piece of metal he could not make out, but it glistened with all the brilliance of the sun and right to him.

"Many Moons?" Cyrus whispered under his breath. "It can't be."

"Buckman!" the man hollered. "Why you call? Stand to me!"

Cyrus could not breathe nor utter a word. It was him! It was Many Moons. His blood was cold and his heart labored to pump one more time. "I . . . I", Cyrus choked. "I'm sorry, sir."

Cyrus ran from the barn opposite end and kept running until he fell into his Grandma Mattie's arms, just at the porch edge and brought her to drop a pail of well water that took ten minutes to draw and tote.

"Child! You will fetch another pail plus one ta boot!" she screamed, before seeing his face. "What the world! Yur as pale as salt. . . sit!"

"Grandma . . . grandma . . . it's true. It's true! There's a . . . there's a man at the barn!" he gasped.

"A man! A man where!"

"Many Moons! I know it was him . . . but couldn't tell. He spoke Indian!"

He lay on his Grandma as she petted him like a lap dog and blowing in his face to keep the fly's from about. He wasn't sure for the time, but it had to have been a spell since the sun was behind the house and he woke flat side in the porch swing looking up at his Grandpa.

"What of this man about the barn? Who was he . . . an *imagine*?" his Grandfather quipped. Cyrus rose from the swing holding the cool compress his Grandma had placed.

"Gimme that damn thing", his Grandfather said, snatching the towel. "I want ALL this imagine crap to stop."

"Grandpa Cyrus!" his Grandmother screamed. "You will not have the *imagines* and I will not have that language about this child." She never stood up to Grandpa like that. Something came upon her.

His Grandpa stood there sweating in the odious aroma of cheap whiskey with a grasshopper the size of soup spoon sitting on his shoulder and staring at Cyrus. But Cyrus knew what he saw and knew real from imagined. It was like it always was; him against the world.

CHAPTER THREE

I t had been a week since Cyrus had summoned the Indian and little time was spent in the barn beyond chores with those done quickly. He had dreams of his brief and real life confrontation with Many Moons, but what was perplexing was why no one believed him when it actually happened. There was a man, and whether he was Many Moons was a valid point, but for his Grandmother to side with Grandpa was a bridge too far. She may not have sided with him totally, but not coming to his defense was a kind of side-taking in his book.

The faithful day drew to its open as Cyrus sat with his Grandmother in church fidgeting with the pencil and drawing characters of an Indian on the visitor's information card. His Grandmother occasionally stilled his hand but he could not keep his mind from the coming day and the anxiety unbearable. He wanted to explain what he was facing, but he was the Lone Ranger in this situation and just like he had always been every year. If even a whiff of his plight got back to his Grandfather there was no telling what ill weather would befall him. The thought of going to

God with this predicament crossed his mind, but he figured He had much greater things to contend with like crops and storms and such than something as banal as this.

"What did you think of the service today?" his Grandma asked while they sputtered down the road from town.

Cyrus heard her but was paying more attention to the air outside the window, holding his hand against its rush, watching it serpentine up and down and how it changed direction when he opened and closed his fingers.

"It was okay I guess. I just don't quite understand why folks get together in a room every Sunday to talk to someone no one can see", he answered with a smidgen of indignity. "Why is it I have to go and Grandpa don't?" There was a long pause.

"Well, the point is that you have 'faith' that there is someone there even though you don't see them", she suggested with hesitation.

"Faith for what?"

"Well, when there is something needed folks go to God for help . . . which is what is called prayer, and when you pray you are showing faith."

"And it's just like that! You get what you ask for?" he questioned with pointed attention.

Grandma assumed his answer would come with a disconcerting shrug or a blah 'Yes Mam'; but no, his inquisition was the last straw for this indefensible day. Maybe there is something about this God thing, he thought; these Sundays that he believed were but a respite from his Grandfather were actually a tribute to this god-guy, this throne-sitter.

"No, no child. God doesn't *always* grant prayer just because you ask . . . it's difficult to explain", she fumbled about in her thought almost as tightly as she held to the wheel. "It's . . . "

Cyrus interrupted, "It's all but a *guess* ain't it Grandma? Whether God is really there and prayin' is no more than barkin' words to the clouds?"

"I suppose, child", she muttered. "You beat all. I can't ne'er tell whether you're cutting hay or plowin' potatoes."

That eve he lay in bed staring at his first day trousers draped over the chair at his desk. He scrunched up into the window box and stared at the Pecan tree, its large branches bowing against science with each gust while its creaks bemoaned the same weight he carried. Why was he here? "What good am I except for chores?" he whispered. "I don't know where I'm from; I don't know who I am, really; and I'm as weak as a three-legged horse."

The morning's breakfast was a big one but he had little more than a bite or two.

"You kiddin' me!" his grandfather snapped. "Cakes, eggs and meat and you ain't eatin'!"

He finished his chores and was in the truck waiting for his Grandma, but the air changed when he saw his Grandpa emerge through the porch gate. They said nothing to each other for nearly the entire ride until his grandfather breached silence.

"You'll be walkin' from now on", he said. "Which means you'll have to start chores no later than 5:30."

"Yes sir."

"I don't want any of this lolly-gagin' and then excuses."

"Okay, sir."

"It meets at the Thompson farm, 'bout a quarter mile down Chicken Ranch road at the cross next to the ol' Burle barn."

"Yes sir, I know where it is."

"None of this shave time on chores neither", he said. "We have a good crop here and I want you handlin' all the necessaries."

Though any trip with his Grandfather seemed an eternity, this one to school came faster than a star's land upon the earth. His heart beat uncontrollably and he began to sweat under his arms. He heard his Grandfather's door slam which brought all the more unease.

"I got it Grandpa", he hollered, running towards the gates of hell. "I'll see ya after school."

His Grandfather stood resting with one arm against the truck as Cyrus turned quickly towards the front door. He had no idea where to go, what room he was in . . . anything.

"Excuse me young man, where are you going?" spoke a voice of authority.

"Uhm, I am Cyrus Walton Buckman the third and was looking for the third grade . . . sir."

"Well that would be Ms Fugate's class, Cyrus Walton Buckman the third, and she is right there", he pointed across the hallway.

"Okay", Cyrus smiled uncomfortably. "I mean, okay, sir."

The man was Mr Burnside, the Principal. He stood tall, though not near as high as his Grandpa by whom he gauged every man's stature. This man was special and Cyrus could feel it. It was strange how this trait beguiled him so because it came without course, rhythm or notice . . . it just happened. He seemed to know folks heart by chance meeting and in just a few moments, sometimes at first word. This man carried himself with a confidence Cyrus had never known before. He looked strong, had a full head of hair that was dark and a mustache with a bit of gray that was neatly groomed and said he could have been a preacher or maybe a government official. Cyrus liked him immediately and he rarely did that with adults.

Minutes after first bell, Mr Burnside brought Cyrus to his home room as most were sitting to their desk's, pulling out paper and pencils, whispering to each under their arms and nodding towards Cyrus in between. This was the kitchen where the heat was high enough that he wanted to get out.

"Ms Fugate!" Mr Burnside halfway hollered with a wave.

"Yes sir."

"This is Cyrus Walton Buckman the third, and a new student", he said.

Cyrus quickly but sheepishly interjected: "I can just go by Cyrus, sir."

They both laughed as with some of the students in ear shot, while they were looking him up and down and as though he were on a carnival Ferris wheel.

As moments of each subject reached their climax, he became more and tense at the thought of recess and then lunch; the two times of the day he would either be embarrassed or wrestled to the ground for his milk money, which would be a fruitless venture since he didn't have any. At his last school they took his pants off at recess and he had to climb into a burn barrel until a teacher rescued him. Covered in ash, he looked like he had fallen down a chimney chute and suffered unforgettable humiliation. Although the culprits were punished it didn't stop it from happening again, except this time he was ready. For the next several days, up and to that very recess, Cyrus had run a gate chain through his belt loops and locked it with a hasp and a bent nail. By the time the yard dogs had begun trying to get it undone a teacher was at his rescue.

"You are a smart, resilient young man", the teacher said in a chuckle, helping Cyrus up. "You're special and I'm going to keep an eye out for you. What grade will you be in next year?"

"Fourth sir, but I'm pretty sure it won't be here."

At recess, Cyrus stayed far from the others, standing out by the water cistern near the road he had been brought in on. He sat down slightly into the bar ditch so as not to be noticed but high enough he could hear the bell. His eyes filled with tears he tried so hard not to let fall while this lonely, so utterly familiar pain consumed him like a prairie. Staring down that road to home, where he wished he was, the tears floated in circles inside his dark blue eyes. It reminded him of the kaleidoscope he got one Christmas and he smiled.

"Hey you?" a voice called from behind.

It scared him immeasurably as he wiped his eyes. His heart began to beat again like a bass drum.

"Yes" he answered politely.

He turned over his shoulder to see a boy who looked like a giant to him. He thought for sure this would be the beginning, or possible end to an already arduous day. The boy sat next to Cyrus and held out his hand. "Jake Thompson", he said. "Whataya doin' way out here?"

Cyrus slowly clasped his hand all the while wondering where the others were and what was to be done; after all, he was far from any aid. Any possible answer stuck in his craw like an over-sized piece of hot apple pie.

"Cat got your tongue?" he asked with this amazing smile that calmed Cyrus' heart in a breeze.

"Cyrus. Cyrus Buckman."

"Well, he can speak. Why are you out here in the sticks; you sick or somethin'?"

"No." Cyrus hesitated, scrambling for a plausible response. Without any to mind, something strange came about him to just tell the truth. He explained in short form that he was too small to fight and everyone knew it at every school he had been; that he was afraid to be around bunches of kids who already knew each other and that made him easy pickin's.

"I'll be your friend," Jake said. At that, the bell was rung and they started back to the school house. On the way, they both discovered they lived but a quarter mile from each other. Jake also explained that he was pretty much the toughest kid in the school that went all the way to the fifth grade. He stood a good hand taller than Cyrus with at least twenty pounds on top of that. You could have taken all the Christmases and all the birthdays with all the presents, even the ones he didn't get and it would not have put as much as a cat's scratch on this very hour.

CHAPTER FOUR

Only two days had transpired and Cyrus' life had taken a whole new perspective; his chores were done before time; his Grandfather hadn't been on him once (at least with the intensity he'd known so often before), and his Grandmother stood astonished when he not only cleared the table but was eager to help with the dishes. On occasion when he had finished his chores long before the bus' arrival, he was running to his stop just to meet with his new found soul mate. He began to see life in an entirely new light. He and Jake became inseparable, at least from Cyrus' perspective, and to a great degree, Jake's. They saw in each other what the rest of the world could not, or did not, what they both innately and silently shared: compassion.

"Hey Pudger", Jake yelled as they both were running to the stop from opposite directions. Jake had but several hundred yards and Cyrus near a quarter mile. They laughed at each others incessancy at wanting to get to school, when it was truly their wanting to talk about the ensuing weekend and what they were to do. "Pudger" had become Jake's pet name for Cyrus but was more a term of endearment and Cyrus loved it. Yeah, he was a bit pudgy about his middle and with what his Grandma termed, baby fat, that Cyrus didn't like whether a term of endearment or not.

"Hey Pudge, ya think your folks will let us tent in the creek on Saturday?" Jake asked.

In between gulps of air, Cyrus shrugged his shoulders, dropping his book's strapped with a saddle girt, placing his hands on his knees and trying to catch what he had lost in the run.

"Got chores in the morning and at night," he answered. But maybe if you can help me get 'em done I can."

"Sure. I got some chores, but not that many since Pa has S.T. to help out."

"Who's he?" Cyrus inquired.

"He's a black man Pa has working for him; been with us since Grandpa past."

"You rich?" Cyrus asked.

"Ain't sure what that is."

"You lived here forever?" Cyrus asked.

"Since I can remember; or since I was born, I guess. It was my grandparents and maybe whoever was before them."

"You're rich."

This was the belonging Cyrus had dreams of; a place where your bed stayed in the same place and the only change came when you made it. This drew Cyrus closer to Jake, closer than he had been with anyone in his short life. An insatiable need to be needed by someone he looked up to, or just looked to.

They sat at the road's edge waiting for the bus. When Jake spoke Cyrus snatched each word like a bird to seed. Jake was much larger than Cyrus and an attractive child in a youthful sense. He was target of the fifth grade girls and much to the chagrin of the fifth grade boys; but, he was never bothered because he seemed to possess some aura; some kind of magic, in a sense, that said he was stronger, tougher, not to be messed with. But nothing was further from the truth. Yes, he possessed these attributes and held them quietly like his father, Sterling Thompson, who was recognized as a genteel man with farming skills and wisdom that cartooned Richard's Almanac and made his whispers in the Two Cousin's Café the talk of the town. Several years after Jake's birth his mother came ill with influenza and died. Sterling raised Jake solo and taught him well: to respect others, love others and give to others, as well as all the necessary secrets to being an excellent farmer. He also carried his father's physical attributes.

He had large brown eyes and brown hair with bangs that shadowed them when he looked downward. When he looked up he swished his head to the side for the rest to see his smile and it brought the girls to giggle and coo. He had teeth brighter than the summer sun and shined like emeralds against his dark skin. What he emanated in character turned the heads of adults: "Yep, that's Sterling's boy alright: fine student, fine son, fine farmer to be. Could the Good Lord give any man more?"

Cyrus saw him as perfect in every form and stood with the same awe. What pained him most was that Jake would lose interest in this poor, chubby farm boy at some point; that their friendship would be as lengthy as his stay, if not sooner, when he'd tire of the abuse the majority would extend for being his friend. That's the way he lost any friend in the past, unless he moved. The energy it took to make one friend was such an imbalance that he'd give up after "Hello."

"You know," Cyrus blurted. "It may bring me a hidin', but you and I *are* gunna tent out in the creek Saturday."

"Pudger! We ain't doin' nothin' that'll get my baby brother strapped," Jake said with a slight smile

"Really?" Cyrus muttered.

"Course, what good would it do? It'd probably close the gate on getting' to see each other."

"No, I mean. . .," Cyrus laughed. "The *baby brother* thing?"

"Well I ain't got one, and you ain't, so yeah. There ain't no one 'round here close enough that I like anyways," Jake replied matter-of-factly.

"Do I have to be *baby* . . . brother?

He laughed, slapping Cyrus on the stomach: "Naw, I was just greenin'! We can just be plain ol' *brothers*."

Cyrus laid his head against his books and stared at the sky. What he just heard was something he felt came from the God he hadn't, or couldn't see. The one the preacher spoke of while he penciled on the visitor's card, yet at moments, listened. The one his grandma tried to explain. All he knew was he had never felt a part of anything as he did at that very second.

"We bes' be headin' home if we're to get chores done", Jake offered.

Cyrus couldn't help but feel the King's presence, as it were, because it seemed his treatment by the rest was directly proportionate to the exposure he enjoyed with his new *brother* and guardian. He cared less for status or any speck of popularity, as he had in his hand exactly what he had dreamed for so long: a friend.

It neared lunch and Cyrus had to use the outhouse something fierce. There were strict rules and certain protocol that had to be adhered to when needing to go: one, a slight, inconspicuous raise of the hand when the teacher was looking your way, and then a vague motion with the eyes towards the door. If one were in decent graces he or she would receive the same inconspicuous nod of approval. Cyrus handled business and was buckling his trousers as he stepped from the water closet when he bumped into Pritchett and Dale Worth, fourth grade deviants known by the town as such along with their families. Story had it that Pritchett's father had spent time in a nut house in Ralls for biting off the upper lip of the bailiff who was carrying him to the courthouse the last day of his trial for manslaughter they never quite proved. His son seemed to be that apple that never fell far from the tree. He was a morbidly ugly cuss. His eyes weren't square on his face; the left seemed a half inch or better lower that the other and his nose was near flush with his cheeks. Kids would josh that he didn't sleep in a bed, that his father had made him sleep in a shop vise since birth and was reason for its lack of contour. His body was shaped somewhat like a convexed hourglass: instead of an 'X' like figure, it came more diamond shaped, pinched at the shoulders and bounced at the gut. There wasn't a tooth in his mouth that was correct or had seen a brushing in their 10 years of existence. All this made little impact, since no one but Dale Worth hung with them; both families being known as pay-backers. Those who crossed any of them discovered little inconveniences like flat tires, missing pets, sugar in gas tanks, etc. Fred Paulson, the town grocer, wouldn't extend the Pritchett's store credit one time and they found Queenie, their in-house tea cup poodle, whacked in a bear trap off Chicken Ranch road. It'd take two men to set that thing and better than a hundred pound weight to set it off. Queenie was so small she had to be weighted at the store. Things like that.

"They grows 'em pretty small outside town, don't they Dale?" Pritchett said to his toadie.

"Sure do, Scoot", Dale answered.

Pritchett edged towards Cyrus until he was backed up against the outhouse.

"I ain't done nothin' to you Pritchett", Cyrus whispered. "I ain't even looked at you or nothing."

"What's that supposed to mean, squat fart!" Pritchett said, exposing those teeth canvassed with food particles from at least second grade.

He had never been that close to anything so ugly. His breath was medieval.

"You think your a big sass hanging around Jake, don't ya? Think he can take me?"

"Why does anyone have to take anyone?" Cyrus asked. "If you don't want to be friends, but we don't have to be enemies either?"

"And your a smart sass too," Dale added.

"Let's just take a leak together . . . "

"Get away from him Pritchett!" Jake yelled from behind, running up with fists balled.

Pritchett stepped back from Cyrus a measure and Dale backed to the side of the outhouse.

"What Thompson, you gunna take both of us? Whataya see in this field mouse anyway?" Pritchett asked, backing further. Jake placed himself between Cyrus and Pritchett.

"What is it with you, Pritchett? You could have more friends than you do, but you seem to want more enemies. This *field mouse* is my friend, my *brother*. I choose to be friends with him. I choose to see the good in him. I choose to have fun with him and not think of how I can hurt him", Jake sighed, putting his hands in his pockets and stirring the pea gravel with his foot. "I just don't get why you look to make folks not like you; don't make a lick-a sense."

They were the same size in height and weight, but not stature. Jake was a giant to his nemesis in that regard. Pritchett stood staring at Jake, his fists balled and with the mock look of a gladiator.

"Boy's . . . boy's!" Ms Fugate yelled from the back window. "Get in here. It does not take this long, not for boys."

Nothing else was said on the way back as each walked in rank, Cyrus in front. This was Cyrus' first episode at this school and it filled him with the same fear as the others, but this time was different; he basked in a security that was as strange as a nestling's first flight. This dream carried him to a dimension far above the earth's plane, a place he'd go when he was scared. He never stopped worrying of the inevitable.

"What's wrong," Jake asked him on the walk home.

"Nothing," he answered in a maudlin tone.

"Yeah there is. Are you mad at me about something?"

"No. I . . . I'm just, you know, kinda tired," Cyrus said. There was silence while he wondered how much easier it would be if he had never been born. It wouldn't have just been easier on him, but on his grandparents, who had to care for him, feed him; on his new friend, Jake, who wouldn't have to be saddled with standing up for him. How . . .

"Hey." Cyrus began. "How did . . . why did you come out to the outhouse? I mean, you couldn't have come out since I was out. Ms Fugate knew I was out. You couldn't have come out."

"So that's what it is? You think too much Buckman."

"Do you think I'm a wimp?"

"You think too much Buckman."

"I'm serious Jake."

"You think too much Buckman. And no, I don't."

They walked towards the Thompson farm in silence again, both wondering why the air so thick.

"Pudger, how you doing in math?"

"Pretty good, but it's my favorite subject, if I had one, of course", he smiled. "Why is it you call me that—Pudger?"

"Not sure. I just come up with names for folk sometimes that seem to fit 'em," Jake answered. "Why—you don't like it?"

"No, I just wondered how you came up with it."

"Don't rightly know."

"I kinda like it", Cyrus shrugged. Makes me feel I've been around you a long time . . . like we are *brothers*", Cyrus finished with a side glance.

"We are *brothers*, idiot! Why'd ya think I came to the outhouse? I saw Pritchett and the goon go out after you did. I always watch you."

"Why?"

"Ain't sure, can't explain it. When I saw you the first day, when Mr Burnside brought you in the schoolroom it was like I knew you before or something—I daknow," Jake conceded.

"Before what?"

"I told you! I don't know! Can we stop talking about this? It's fun being around you, but not when we're talking about this all the time. What are you so afraid of?" Jake finished. Cyrus stopped and they stood facing each other.

"Everything you're not."

CHAPTER FIVE

Both were in another world when they were together; a convergence of two souls that opened their eyes to the other's unknown. Jake came over that Friday after school and was properly introduced to his Grandma Mattie and later to his Grandpa Cyrus, who had been in the field and was concerned more about young Cyrus' chores and their completion than who Jake belonged. Cyrus didn't have to draw a picture of who his Grandpa was, Jake knew. Grandma Mattie hugged him like a stuffed doll and doted on him as one might a foundling and this brought Cyrus to smile.

"We happy ta have ta you supper, child?" his Grandma said.

"I'll have to ask ma Pa", he answered.

"Grandma, reckon he can do a stay over? He can help me with chores tomorrow and we'll be awful quiet", Cyrus asked. His Grandma twisted her napkin around her finger several times then nodded, "I suppose, but I'll have ta mention it to yur grandfather, seein's he may have somethin' special ta do at light."

Jake nudged Cyrus with his knee.

"Grandma, think we can tent outside?" he asked.

"Oh child, where? ."

"I da-know, maybe out buy the creek or maybe the barn?"

"Oh my! You know how yur grandpa doesn't like you in that creek none. If you was ta get snake bit or it goes ta floodin', he'd be beside himself. Besides, that wet ground will have ya all stove up and wheezin' by morning"

"Grandma", Cyrus began as they followed her into the kitchen. "First of all, Jake here is a snake charmer of sorts, he's killed a passel of 'em by his lonesome, and next place, they let the sirens off before they flood that thing, and I ain't never recalled them doing so at night anyways."

"Well, you get your grandpa's okay."

There was little Cyrus expected from his grandfather. With several hours of daylight they headed to the barn for his chores.

"Whatdaya think he's gunna say?" Jake asked.

"No. But you'll be able ta stay over . . . just not at the creek. He'll never agree to anything that I would care doin'. It's his way about me." Cyrus set against the forbidden hay bin twirling a piece of straw between his fingers like a circus baton, staring at the horizon through the loft door. "How are you and yur Pa with each other . . . I mean, do you like each other?"

"Kin always *like* each other, Pudger, just on occasion don't like to be around each other; guess that could be the way with yur grandpa. I know it's . . . what about the barn?" Jake said abruptly.

"What about it?"

"Can we tent in here?"

Cyrus bellowed a laugh, "Have you fallen on yur head! This would have to be heaven and we're Jesus before we'd get to tent here!"

"What's so special 'bout here?"

Cyrus reached behind himself and fumbled through the loose hay in the bin until he stopped and with a slight grin brought his hand forth and a bottle. Jake shrugged his shoulders and said matter-of-factly, "So".

"You wanted to know why." Cyrus rebuffed.

Jake took the bottle and held it to read the label, then pulled the worn cork and stared at it while he rolled it between his finger and thumb, occasionally sniffing it.

"What?" Cyrus queried.

"Nothing, except this ain't the label . . . what's in it ain't what the label sez."

"And how do you know?" Cyrus asked, squinting at the cork.

"Jus' do. I need to ask my Pa if I can stay over. Should we do it now or after chores?" Jake finished quickly.

"I'll get started here and you go ask. By the time you get . . . what if yur Pa says, no?"

"He won't. We gotta a barn too."

Cyrus watched his buddy head down the road until he was but a dot on the horizon. "Brothers", he whispered.

He'd just finished haying the plow horse's stall when he heard Jake's yell. It was more inviting than a supper call to a battalion of Indian hunters after a day's chase. He began to pull the doors to when Jake again hollered: "Whoa, whoa I wanna see where first."

"See what?" Cyrus asked.

Jake squatted forward a measure and made a suggestive dance in a circle, patting his open hand against his mouth again and again. Cyrus looked at him with a grin of embarrassment.

"What in hell's name . . ." he said chuckling. "You know what an ass you look like?"

"Okay, but I wanna to see where you saw him."

"Who?"

"Now yur greenin' me. That Indian you saw back a spell."

"Oh," Cyrus said sheepishly. "Yur funnin' me again, ain't ya? You think I was greenin' ya when I told ya, and you think it now . . . like my grandpa; it's just my *imagines*."

"Not at all. I believe you, but I also like funnin' ya too."

"Yeah, but you thought I was full of beans when I first told ya."

Jake stood staring at him with his hands on his hips until Cyrus walked the door back open.

"It was right here," he said, tapping the ground with his foot. "I was over there by the hay bin, kneeling and playing like I was, you know, fightin' Indians and stuff."

Jake's demeanor changed as he walked past Cyrus and into the barn. The doors at the other end remained open so his grandpa could lead Dud in without having bother. The barn was huge and unlike most he'd seen, especially now, in the half light of the dusk, the day's remnants stretching into its darkness with the last of its strength. The studs that held the loft and roof in place were ominous in width and tall enough to hold the sky in place. It was immaculately clean: the tack hung neatly in measured precision; the dirt floor level and smooth as concrete; the square bales of straw and hay stacked perfectly along the loft's edge in a fashion that would rival the Inca's.

"It must be near 20 feet up there", Jake muttered.

"Twenty-five", Cyrus said, easing his way inward and amazed by his friend's inquisition.

"This is where I spend all my free time", he said through a sigh. "All my time."

Like from a trance, Jake walked over to the hay bin and asked as he squatted, "So you were, how . . . like this?"

Cyrus stepped back some and poised himself in a posture that was uneasy. "No. I was like this," Cyrus squatted on the opposite side of his buddy. "I was lookin' that way and . . . "

Jake interrupted, "Were you holding a pistol or anything?"

"Well kinda, I was . . . you know, playing like I . . . "

". . . What were you wearing?", again he interjected,

"Well, I was wearing . . . "

"Can you remember what you . . ."

"If you will shut up!" Both stood there a second waiting for the other to speak.

"You think I'm an idiot?" Cyrus whispered.

"No," Jake answered. "I really do believe you. I know it's important to be believed."

"I . . . oh crap!" Cyrus shouted. "We gotta get, Grandpa's comin'. He don't know you yet and it will be a strappin' for sure if he catches you here!"

"How in hell's name did you hear him?" Jake asked as they pulled the doors to.

"Are you kiddin' me! I stay alive by knowin' where he is."

They scurried the fence like spiders dodging a broom and made the porch front just as his grandpa was coming around the turn-row at the end of the field. The barn could never be in perfect condition, but had to be in grandpa's condition, which was a notch past. They sat inconspicuously in the porch swing and acted as though they had been discussing the day's events when Cyrus Walton Buckman the first was closing up the barn doors.

"I get hided once in a while and it ain't that bad," Jake said through tight lips.

"You ever had one with the back cinch off a ropin' saddle from a man that big?" Cyrus asked with a nod towards his Grandpa.

"Uhn uh."

"You get more than five you won't set for bes' of three days."

As Grandpa Cyrus ambled towards the house Cyrus was going through the list in his head of all the things he could have either left undone or made a mistake on. The closer he approached the larger Jake's eyes opened to take him in.

"Afternoon young-in's," he said. "Who's this?"

"It's a friend of mine from school, Grandpa, and I was wonderin' if he could stay over and tent out tonight; all my chores are done just like you like 'em and he's gunna help me straighten up the loft in the morning early, if he can stay." Cyrus had become a magician with his grandfather in this regard. There was a specific protocol, along with nuance and deliver that had to be executed as perfectly as his chores when *I would like to's* were presented.

"Jake Thompson, sir," he said, standing with his hand extended. He exhibited the same brazen self as he did in anything. Cyrus smiled inside at how forward he was.

"You're Sterling's boy."

"Yes sir."

His grandfather shook his hand, stared at him a brief moment, nodded his head and walked into the house all the while mumbling.

"Grandpa", Cyrus hollered from the porch swing. "Care if Jake and I tent out tonight?"

"Chores done!" he hollered back.

"Yes sir! Jake helped me; he's good ta have around." They waited for a response to the previous question and none came, which in most instances, a part from the times he didn't hear, meant a 'no' vote. The question was again fielded at the supper table as Jake had his head into the pork chops and potatoes with all the fervor of Grant in his march on Vicksburg. He and Cyrus' grandmother were in intermittent conversation between bites and it appeared she was fond of Jake and his presence since no one ever came over, especially for supper. His youthful face was an uplift in several ways, but the most important being that Cyrus had a playmate and she could see the difference in his demeanor tremendously. She knew something had been happening in his life, but he never said what it was. He never mentioned Jake at all, except maybe a time or two when he had said, "my friend and me . . ." She couldn't remember him ever having someone over. Now and then he had occasionally been to another's house and the very thought made her wonder why. She looked across the table at her husband of 52 years and nodded quietly.

Cyrus had his grandfather's idioms down to a science. He waited patiently for him to finish his three finger shooter of bourbon, strike the match underneath the table top, lite his pipe and then after the third draw, "Grandpa, me and Jake are gunna tent out tonight, if that's okay." He waited a moment, exhausted most of the smoke and said, "No, to many snakes out right now." The last of the smoke bellowed from his nose and mouth with each word, a bit like you would imagine from a dragon's. Cyrus caught Jake's mouth cocking to say something and he kicked him under the table, ever so softly, of course.

"He's welcome to stay the night, but not outside", his grandfather added.

One must pick and choose their battles, but Cyrus didn't care for a battle with his grandpa at any turn. If Jake had had the chance to spout off even the most spectacular of rebuttals it would have inevitably shot down any chance for him to stay over, period. The adage, *children should be seen and not heard*, was not something grandpa espoused; it was his fervent belief children shouldn't even be seen. He didn't like children except for chores.

Even if this were the last time he had a sleep over it didn't matter. If life ended that night his destiny was complete. Not only was someone staying over this night, but it was his best friend. It was his *brother*. Cyrus' passion for Jake was far and quickly becoming what he had been looking for all his short tenure; someone who not only heard him but listened; who not only saw him but noticed him.

Lights out was another thing his grandpa enforced with military precision. This was pretty much a half hour after sundown. It took a while for Cyrus to piece together why this had been such a regiment in life, thinking in principal that it had to do with the time they arose; but, not really. Cyrus snuck down to the stair bottom an evening not too far back and found grandpa asleep in his rocker with a bottle at his side; the radio playing piano music so low it was near inaudible, while his grandpa snored, only to stir on occasion to lift a glass to his mouth. As with most things in life, especially in youth, questions seem to answer themselves and at moments when they were not asked.

Cyrus' bed was a high feather bed double that belonged to his father in his youth and became Cyrus' when he was three. Cyrus weighed all of 85 pounds soaking wet so he hardly made a dent in the mattress, but when Jake sat down on its edge the pile of well sown feathers took a nice fold. When Jake laid down the opposite side lifted considerably. Cyrus laid on the rise and it flattened neatly.

"Geez, this is the softest bed I have ever laid in. It's like a cloud", Jake sighed.

"It is, ain't it", Cyrus added, not knowing any different.

"I don't think I'll wake up", Jake said.

"Oh yeah you will, or you'll get a pail-a water."

"Pail-a water? You mean he'll pitch water on ya if you don't get up?" Jake asked.

"Yep."

Jake lay there while he pieced Cyrus' puzzle as it came to him. His life was not anything as cumbersome as his and its reality brought answers to him in snippets that painted a picture of why Cyrus was so timid and afraid—he learned his fear at home, and if you couldn't be safe there, you couldn't be safe anywhere. This view into his little *brother's* life was unlike anything he had experienced; this feeling of protectiveness was so salient and vivid that he wanted to be around Cyrus all the time. He wanted to be big enough to quell his grandfather's abuse and at the same time bring him to realize what a gift he was. All these feelings welled inside him and brought anger.

"Have you ever thought of runnin' away?" Jake blurted.

"Run away?" Cyrus whispered.

"Really, if you ran away you could stay in our barn, and it would make your grandpa realize what an idiot he is treatin' you the way he does."

"Have you took leave?" Cyrus asked. "I'd have to come back some time; it'd be the same all over and worse."

"I thought about it before." Jake murmured.

Cyrus stared at him blankly and couldn't believe what he had just heard from the boy he envisioned perfect; who lived the perfect life with the perfect father on the perfect farm that belonged to them.

"What?" Cyrus muttered.

"You think about me like everyone else does; that everything rolls on at the Thompson farm like my Pa is God and I live in heaven? It ain't that way, Cyrus."

Cyrus was confused beyond thought. He sat up on his elbow and stared at his mentor, who lay staring at the ceiling.

"Nothin'", Jake said. He rubbed his eyes and smiled. "Nothin, it's nothin'."

"How come everyone thinks you're so tough and you never have to prove it? Is that what bothers you . . . like right now?" Cyrus asked.

"Cyrus, you think too much! God! If you would jus' not think so much you wouldn't be so scared all the time. That's why you see me like you do. I don't look away when something happens; I run at it and don't think about what *could* happen. Goddamn it's hot in here!"

Jake sat from the bed and pulled off his shirt, then his pants and Cyrus did the same while he chuckled; he'd rarely heard cussing from a peer before, and never under his own roof.

"What!" Jake quipped.

"Nothing, except I'm so used to it. Kinda like what you were talkin' about. You're used to what you're used to, being strong around other folks and stuff . . . anyway."

Jake sat in the window and stared at the full moon coming through the giant pecan tree's branches. Cyrus eased over and sat the opposite end, placing his feet atop the window box, his arms around his legs. The moon's reflection glistened off the moisture in the craw of Jake's nose and mesmerized Cyrus to a lull. It was on his eyelids too. They were long and dark and beautiful yet as mysterious as who they came from now. He did not know if he had been crying, and if he had from what?

"I sleep here most nights because it is pretty hot. Before it rains it gets real cool, almost cold and I sleep great."

"Huh?" Jake replied, stirred from his own thought. "It feels kind-a cool right now, cooler than over there." Jake motioned with a nod. "Let's tent here", he smiled.

"Dang Jake, it's barely big enough for me."

"Yeah it is, we just put our legs beside each other like this."

They both lay at opposite ends and put their legs to each side. Jake chuckled as he put his hands around Cyrus' feet and squeezed them. Then he began to tickle them with his thumb. Cyrus giggled and said, "You're gunna be sorry."

"Why, I'm the tough one remember?"

"You're hands are gunna stink; I got the worst feet in town, maybe the world!"

"Holy crap! You are so right. Love's sow pastures don't smell that bad."

They laughed aloud and began wrestling, one working to knock the other out of the window box until Cyrus hit the floor and shook the wood frame dwelling to the foundation.

"What in hell's name is goin' on up there!" his Grandfather yelled from below.

They both jumped into bed; Cyrus hit the light in flight. His grandfather' burly and awkward step banged against the steps as he came up the stairwell. The knob turned and the door opened. His massive frame filled the doorway from jam to jam as the smoke from his pipe billowed around his head and brought him to look more like the giant in Jack's story. The smell of cheap tobacco and whiskey swilled their heads while his grandfather stood the door-way for a moment.

"I don't want to hear anything else coming from this room un-til the mornin' sun."

"Yes sir", they both chimed in unison.

They spent a measure of time talking about their teacher's backside and other physical detriments of various and sundry school employees as well as some of their friends. Laughing with pillows over their faces, their spirits came closer as both began to risk trusting each other's hearts and souls and in the distance their youth would afford. As the moon rose higher and the blue horizon dimmer, they both dozed off and to a place where they lived together in dreams; where there were no rules, no sadness's, no tears and no fears; where each relied on the other alone: where they were truly *brothers.*

CHAPTER SIX

J ake woke to the birds reveille from the pecan tree as the cool
breeze of the Alabama fall gusted through the open window
and over their uncovered bodies. Cyrus was half on top of him
with his arm and leg draped over one side, Jake's hand against
Cyrus' back. He must have held him all night, which was just fine,
the position of *big* brother suited him well. He dragged his finger
down the middle of Cyrus' back ever so lightly, making him wince
and squeeze Jake's hand tighter. He chuckled quietly as he did
it over and over, finding the comedy in Cyrus' grunt and the way
he'd pulled himself closer to Jake.

"Whatdaya doing?" Cyrus asked.

"Nothin'," he answered with a smile. "Just funnin' with ya."

"Funnin'?"

"Yeah, don't act like you don't know what I'm sayin'."

Finally waking to where he was and his position he pulled back
quickly and with a look of embarrassment, "Sorry," he said.

"For what? I thought it was pretty nice; my little brother all
scrunched up."

"Now yur greenin' me and havin' a time with it. We better get chores handled and then . . . "

Jake interrupted, ". . . and *then* go to the creek and catch crawdads."

"You gotta thing about that creek," Cyrus said. "I don't care about getting' strapped ifin' Grandpa catches us. All he has to do is hear us and believe me he has ears like a hawk has eyes."

"There ya go again, being afraid of the future before it comes the present and then you're ruled by the past," Jake stated.

Cyrus climbed from the window box and put on trousers, all the while Jake lay with his hands behind his head instructing and dictating the day's itinerary.

"Okay, what if we do chores, and I mean everything, and then conjure up Many Moons—and if he don't show, I'll be Many Moons and you be the solder guy," Jake posed.

"The solder guy? You still think that what I saw was what my grandpa says—nothing? An *IMAGINE!* And it's Lt Col Cyrus Buckman, not the *solder guy!*" Cyrus screamed.

Jake sat up to the edge of the bed and relented, "I believe you Pudger; I said I believed you from the start, but what if he don't show because I'm there?"

They dressed and headed to the barn, but not before grabbing a couple of pieces of Mattie's pound cake and a swallow of milk from the bottle; a deadly offense in itself. Cyrus pitched the hay from the loft and Jake portioned it to the various stalls as instructed. They were a seamless machine when together, working like juggernauts with the rhythm of a marching band. Not a word was said that didn't pertain to the immediate task; Cyrus pointing and nodding and Jake throwing and shoveling. In half the time it took Cyrus in his lonesome to do his chores they had finished with plenty of time for eggs and bacon and a lot of Indian conjuring.

The barn was in tip-top shape while they both stood back and reveled at what might come from Grandpa's mouth on their diligence, and how he might just *require* the necessary presence of Jake Thompson at every weekend he was available.

"You boys hunger for some breakfast", Grandma asked.

"Yes mam", they answered in unison.

"How was your first stay at the Buckman home, Mr Thompson?," she asked, setting dishes to the table.

"It was the best night sleep I ever had, Ms Buckman."

"My name is Grandma and that's all I go by, youngin," she quipped.

They sat eating their breakfast with nothing said, but Cyrus could do little less than stare into his mentor's eyes and bask in the dream that his prayer of prayers had been answered—there was truly a God who made these things come true; the real things that are so badly needed and not the foolish requests for a new car, more money or a bigger house. Those things, as he saw it, were frivolities that held no substance and did more to diminish life than augment it. But to get a blessing like Jake was far and above anything the Lord could manifest that Cyrus so badly needed. Only God could have known that. Only God could have done it.

After their morning fill they sat on the porch front contemplating the day's agenda—should they begin the perilous war between Many Moons and the Buckman brigade, or should they visit the fort made by Jake in no-man's land set forth by Grandpa Cyrus— the treacherous creek a short distance between both farms. Young Cyrus' fear of his Grandpa and his retribution for any wrong hovered over him like a hawk its prey—unnoticed, unrecognized and inexorable. This was the point that shamed Cyrus because it dwelled in the very arena that Jake was so adamant about; Cyrus' fears of tomorrow that robbed him of today.

"Pudger, let me show you *the fort*. I know you'll love it. I've spent many a night down there and n'er saw a snake one", Jake muttered.

"Okay", Cyrus answered begrudgingly.

The closer they came Cyrus felt more uneasy. This was the part of fun that wasn't. Disobeying his Grandfather with intention was worse than accidentally. At least the accidental wrong was enjoyed. Knowing he was in the wrong robbed any bit of fun that may have been had. That was the biggest part of Jake he admired, but Jake also had never felt the back cinch of a saddle against his fanny with Grandpa at the other end. There were on occasion minuses for Jake's pluses, and this was a prime example; the moment of clarity Cyrus brought to this table of brotherhood that Jake seemed to miss, and that made Cyrus proud that he understood something his mentor didn't.

They walked a measure down the side of the creek that was awfully deep and dark at points: fallen trees, big ones that stretched the width of the creek and boulders the size of a plow horse. They came to a large bend, nearly a horseshoe turn where a huge live oak lay across from one side to the other in what seemed near thirty foot or better. At the base where the roots were turned up towards the sky like a giant spiders legs was a hole underneath— and it was some kind-a dark in there. It gave Cyrus the willies.

"Here we are", Jake said. "Nice, huh?"

"Yep, I guess"

Jake traversed the length of the tree to the other side, making the bark crack and the tree moan with each step, "Com'on", he waved to Cyrus. "You'll like it, I swear."

It was awfully dark and smelled of rotten wood and possibly dead bugs and a rat or two. They climbed down under the giant base into a world that could not be seen from above. Jake had turned this dungeon of decay and death into a palace of serenity and silence. He had candles placed in spots of abundant darkness, pieces of carpet he had procured from the town dump that lined the cold and mildewed ground, slats of two by twelve's for a table of sorts with trinkets and memorabilia set here and there that put his signature in place and told any would be passersby that this cave was taken. Of course no one in their right mind would ever find this spot, and if they stumbled on it they would never have cause to enter it. It was perfect!

"Wow!" Cyrus muttered, sitting on the hand laid flooring and against the night stand made from a wire spindle quaintly covered with a purple terry cloth bath towel. "I could definitely spend all my time here."

"Told ya", Jake said "Yur probably the only one I'd ever bring here, since yur family and all."

"What happens when they open the dam?" Cyrus queried with a nervous smile.

"Da-know, never has happened since I came on it end-a last year. If it does happen I have only three to four feet to climb out, and that's if I'm here. Guess I'll lose what I can't grab."

"How often you stay here?"

"Mostly on the weekends, when Pa gets into the bug juice . . .", Jake stopped abruptly and stared distantly out across the creek bed. Everything slowed in the pale silence that overtook this home-away-from-home while they sat motionless and basked in the comment they both knew all too well.

"Is it the same at your place?" Cyrus whispered. Jake sat looking out across the creek bed in silence.

"Cyrus Buckman the third, we're campin' right ch-ere tonight. I don't care ifin it brings a hidin', which I don't think they'll ever find out. I'm gunna show you how pretty the sky is at night and when you hold yur breath you can hear you heart beat. We can laugh as loud as we want and cat around til the moon falls, but this night *we are* stayin' here", Jake mandated.

Cyrus rarely bucked what Jake said and this was one of those times he would have but in his old scared self, strangely this time he chose to let it ride. He was beginning to see weakness in his character by the light that Jake emanated. Somewhat of a beacon in a dense fog and it was the first time in his puny life that he was beginning to feel autonomous from the ropes and fears his grand-father had bound him. Good or bad, Cyrus was trying to stand on his own and much like his mentor had wanted desperately to discover his strengths, discard his weaknesses and become his true identity; the image of himself his grandfather labored so strongly to conceal.

"I'm for it, Jake, but I don't want to do it just to get a hidin'. It'd take all the fun out if I knew what was comin' the next mornin'. How can we do it without both kin knowin' we're gone?"

"You're funny, Pudgie . . . so busy being afraid of getting caught that you pass right by the way to do it", Jake said with his smile of genus. "You ask ta stay with me and I'll ask ta stay with you. Both will be so glad ta rid us for an evening that they'll say 'yes', and we just meet here."

"Dang!" Cyrus said, shaking his head. "Guess that's why you're you and I'm me. Someday I'll be a *you* though."

They spent the better part of the morning reminiscing and planning their evening in the throes of the temple creek. There were cubbyholes all about the fort made by the creeks raging cur-rents. Each one had a candle, a knickknack or a play item that suited a third graders preference. Both had yet to see the creek at its thrust, but the entire farming community, new and old, told of horror stories about victims the creek had claimed even after the sirens had been put in place. It was truly a no-man's land, and yet in a sense, a red badge of courage for Cyrus and a sort of hospice for the resurrection of his timid soul.

Vaguely and from such a distance that one could have pre-sumed it was the siren going off, both struggled to gather the di-rection and source of this wail; but, after the third screech Cyrus figured it was his Grandma Mattie heralding them for lunch. If they ran straight to the house from the creek side it would have been extremely incriminating and possibly a deal-breaker for their ingeniously conceived plan for that eve. To appear from the backside of the barn as though they had been playing in the corn rows was the safe bet and they had to high-tail it to get there before Grandpa. Out of breath and laughing in between gasps at the barns edge, they kept spot glancing each other as though each knew something the other didn't.

"Being bad feels pretty good, don't it," Jake muttered.

"We ain't really done nothing bad; we just made plans to be kind-a bad," Cyrus interjected.

"We both deserve ta get away from our bosses once in a while—I mean, they hide stuff from us so I see no problem hiding somethin' as little as tenting in the creek from them. Snakes! What a crock," Jake added. "Cyrus, I ain't a bad guy and I don't look for trouble . . . sometimes my life gets crazy enough that I gotta be by myself if only for a night. There ain't nobody I really care bein' with 'ceptin' you because I know you to be real—I knew that the second I saw you come in ta Ms Fugate's; that you and I was gunna be best of friends."

"You knew that, huh?"

"Yep, every time I tried to set with you at lunch you'd pick your sandwich and take off like a bat out of a burnin' stump!"

Cyrus chuckled, "I thought for sure you was trying ta find out about me so you and your buddies could pants me at recess."

"Pants you?"

"Yep; last year at Horace Mann Elementary they not only got my britches off but my under britches as well. I was buck naked from the waist to my brogans—ever tried runnin', pullin' up your britches and working to hide your dinker at the same time?"

Jake tried to be serious but the visual was just too funny.

"Weren't funny, Bruiser."

"Bruiser?"

"Yeah", Cyrus smiled broadly. "That's *your* nickname."

"How'd ya get to that?"

"Don't rightly know, but it fits."

"Were there chickens watchin' when you lost your britches?" Jake asked.

"Chickens?"

"Girls, dummy."

"Oh, I reckon. I didn't stand to gaze about though. I dove into a burn barrel head first; a teacher fetched out me and helped get my britches back in place. I was black with ash from head to toe—looked a bit like Sambo."

Jake roared and Cyrus had to find humor too. He never told this story to anyone, even his Grandma when she had asked, "Child, what in the world did you get into? There's smut all in your trousers is like you was throwed head first into a burn barrel."

After lunch which was last night's greens and ham hocks with a smatterin' of mashed potatoes and gravy and a piece of Mattie's pound cake, they set out for the barn 'to get a head start on the evening chores', as they dictated to Grandpa Cyrus in loud unison at the dinner table.

"What in hell's name are you both high voicin' at the table for? Chores are chores and I could give a lick if they were started yesterday as long as they are done when due. From now on, Cyrus J., you need to have your guest filed on that point, hear!" Grandpa roared.

"Grandpa, please! Not in front of Junior's friend!" his Grandma scolded.

It was unusual to witness this "standing up" to his Grandfather; beyond unusual it was downright bold, all these initiatives being aired by the once silent majority. While they sat on the porch swing waiting for Grandpa and Dud to take back to the bottle and plow (not necessarily in that order), Cyrus eyed his mentor with intermittent glances, smiling at the suggestion that there was some kind of magic about Jake Thompson that was empowering and reassuring the lowly of the Buckman family. Grandma Mattie never, never stood up to Grandpa concerning his comment or ruling unless she truly saw the chuck wagon nearing the bluff—more than once did she intercede to stop the irreversible from occurring, like when she pulled the .30-.30 from Grandpa's drunken arms as he was beading down on a river dog he believed to be the chicken killer of Fayette County, when in fact it was just Cyrus on his wooden pony chasing Indians. It was one of the umpteen times he would swear off liquor.

CHAPTER SEVEN

Grandpa hadn't been out of sight more than a handful of seconds before Jake was dragging Cyrus over the fence and into the barn.

"Dang Jake! Hold up a sec'", Cyrus bellowed. "We got plenty of time."

"I wanna see if we can conjure Many Moons", he said excitedly. "Been waitin' for this all day long; I showed you the fort, now I wanna see Many Moons."

"I tell ya, Bruiser, it ain't that spectacular—it's pretty scary—if he comes."

"Why would it be scary?"

Cyrus didn't know how to explain what he saw, or if what he saw was really what he saw. Even if he could explain he wasn't sure he wanted to on account that his trusted friend and brother might decide he was a little more off balance than maybe. No matter who you were seen as or how popular you might be, everyone outside your world had some measure of reservation about you; whether you were complete, two bricks shy or if your whole load was gone.

You see, Cyrus' fear was not really of what people thought of him; his truest of fears was that he would lose what he had: Jake; his brother; his guardian. To lose Jake would be to die, especially if Jake traded him for the other side—for the Pritchett's and the Worth's of this life.

They pulled the giant doors back that partially lit the long and darkened barn floor to the forbidden hay bin. Cyrus ran to the other end and opened those doors, fully exposing the ominous theater and its magic. In the full of day this place was gargantuan. Jake had privy to its view at the brink of dusk, but now the sun's beams shot through the loft windows and spaces between the slates and brought this so called barn to an ethereal sense of being. Cyrus was amused by the awe-struck look on Jake's face as he twirled in circles, glaring at the massive cathedral beams across the roof's base that seemed to suspend the heavens and yet only held bales of hay.

"There's magic in here", Jake whispered to himself.

He held his hands outward as though stretching to touch something, or to feel the coolness of the musty palace and its aura that so impressed him. Cyrus had seen the inside of this place more often than he cared to, and not once did he ever feel anything more than a desire for its timbers to be ablaze.

"You okay", Cyrus asked sheepishly. Jake didn't answer, mesmerized in thought. "Why don't we just start us a little fire right over in that hay bin and burn this dung heap to the ground?"

A moment after Cyrus' comment reached home, Jake looked at him like he'd tinkled in his Post Toasties, "You outta your mind, swamp rat!"

"He's alive!" Cyrus muttered.

"This is a special place, Cyrus; a real special place."

"Special?"

"I believe you, Cyrus. I believe you did see Many Moons." Jake said, turning to the hay bin. "Show me what you did exactly when you saw Many Moons at the barn doors."

"Look Jake, I might-a been seein' things, or maybe wanted to see Many Moons bad enough to believe it."

"Jus' show me, Pudger."

Cyrus knelt next to the hay bin opposite where Jake was standing. "I was like this and I . . . I said something like . . . Jake this is sooo stupid."

"Cyrus! What's stupid about it? Now you aren't believin'."

Cyrus sat down with his arms across his knees. "Jake, I don't want you to think I'm a squirrel or especially a lyin' squirrel. If he don't show then that might make you think ill of me."

"Lord! You are such a squirrel", Jake laughed. "That's what you really think 'bout me? That I'm your friend 'cause . . . 'cause what; you're the most popular guy at Fayette County Elementary? No, 'cause you care 'bout other folk more than you do you . . . and that's some kinda special."

"Jake, how old are you?"

"Why?"

"You're different than anyone I've ever know'd my age; you see things, know things and explain things no one my age is able."

"I'll be eleven in four months."

"Eleven!"

"Yeah, papa started me out schoolin' when I was eight. He needed me 'round the farm to do the little things he couldn't get to. A bit after my eighth birthday, S.T. came along; he was without a place and papa made a deal with him that he'd feed him and give him a roof over his head in trade for chorin'. He's been with us ever since. He and papa set up nights jawin' and passin' the bottle. I never gave it much mind 'cause they watch each other, but there are times they'll pull the cork in the mornin' and it makes it strange for me."

"Strange?" Cyrus inquired.

"Yeah", Jake whispered. "Can't put a finger to it, just that Pa's different. Bit like there's Pa and S.T. and then me."

Jake's eyes watered and his voice cracked; the nuance of his brother's strife covered him like a wet wool blanket. Jake rubbed his eyes and blurted, "Pudger!, let's get this Indian's butt in here and do some battlin'!"

"I'm-a hearin' ya Bruiser!"

"No! it's Colonel Thompson", Jake commanded.

"Colonel?" Cyrus whined, "Guess you gotta be a Full Bird co-min' into this war!"

"Gotta go with the stout", Jake mused. "We can always Indian wrestle for it."

"Naw, but if he does show know that you are the one in charge—stout bird."

Cyrus brought Jake up to speed on the position and condition one's state of mind had to be; you had to believe that you were the despised adversary of the combatant, Kiowa Chief Many Moons, and that his presence is as real as your own. You had to feel your weapon, your uniform and your commanding position . . .

"Wait a minute, Pudger, you're makin' this way too . . . "

Cyrus interrupted, ". . . Lt Col! And that's the way it happens."

"Okay", Jake relented.

Cyrus knelt to one knee and leaned against the hay bin while Jake knelt behind him. Staring at the barn entrance he summoned the Kiowa spearhead, "Many Moons! This is Lt Col Buckman, the bluecoat who has come to take you, but I have not come alone this time; I have another warrior with me who is fiercer and mightier than me. Will you show yourself for battle?"

The barn remained silent. Jake was so close to Cyrus that he felt his breath against his neck. It was the first Cyrus had ever felt in command, in command of anything. He wondered though if this was a good idea: if Many Moons didn't appear his idol might see him in a cynical light, and if he did, there could be more to deal with than proving a point true. The abject fear that overcame him at first glance of "the man" in the barn doorway, as with the verbal communication he had with him was so real that . . .

"Cyrus look!" Jake whispered, pressing against him.

There was movement of a shadow against the ground immediately outside the barn door and to the side of the sun. The movement was slow and agile like an object fluttering in the wind.

"Is it sunflowers, maybe?" Jake asked.

"No. Not on that side of the barn", Cyrus muttered.

"Call him again."

"No, let's wait a spell."

"Many Moons!" Jake summoned loudly. "This is Col Thompson of the fifth Cavalry and we have you surrounded!"

"You idiot! This isn't a joke!"

For the second they sat spinning in youthful argument until both glanced back at the doorway to see the shadow had vanished. They looked at each other with bewilderment, each running through their tiny mental rolodexes in search of a plausible reality of the shadow's presence then disappearance and nothing fit except one. At that moment there was a hinge squeak behind them at the back doors. There stood within feet from them the largest man they had ever seen in flesh. He was dressed in deer skin leggin's, bare chested with a thin fur-lined vest that was garnished in necklaces of claws and shiny trinkets; he donned a leather headband inscribed with strange markings and a long train of feathers that came to the middle of his back. On his waist was a scabbard that held the longest and shiniest knife they'd ever laid eyes to. They were frozen in space and time. Neither could swallow nor breathe.

"Two blue coats who call for battle, but no weapon", the man said.

"When I say 'now', you run for the loft and scurry down the hay rope", Cyrus whispered. "NOW!"

Just as Jake bolted over Cyrus' shoulder, Cyrus leaped over the hay bin and darted for the front door of the barn.

With his knife unsheathed and glistening off the sun's beams, he lunged at Jake who was near the top of the loft. Tumbling over the top of the ladder he kicked it hard enough to push it off balance, crashing to the floor. Jake dove through the loft doors in midair that was better than twenty-five foot up, grabbing the rope that hung from the block and tackle and sashayed to the ground, landing in a pile of hay. Cyrus was already standing atop the fence watching and making sure his brother was in the clear. When they made it to the porch front they grabbed each other in a collision and neither let go, breathing, gasping.

"It was all in our mind, Jake. We'll never do it again . . . but it was really all in our mind."

"Not sure 'bout that", Jake said slowly easing his grip on Cyrus and sitting to the porch steps. "How might it in both our mind's at the same time? Look", Jake finished.

Jake turned his right calf around to an upward position and his trousers were ripped from the back of his knee to nearly his ankle in a perfect cut. Cyrus pulled the rip open to see blood oozing from a gash about six inches long and some of it deep. Cyrus had watched his Grandma patch up his Grandpa so many times. Taking Jake into the house, he pulled off his trousers, washed the wound thoroughly with soapy water and a hint of bleach; made a poltis of mustard root and salt, bound the wound together with baling string and then wrapped it with bed linen.

"There Col Thompson, good as new. Gunna be sore for a spell, though. Guess that'll teach you to pay attention to your junior officer", Cyrus laughed. Jake didn't. He sat staring at Cyrus like he was a god. His eyes began to swill with moisture through his smile of adoration and wonder; he could see what Cyrus hid and feared yet was the most beautiful: Himself.

"You are the stud horse here, Mr Buckman. I believed you, but now I *believe* you. You were so cool-headed, Pudger. We might have died in there if it hadn't been for you."

"Ya know Jake, you could-a caught this on a bent nail off the hay bin."

"You're joshin' me, right! Are you saying there wasn't a man in there who spoke to us, and that you did not tell me to run to the loft? Tell me I ain't hearin' this. I was there buddy boy!"

"Tell it to my Grandpa then", he sighed. "I'm so tired of being took for a no-account, Jake. If it hadn't been for you comin' into my life I may have just found a place and laid down for good."

"Your Grandfather is a lonely burned up man who is jus' like my Pa in many ways—my Pa never got over losing my mama and your grandfather never got over losing his son—it's like no one is ever satisfied with what they have."

They were still for a moment, staring at each other.

"What?" Cyrus asked.

"It was meant that you and I are friends; we became instant friends out of all those kids and we live right next door. We share this magic that *no one* would ever believe, and it doesn't matter if they do or don't because it was meant for us! Cyrus, what just happened to us?"

"You mean in the barn?"

"Ah, yeah.

"We were chased by Many Moons", Cyrus laughed loudly, "And . . . my brother Col Thompson got whacked!"

"What was he wearing?" Jake asked.

"Ah, leather leggin's, a furry vest made from a milk cow— Holstein, I reckon—that had shiny buttons with leather strings in the middle . . . ah."

"What was around his neck?"

"Necklaces made with claws and beads, and he wore a leather strap 'round his head that had funny marks on it and yellow hawk tail feathers all down his back."

"You saw, I mean we saw something that nobody would believe we did because we're a couple-a dumb kids. But we did see him, right."

"It's kind-a funny, it doesn't really scare me anymore. If he wanted me or you he would have been able to get us. Did you see how big he was!" Cyrus bellowed. "And even more strange is that he looks exactly the way he does when I play . . . well, when I play like I'm ridin' my horse and stuff", Cyrus diverted quickly not to give way to still riding Cid.

"Yeah", Jake muttered. "Hey, let's plan tonight."

"I gotta get Cyrus an' Mattie to agree first."

"They agreed for me to stay over here once, no reason why they wouldn't agree for you at my place, and I know Pa will say yes."

"Maybe someday I'll get it", Cyrus said.

"You will", Jake chuckled.

"You don't even know what I'm talkin' about", Cyrus muttered.

"Confidence."

CHAPTER EIGHT

J ake was right, as usual, there was an atypical air about his grand-parents by how easy it was to get their approval for the over-night—way too easy as a matter of fact: no questions, no demands or commands about chores and what would happen if they weren't done and as though that would have slipped someone's mind. After its daily recitation for the last nine years and four months, how dense would one have to be? Life was taking on a whole new perspective for young Cy and the only thing he could blame it on was his new buddy and soul mate, Jake Thompson. It appeared there wasn't anything Jake couldn't accomplish, no ill feelings that weighed him down, no sudden occurrences that placed him at guard and no fear—no fear of seemingly anything. It was as if he were of divine province; a guardian angel of sorts. Yeah, that seemed to hold water: His prayers, the prayers his grandmother prompted him to consider, as with Brother Higgins, his tiny preacher with poor lungs, and it looked as though they were right.

"Hey!" Jake blurted. "Snap out of it. There're some things we gotta get like eats, a blanket or two, maybe a pillow . . . Oh, can you get some matches?"

"Ah yeah, I can't get everything though, they'll begin to wonder what's goin' on. They may be idiots but they ain't stupid."

"Get what you can and I'll do the rest."

"What'd yur Pa say?", Cyrus inquired.

"What I told ya he'd say", Jake replied incensed.

"What's with you, Pudge? You gettin' scared again?"

"Naw . . . but I do feel a bit like a dog out of his pen; not sure how ta feel I guess."

There was newness about Cyrus and the way he was beginning to see things. Jake was absolutely correct in his chronology of events, how Cyrus' grandparents would nod their heads without second thought at his request for an overnight; nod their heads at just about anything it appeared. Just as anyone could see a storm's break in the distance, a tiny sliver of Jake was coming alive in Cyrus. Watching his mentor gather knickknacks about his barn and the way he methodically made things happen like Santa's checklist, he realized he had found his liege; his king of sorts. Every one of Jake's suggestions, once met with a measure of contemplation and pragmatism, now materialized as normal and as fluid as breath. There were no questions or concerns, only a smile of acknowledgment. It was funny that way, the way Cyrus cared for nothing except Jake's approval. The hierarchy of his position in their makeshift regimen meant nothing; all he cared for was one affirmation and only one—Jake's.

The light that had once assisted them in their fort decoration was now below the creek bed and nearly to the horizon. What was left of the sparse sun beams that illuminated their earthen shelter, glowed against their boyish overnight necessities that supplanted more now a security than a purpose—a handful of comic books never afforded Cyrus; a wooden toy here and there; homemade candles in every cranny that flickered with the same reticence Cyrus' heart labored to hide behind this loneliness that, with each thought, became worse and seemed only to synergize the uncertainty of his decision: he could not seem to find comfort in the fact he was ready for this large an adventure. Cyrus mirrored his mentor's every move in hopes that this insecurity would disappear as quickly as the courage before had arrived.

After the evening meal that had been brought gracious by a church key: a can of sardines, a handful of soda crackers and two bottles of warm cream soda, they lay back on the double-quilted blanket Cyrus snuck from the attic hope chest that belonged to his mother and awaited the day's disappearance under the weight of night. It was a young boy's Utopia when he wasn't alone.

"Hey, you wanna conjure Many . . .", Jake began.

Cyrus interrupted, "No!"

Jake laughed and poked at him, "What?"

"Did you really see him, Jake?"

Jake stared at him a moment and shook his head, "No, I didn't."

"Why'd you say you did then?"

"I daknow, I guess I didn't want to see you feel bad."

"How'd you get cut?" Cyrus asked.

"Just like you thought—somewhere between the hay bin and the top of the loft by a nail or something. I felt it was real, Pudge; I mean, I wanted it to be and it was fun."

Cyrus lay there next to his buddy feeling empty, but not as much as he should have. He realized Jake had done what he did for him and not to make light of him. He also realized his grandfather was most assuredly correct in that all of his experiences were nothing but *imagines*.

"Pudger, please don't be mad at me. I wasn't greenin' ya, I just wanted to believe in what you believed in—and who knows, maybe you *are* the only one who can see Many Moons, and he was there."

"It ain't that big a deal, Jake," Cyrus added under a cloud of disappointment. "Whether he was or wasn't is okay—I know now a lot of my stuff ain't real—at least real to other people, and what's so bad 'bout havin' some dreams or things to myself, right?"

"Cyrus, you're my best friend; the best friend I'll ever have. I remember the first time I saw you when Mr Burnside brought you into class. Being eleven in the third grade I see folks in a different way and guys see me different. Sometimes the guys I think are my friends aren't—they just like being seen with me or something."

Cyrus chuckled a bit, "Me . . . me too, in a way. You make me feel like everything is okay. Every morning I get up the first thing in my mind is seeing you in front of the Burle farm. In the beginning it was because Pritchett and his toadies left me alone, but soon enough I knew it was because I wanted a big brother so bad I could taste it. The day you called me your *brother* was the best day of my life; I also saw things I never noticed before."

"Like what?"

"Oh, why people like Pritchett are as ugly inside as they are out; why they can't find someone like you . . . like I did."

Jake rolled over, put his arm under his head and stared at Cyrus until he turned his head.

"What?" Cyrus said.

"Pritchett loves to be Pritchett. I've tried to be his friend just so I wouldn't have to fight him, but he won't have it", Jake said matter-a-factly.

"I've always lived in a place I made for me, where things might not be real but it gets me from one chore to the next. I ain't big or strong, jus' scared and folks know it; my grandpa can't stand me and I'm hard on my grandma. It would be so much easier if I was outta the picture; really, if I never was."

"You don't know what you have that others see—Pritchett would kill to have what you have. Cyrus—you never know who's watchin'."

"Me! What would I have that someone like Pritchett would want?"

"More than you would ever know," Jake answered solemnly as he lay back against the quilt and stared at the night.

Several moments of silence past, something that was uncomfortable for Cyrus: the quiet. If there wasn't noise of some kind it left in the air that something was amiss; that his grandfather was lurking in the shadows, watching, waiting for a reason to climb down on him. There were no bones about it, he was deathly afraid of his grandfather and had forever imagined there would come the day he would kill him.

"Jake, do you like yur Pa?"

"I daknow. I can only remember my Ma when I see a picture of her and it makes me forget my Pa. I really don't think he likes *me*. I feel it sometimes when he looks at me—kinda like he's looking through me at something behind."

"When he hide's ya, does he do it like he wants ya dead?" Cyrus inquired as might a blind man looking to cross a road.

"He . . . he doesn't hide me that much. I mean, he has, but I'd rather him do that than what he does."

"What?"

"He doesn't talk to me. I can go days and he won't say anything and it hurts so bad," Jake said, his voice strained and tearful. "He'll talk to J.C. about me right in front of me like I ain't there. He even said before that it shoulda been me that passed instead of my Ma."

Cyrus rolled towards him, placed his head in the nape of his neck and hugged him. The creek's evening song of cicada, crickets and occasional bullfrog lulled them to a slumber they had not known before themselves. They held each other in a protective covenant that was not of word or measure but of innocence as subtle as their existence.

CHAPTER NINE

The accomplishment Cyrus had achieved for his night in the creek was larger than anything he'd ever known: a portion defiance and the balance, the absence of fear, which if he was brutally honest, was due to the sanctuary of his benefactor: the one he lay next to while he basked in the dawn's quiet. Mesmerized by his slumber, Cyrus wiped the drool that puddled in the corners of Jake's mouth and then to his own, as a derivation of the Indian ritual he pretended—blood brothers, but in this instance, saliva brothers. There was little about each other that wasn't in some way intertwined, shared or possessed, even moments where their idioms blurred personalities. It was difficult at times to determine where one stopped and the other began.

He opened his eyes a moment, smiled and leaned close to Cyrus' chest, curling his hands into a fetal position while Cyrus smelled of his hair. Strange? Not really, if you were as far from the world as they were and your only association to a caring soul was at the swinging end of a saddle's back cinch.

Cyrus wasn't sure who was holding who and if it mattered greatly. If he was holding Jake that meant he could be as much a caregiver; but, if it was Jake holding him then that surely proved Jake's love for him was as true as the protection he freely extended. It was a youthful nuance that was extremely important, in fact, near critical at this juncture. Their young friendship was as soft as wet cement—everything that happened had to have meaning whether it was there or not. Neither had ever felt for another human being what they were discovering. The only thing Cyrus ever cared for had been a broken wood pony. As much as it meant for Cyrus to wake on a Saturday morning at the thrill of a battle with Many Moons, it now took a back seat. His new kinship surpassed anything his tiny, inexperienced mind could fathom, and it consumed his soul. Jake wasn't some inanimate object carved from a tree stump, donned with artifacts from various state fairs, plow fields and attic sales, this was his brother . . . his *brother!*

The chilled morning of dew and creek covered both of them along with the remnants of the eve's campfire. Cyrus lay huddled to his brother as close as he could. "Turnabout fair play", he thought with a giggle—he ran his finger down the middle of Jake's back, slow and deliberate. Jake bowed his back and drew closer to Cyrus, letting out a sigh and putting his arm about his waist. Cyrus did it again and again, finding not only humor but the warmth of his buddy. Jake woke with a broad smile.

"You! You knew I was doing it all along", Cyrus laughed.

"You know better than to try and dog me."

Save for what was left of the sardines, a few soda crackers and a swallow or two of crème soda, breakfast was scant pickin's unless they cajoled Grandma Mattie into a hot sit down. They catted back and forth awhile until they remembered: chores.

Collusion and pooling of their resources quickly became their way of life with no parental opposition, because the folks were happy beyond definition; these two "youngun's" had not only found each other but were out of their caregiver's hair and handling chores. There were other benefits as well. Cyrus moved from poor marks in school to satisfactory across the board, and Jake, well, his relationship with his father seemed back on the rail. None of these by-products meant a hill of beans to either Cyrus or Jake because they expected nothing more and wanted nothing more than what they had—themselves. They depended on no one.

They continued in this subterfuge about the creek and as long as they had their chores done in a timely manner, who cared? Cyrus knew though that if his grandfather ever discovered the truth about their deception it would be the end . . . the end of a lot of things, up and to his life and so he lived it like that. He believed deeply that his grandfather despised him, despised his very existence.

"Pudger, there ain't anyway yur grandpa would kill you. I just ain't believin' it."

"Jake, every night he sets up in his rocker sippin' whiskey and staring at a picture of my Pa and Ma . . . every night."

"So what. My Pa always talks 'bout my Ma and how special she was and all."

"Has he ever told you it would have been better ifin it was you that died?"

Jake stared at Cyrus unable to answer his out-of-the-blue comment, even though he had walked the same path with his own father. More than once he had stumbled onto his father's sadness and knew just to listen. Hurtful things said he did not take to heart but rather set them on a shelf, and in some uncanny way knew they were not said of spite or malice but of grumblings too deep to soothe. Maybe it was the added years that propagated such maturity in Jake, but Cyrus could see only what was in front of him, and oddly enough, through Jake, but a child himself, was beginning to revel in life. It was more than just a composition of chores, fears and heartaches. He was learning there were things that came without recompense—things that were completely free.

The fort lay dormant for several weekends because cropping was at high swing and it was near impossible to play the parents against themselves, since being in the field precluded one from the other. Even though there weren't phones, it wasn't difficult to look across the pasture and wave at the other party—"If they aren't with you and they're not with us, then where are they?" It was Jake who could be thanked for this aversion.

Between the cornfield, sleep and school there wasn't much time to enjoy the finer points of life and it was wearing on Cyrus. To aggravate the situation further, other elements were becoming more tenuous as the holidays approached. Cyrus' struggles with Pritchett and the others were coming back into play and he didn't understand why. Actually, there wasn't any reason, excepting the out-right meanness of these boys. Confrontations began to materialize on the bus and at recess, and Jake urged Cyrus to just ignore them, but that only served as license to ramp up the chastisement. Although Cyrus continued to bask in the protection of his big brother, for whatever reason, Pritchett and his gang had become desensitized to Jake and his somewhat obscure authority.

"Cyrus, don't bother with 'em. They're nothin' and will do nothin' if ya just don't pay any attention to 'em."

"Why do they jus' pick on me . . . I have never done anything to any of 'em? When I see 'em coming I go the other way."

"I daknow. I can get Pritchett off to the side, but that'll probably mean I'll have ta fight him, and I jus' don't want that kinda trouble."

With those words Cyrus began to feel that all too familiar pain; the pain of being alone in his world of make-believe; the pain of being in constant fear, fear of life, fear of his grandfather, fear of just waking the next morning and he was sick of it. He was shown a side of life he had never seen or experienced and he was not going to give back to the old way.

"I'm gunna do something 'bout it, Jake. I'm gunna do something 'bout it on my own. I ain't livin' scared like this ever again because someone can make it that way and for no good cause."

"Like what?"

"Not sure yet, but if you can't help then it's up ta me, ain't it?"

"They'll kill you Pudger, or at least make you feel like dyin'."

"Naw, I'll make the ground even."

"What's that mean?" Jake asked sheepishly.

"I'm sick of being the kid everyone picks on because he never does anything back. I may get banged up and even hurt, but they're gunna know I ain't takin' it anymore. They won't forget me."

Cyrus' attitude swept over Jake like a warm prairie wind, new and inviting to a point but alarming. He wasn't a fighter or even a bluffer as a fighter. He had been under foot for so long that his signature was known; a porch dog that had been whipped so many times that all one had to do was stomp their foot and he was long gone into hiding. Then there was something to say about that. Any person, even the strongest of links, can reach a breaking point. Cyrus witnessed Jake's magic but had not truly examined the physical attributes that were the pillar of his position in this vast menagerie of elementary school tough guy. The fact that he was eleven years old, twice the size of any of their peers and wielded a mystic that brought some adults to scratch their heads was what he wasn't seeing in full light. Cyrus saw only the product of Jake's persona and not the formula and this worried his mentor. He could get into some real trouble.

"Why don't you say something to your grandpa?" Jake mentioned.

"Oh, why didn't I think of that . . . you gotta be kiddin'. First, even if he did act like he cared it would be to see me get my butt kicked, and second, I don't think he'd even act like he cared."

"What's this *even ground* stuff you're talkin'? What's that mean?" Jake asked.

"Not sure yet."

Cyrus' entire demeanor for the balance of the day was immersed in thought and contemplation. That afternoon as usual, on the walk home, Jake followed him but said nothing. Pritchett was behind and began the heckling from where he had left off at lunch.

"Hey, squat-ta-piss-sissy, you ever gunna stand up for yourself or jus' stand behind your bodyguard the rest your life?" Pritchett muttered to the laughter of his entourage.

Jake turned to say something but Cyrus jeered at him in opposition.

"What?" Pritchett responded. "You gunna pick up his leash again, Thompson? I gotta a surprise for you tomorrow, squat-ta-piss. A real surprise."

He did as Jake originally instructed, even though it proved fruitless, and did not pay Pritchett any mind. It was comforting in a way, averting the pressure of having to rebut mindless comments from a mindless individual of a mindless world. Cyrus sat quietly counting the passing fence posts with a bob of his head, occasionally murmuring inaudible things that brought Jake to lean in and eves drop without avail.

"What the hell is going on with you", Jake whispered.

"Nothing. Jus' doin' as you instructed me—not payin' goonhead any mind."

"You know . . . you know I'm worryin' about you already and I don't cotton to it", Jake muttered into Cyrus' ear.

The care and feeding of Jake was becoming more fluid with each day they spent together, and as sharp as Jake was it was peculiar he didn't pick up on it, or did he? There were times Cyrus was deliberate about his actions he knew would fall uneasy with Jake but not even he truly knew why; only that a need deep inside would wake on its own, uncontrollable, unquenchable and most of all unexplainable. To harm his brother with any intention would be more than his heart could ever bear, but when he felt Jake's attention wane this *thing* would consume him with a blindness to anything but what shook the status quo. He couldn't handle it and worse than that, couldn't explain it. He only knew he needed Jake and so badly did he want Jake to need him.

They stopped at Burle Barn to pitch stones at the crows while Pritchett muttered on with hometown epithets from the background. Cyrus paid little attention because most of what wasn't muffled by the plumes of rural road dust was by the monotonous buzz of cicadas. After a stone or two, they were alone and on a slow plod towards home. While both wanted badly to speak their mind, this worry that something errant might be said brought tenseness about Cyrus and made it difficult to breathe.

"Hey", Jake began. They stopped and faced each other in the quiet for a moment. "I have to know if you're mad at me for somethin'."

"I ain't mad; I ain't mad atoll."

"When you don't say nothin' to me, like it was all this day, it scares me . . . it scares me bad, Pudger."

Tears welled in Cyrus' eyes. He glanced to the corn rows opposite Jake's view and when he tried to speak each word hung in his gut as if one came, they all would in a giant explosion. His lips quivering and tears down his cheeks, he turned to face the music.

"I . . . I get soooo scared when I'm not 'round you and I think about Pritchett gettin' a-Holt of me. I know I should be stronger, but I ain't. Just a fact."

Jake moved to him, put his arms around him and hugged him.

"You're my brother, Cyrus. Always and forever."

He cried.

CHAPTER TEN

The solidarity between these two became like the strength of ten men in spirit and soul. Cyrus' view of himself, once that of an oak sapling that could be brought to the ground with a slight wind, was coming to stand tall and strong enough to face Pritchett solo. These times seemed to be a "God" thing, as his Grandma referred to stretches of darkness until the light, where his strength was being tested on varying plains. Visibly he was growing in character, but bodily? His build was actually taking on a likeness of Jake. He cut and combed hair like Jake, he walked and spoke like Jake, his wit, humor and smile were like Jake. Their affection was as pure as the driven snow, and it confounded Grandpa Cyrus to the point he made comment: "You two need some time apart . . . folks in town are talkin' and it sticks in my craw", he'd bellow.

"Talkin' 'bout what?" Cyrus inquired, in his makeshift lower tone he'd supplant to augment this manhood he was trying on.

"Like that damned phony voice you're workin' so hard to tailor; you ain't there yet boy and folk make light of it!"

"Cyrus Walton! I will not have that language at this table, or pointed at your grandson!" Grandma Mattie scolded. Seldom as snow in Tuscaloosa did Miss Mattie ever raise her voice to Grandpa Cyrus, but she seemed to gain this divine providence when young Cy was being whacked injudiciously.

"There ain't a tick's blemish on this baby's soul, and what he's learned without us workin' to wreck it has been straight from the Lord's hand!"

Grandma Mattie could stand toe to toe with the stoutest when it came to chanting praises for the Lord and correcting the errant ways of non-believers; but, she was never more sure of her position than when pointing out blatant transgressions against the meek, like her grand baby. Cyrus cringed at the embellishment: "grand-baby", a salutation that occurred only at church and associated functions but became more intolerable with age and impossible to avert because of hers.

"Gran'ma, Please! Please! Please! Do NOT call me your grand-baby", he pleaded on their rides to and from town: "to" as a reminder and "from" as a scold. She'd gently and quietly blush from his command, but heeded it only for a time. It was an expression of hers; a term of endearment that was in a solemn way the acknowledgment of the love for her own son. Cyrus' intuitiveness about people saddened him on occasion, especially so concerning his Grandmother and how he exploited her age when he corrected her openly and got away with it.

"Gran', I'm sorry. You can call me whatever you want."

"Sweet child, I know I do embarrass you at times. I certainly don't mean it."

The sun's rise gave call to another day as the warm rays edged their way through what was left of the leaves on his pecan tree and into his room, against his face and then his eyes. Slowly and without regard to time or chores, living arrangements in the Buckman household were changing with little notice until now; Grandpa Cyrus had not bellowed out anything about rising and shining or how much money was to be lost in the process. It must have been about five-thirty, which is when he would be haying Dud and laying out his rigging and checking on the goats on his way to get water for both.

He hitched his overalls as he flew down the stairs and out towards the barn, careful not to sound late or reveal that his Grandpa had himself overslept. Just the thought that could have happened was not only against science and probability, but had to be somewhere in scripture—it wouldn't happen.

He pulled the barn door open, breaching the darkness to the forbidden hay bin. He could vaguely see a brogan sticking out from under a pile of hay. "What on earth." As he approached the bin it came clear what was hooked to the brogan—his Grandfather. He uncovered him. In his hand was a bottle of corn mash, some seriously bad breath and a curse word or two when Cyrus tried to take the bottle. He was better to fetch his Grandmother who, was up building breakfast when he entered the kitchen. A part of him was amused at the fact that the Great, Cyrus Buckman the First, was out cold on the barn floor, hammered, smashed, plowed— whatever adjective might befit the situation.

They both went out to the scene while young Cyrus summoned all his elementary strength to get his Grandpa to his feet and Grandma guiding the way like a cheerleader. He was certainly drunk but not so much that he wasn't aware of what was happening, who was there and how he was going to explain it— not to his wife, as this was but one in a thousand times she had dealt with an episode, as she referred to them—but to his young boy, who might have known in some vague sense that he hit the bottle on occasion, but not like this; completely incapacitated, unable to utter as much as a single-syllable word without deliberate concentration.

They laid him to bed in his overalls, dirty, sweaty and intermittently conscious. As much as he tried to sit straight to remove his clothing it wasn't going to happen. His Grandmother glanced to young Cyrus with a depth of embarrassment that brought tears to her eyes, the kind he was so familiar with—frozen ones, the ones that never fell. This did not shock or bother little Cyrus at all. It bothered him though that his Grandma Mattie had been burdened so long with what he pretty much had known most his days and that she felt she had to keep him sheltered from it.

"Gran' I've knowed this a spell; ain't nothin' 'bout it that moves me either way. I am sorry you've had ta handle it all these years."

She smiled at him and kissed him on the cheek, reveling at his maturity and glimpsing his manhood that was not so far off.

"You bess get ready for school. I'll handle what's left. Go on."

Cyrus met up with Jake at the Burle crossing a couple minutes behind schedule which evoked the question: "What happened?" Jake inquired.

"What time is it?" Cyrus asked.

"A bit past seven."

"No, exactly", Cyrus commanded.

"Hmm, eighteen past."

Cyrus smiled broad and chuckled: "Two minutes late and you ask, 'what happened'?"

They were funny that way. The slightest, minuscule deviation from schedule, a verbal nuance or an unusual facial expression would bring concern and then confusion. Jake would begin laughing because he was expecting it from Cyrus (like he was supposed to know something), and then Jake would laugh louder because it was funny that Cyrus was clueless about what he was laughing at and that brought both of them to an outrageous roar. Funnier yet was that if a associated party was in ear shot, they found themselves laughing because the boys were, which made it even more funny to Cyrus and Jake—everyone was laughing and not a soul knew why.

"What? What is it, goon-head?" Jake asked playfully.

"Can't ya see it? We're sooo close that we see each other's rain clouds before the guy who's gunna get rained on does."

"You been at the hay bin?" Jake said drolly.

Cyrus raised his brows a bit, put his hands in his pockets and let out a sigh: "Naw, but Grandpa was; found him in the barn this mornin'. He was more out of it than I'd ever seen. Grandma thought I didn't know 'bout it."

"There're lots a folk who believe one way 'cause they think one way and that's the way everything is, but it ain't true is it?" Jake mumbled. "The old un's are s'posed to be the ones who show us the road, the way to go; but they're too busy loadin' us with feed sacks an' makin' us keep our head down."

Jake paused a moment while he stared at Cyrus' middle. They looked up at each other and smiled.

"What's that?" Jake inquired, motioning to Cyrus' belt that wasn't the usual piece of tanned leather.

"Mr Pritchett's surprise for my surprise. I told you I was gunna even the ground."

"I know, but . . . I mean, what's chainin' your britches together gunna do for ya?"

"Pritchett is easier to read than one of your comics. I know 'exactly what he's gunna try for. He's gunna make a run at pantsin' (termed pants'd having *your britches removed without consent) me at recess, maybe after lunch.*"

Jake laughed more at his ingenuity than the picture of Cyrus fighting to keep his pants up.

"How's . . . ", Jake began.

"Believe me, been here before and know what happens. After he and his cronies think they got the best of me, I unhitch this lil' hasp here and the chain jus' slides right out." He continued.

"Before any of 'em know one damn thing of what's 'bout to happen, I have beaten Pritchett like a plow horse to near death. His own ugly-ass mother won't know 'him."

Jake dropped his books and grabbed Cyrus by his shoulders, forcing his face to his and shaking him, "Don't do it, Pudger! I'll be with you and we'll work it like we do, if you whomp him with this chain the whole Pritchett gang will be a lit fire."

Cyrus looked into Jake's eyes while tears came to his own. It was as though everything piled on his shoulders was screaming for reconciliation: his Grandfather and his plight, his Grandmother's plight with his Grandfather's, and to top it off, his part in his Grandmother's plight and the rest of the world. Nothing appeared to have either a solution or an end—nothing!

"I can't do this anymore, Bruiser. I can't be scared like this anymore."

"I know", he said, pulling Cyrus' head to where their noses touched. "We're gunna fix it, fix it for good but not like this."

Cyrus smiled and caught himself laughing: "You ain't never lied to me—because of that everything you say we're gunna do I know we're gunna. Just us. You—and me."

CHAPTER ELEVEN

They climbed onto Mr Love's summer time pig-hay-moon hauling truck and found themselves a milk crate. They had to pass by Pritchett who gave both of them a good long eye contact that said little to either. Cyrus was ready. It didn't mean squat to him if he was banged up some, not anymore.

"So what's gunna happen?" Cyrus queried.

Jake shrugged his shoulders and turned back to thinking while Cyrus kept jobbing his thigh.

"I don't know right this minute, Pudger, so please leave me alone."

The thoughts of going through with plan A still maintained a course of its own and Cyrus hung to it as safety net. Taking some blows with a fist or a knee to the groin was not even a contingent worry—his fear at the immediate was losing his britches on the playground in front of God and all the pullets. It had happened before. Even some of teachers laughed.

First bell rang a minute or so after they arrived and Jake had already vanished. The only time during school they weren't together was when they were at their cubby holes at opposite ends of the five room school house. When Pritchett walked by Cyrus he slapped him on the back of the head so hard it knocked him to his knees. Several 'Ooooo's and 'Ouches' where muttered between witnesses, but other than that not a soul paid any more attention to Cyrus or assisted him. He came up watery-eyed and rubbed his head but just once. On his way to Ms Fugate's room he was deep in thought concerning Pritchett and what he was owed. This "thing" had never become physical until now. There was no way, no way in hell he was to turn the other cheek here. He set his books to the floor next to his desk and ambled over to Pritchett slowly, who at that moment stared at Cyrus with this vacant, no-nothing, squat-ta-piss look that had been there all this time but he just hadn't noticed. He knelt to Pritchett at eye level, his nose inches from his. Pritchett's expression went from big-man-on-campus to that of someone trying to hide a big bite of apple-crap pie.

"If I see ya at recess, I'm gunna screw ya into every color I can come up with. Even that sow of a mother won't recognize ya. The cops are gunna come . . . and I'll go with 'em, but not without yur red all over me."

"Ya think yur gunna take us all down? Pritchett answered with a quiver of utter embarrassment and shock. Cyrus had caught him so off guard that it even unnerved his backup squad, the bulk of who were speckled about the room and staring with open mouths.

"No, just yur ugly ass." He vaguely whispered as he walked to his desk slowly, assuredly. He was just short of pissing his pants though. Never had he ever done anything like that. It all happened so quickly that he didn't have time to think what he was to say—it was pure, poly-unsaturated, lard free emotion—and some high-dollar acting as well. When Ms Fugate began class her voice rolled around his ears a little less than an echo as though she were speaking from the backside of a barrel. His heart raced and he was troubled slowing his breath. Please don't let me pass out, he thought.

By third period bell and an hour from lunch, Cyrus's mind remained stuck in first gear since his impromptu and all he could think about was finding his Merlin. He caught a glimpse of Jake at his cubby and ran to safe-harbor.

"Oh my God!" Jake screamed, rushing at him.

"What?" Cyrus shouted back befuddled.

"I can't believe you! You stood up for yourself and ya have Pritchett so undone he's with Mr Burnside." Jake had already been told by at least half a dozen on-lookers moments after second period bell.

"What? He's *undone?* What's that mean? What's *undone* mean, Jake?"

"What did you say, Pudger? heard bunches a stories, but never got the same one twice—some said ya told him you were gunna kill him; some said ya told him you were gunna kill his family and 'bout being bloody and fightin' the police and everything . . . "

". . . fightin' the police?" he whispered, standing speechless and staring into a dense chasm of gawkers behind Jake, like reporters waiting for a salacious bit of inflated story that they were to cut-n-paste however they believed it happened anyway.

He leaned to Jake's ear: "Meet me at the cistern."

Another fine element of Buckman spontaneity because getting there without being noticed by faculty or Pritchett would be impossible. Passage was through the middle of everything—but, whatever. It was a huge deal and he was in a huge place.

He was at the cistern first, not half a minute after the lunch bell, but Jake took longer as usual and kept Cyrus wound tighter than an eight day clock. He was a basket case.

"How the hell can I get here five minutes before you and we're in the SAME CLASS?"

"Be calm baby brother, I got us faded."

Just below view from the lunch arena, they sat hollering and spitting in each other's face for a time until his presence was felt. Yep, Mr Pritchett and then some—more than before like he'd been combing the town, maybe outside too. There was a face or two of unknowns.

"What say there, Buckman?" Pritchett gummed in his semi-toothless grin.

Cyrus edged his hand to the hasp on his belt. He glanced over to Jake who was sitting there unfettered, cool and calm as any garden vegetable with his arms around his knees and rocking back and forth.

"I ain't got no truck with you, Thompson, so you can go . . . unless you want to join in."

"What is with you, Pritchett? It's like you live to be hated by your own."

"I got friends, Thompson, jus' look 'round ya." Pritchett said, waving his hand about.

"Yeah, well so do we."

With all the timing of a conductor's baton roughly a dozen fifth graders and a half dozen sixth graders surrounded the caucus, stopped, stood and folded their arms. Farley Thompson, Jake's first cousin, who was the sixth grader everyone spoke about shaving after gym, was the one who rallied the group for his baby cuz. He threw in a free-bee too. A get outta jail free card of sorts:

"Any you stump breakers from the other side even let it cross your mind 'bout bothering these two—EVER again! The pretty shades of red and pink will be your favorite colors for a long spell. Now y'all know me. Ya know ma family. We don't look the other way anymore."

Well, lunch was over and Cyrus was stupefied by what he had witnessed: someone had just averted the Black Hand from executing Ferdinand; WWI was over before it began and all the soldiers just went home. Wow! Just like that; how life imitates history.

"Hey", he hollered to Jake. "Is this done? Is it over?"
"I 'magine", he smiled.

He should have never doubted him, but he had and it pained him; pained him to the point he had to tell Jake if there were to be a real, straight-up brotherhood. Though not as big a thing as he made it, it did set his integrity back after he had struggled the time to get it as close to parity with his brother's as he could. It's how Jake taught him.

It was Friday, weather was a bit brisk but workable, bondage from Pritchett had been expunged and Halloween was next week—tent out tonight! It would be okay on all sides and by all parties. Ever since the "barn incident", as it came to be referred by Grandma Mattie, his Grandfather placed resolve for anything concerning Cyrus in Grandma's lap, jurisdiction that included chores, school and over-nights. It stood fine by Cyrus not to be watched, cajoled or occasionally whacked for missing a chore or leaving a gate open.

The afternoon ride to the Burle crossing from school was as quiet as a library. The whispers overheard concerned mostly Mr Buckman's soliloquy at first period. Even the girls were cooing over Cyrus' bravery, which at this immediate posture was of only slight concern to him; slight meaning that Cyrus was interested in only one girl's attention: Cheyenne Hold. The bit of gristle here concerned the fact that Cheyenne was blood kin to Pritchett, like a cousin of sorts, but distant enough that lineage didn't extend to holiday gatherings and such from what Cyrus had pieced. Didn't matter though, Cyrus liked someone so secretly that not even Jake had wisp of it, for a couple of reasons, with the most important just identified.

They sat next to each other saying nothing or even paying any attention to what was quietly transpiring around them and concerning them. Although it was hard for Cyrus not to look around the bus and take in a little bit of this hoorah, it was enough to know that the "Pritchett Affair" was now a memory and he was free. His thoughts waned towards that evening and the time he was going to spend with Jake; his Zeus. Every pistol had been loaded ready to fire and weren't; they never left their holsters and all because of Jake. Life had never been as rich as it was at that moment.

Cyrus was in a scurry to get to the fort before dusk. He wanted a real fire this night instead of the usual, quaint, squat-ta-piss marshmallow makers. In fact there were several deviations from the norm Cyrus had planned and a couple he knew Jake would buck the bridle off on; but, the event that occurred not a handful of hours prior could not go without an honors court he felt.

He toted a larger sack than usual for an evening in the creek, one Jake could see from inside the washout where he had arrived first this time. This really jerked Cyrus' chain because Jake was never on time to anything of importance: "Un-stinking believable", he muttered.

Though it was more difficult yet safer to come by the creek's bottom, with its unsettled rocks, washed up brush piles, and having to slide down one side then painfully back up the other, Cyrus still chose to navigate the weathered oak that lay across from his side to the fort's entrance, and with every step bemoaning permission just to snap in two.

"Yur gunna be sorry the day that rotten tree gives and ya hit that creek bottom and those boulders", Jake poised.

"Yeah, but totin' all this down and back up don't seem as fun as searchin' out the hard spots and getting' here lots quicker."

Jake gathered some branches and brush for the fire before Cyrus got there, but not enough for his call. When he was through collecting and piling it near covered the entrance.

"No, you ain't firin' that thing up all at once, not while I'm in here", Jake commanded. "Not only will it be seen for miles, we won't be able ta get out."

"Okay, I'll make it smaller, but want somethin' bigger than those teacup warmers like before."

With the fire working to its zenith, Cyrus set the bedding in the hole while Jake lit candles and laid supper out on a tissue—deer jerky, two apples and two bottles of crème soda.

"Bes' save yur apple for breakfast", Jake said.

"Naw, I got breakfast—sardines, lil' bit-a Mattie Fay's hot water cornbread and . . . this for you and me after apples and jerky", Cyrus added, pulling a pint fruit jar from his burlap sack that was half full of a brown solution.

"What's that?" Jake asked.

"Whatdaya think?"

Cyrus opened it and took a small sip. "Wow! It don't burn as much and ya won't get sick if ya jus' sip it."

"Is that . . . is that whiskey?"

"Yep, just a tad for celebration."

Jake lay back and stared at him with bewilderment. "After all you've seen with yur Grandpa and yur doing' the same?"

"I knew you'd go south 'bout this", Cyrus shook his head. "I don't care anymore Jake, 'bout anything more than you and me and I want this tonight. I want you and me ta sip down this bit-a mash and jus' talk and laugh and not think . . . jus' this one night."

Jake nodded, got up and walked to the entrance of the fort and sat down on a limestone slab.

"You mad at me?" Cyrus whispered, sitting next to him with jar in hand.

"No."

The fire behind lit the creek bed and cast their silhouettes on the opposite side as though two giants were communing. Cyrus held the jar overhead and its shadow made it a barrel. They marveled at the gestures and dances their figures made. Jake reached over and took the jar from him.

"Don't smash it", he pleaded.

He eased the lid off, took a sniff, made a face and then took a sip.

"Hum, ain't all that bad. In a way it tastes pretty good."

They sat for the better part of an hour, passing it back and forth, commenting how the burn became less with every swallow and the warmth from the inside increased.

"Wow! Look at the sky", Jake pointed.

Cyrus leaned back to look and fell off their perch. His head struck a stone from behind that dazed him and he was at such an angle that he couldn't sit up. Both laughed like new found drunks, as oblivious as they were unencumbered by their discovery, and incensed towards the adults who had kept it from them for so long. How much easier would had life been?

Jake pulled him up right and they stumbled into their crib where both lay semi-conscious and murmuring nonsensical about the day; you know, about Pritchett and being brothers forever and all. Jake pulled off his shirt, rolled it into a ball and placed it behind Cyrus' head.

"Why ja do that? You're gunna get cold", Cyrus scolded.

"Naw, got a quilt and I got you", Jake smiled. "I love sleepin' by you Pudger, besides you gotta knot on your skull that's gunna be sore as hell in the mornin'."

"Hey Bruiser, is there anybody you really like at school?"

"You're kiddin' right?" Jake chuckled.

"No, I mean besides me, like . . . "

". . . A girl?" Jake interrupted.

"Yeah."

"Yeah I do. Never said nothin' to her though. Never done much but look. I never been real easy with girls, and besides, never thought too much of ma-self neither."

"Are you kidding? Girls are talkin' about you all the time."

"Don't be greenin' me, Pudge."

"I ain't. I hear 'em all the time at my cubby."

"Who?"

"Couldn't say to a pinpoint, I jus' hear 'em gabberin' about how you're strong an' big an' all—you know. Who do ya like?"

"Ah, ain't no account."

"No, who is she?"

Well, I jus' watch her from a ways-a-way kinda. She ain't got no reason at all to know I fancy her. I just think she's real pretty."

"Who?" Cyrus asked eagerly.

"Cheyenne."

Cyrus' expression drifted from excitement to maudlin. "Cheyenne", he gurgled.

"Yeah. What's wrong?"

He lay back and shook his head in a bit of disbelief, but it truly didn't hit him all that roughly. Cheyenne was a popular girl and somewhat the kind who was unattainable, so he personally had her high on his shelf just way in the back. If any guy could be friends with her it would be Jake. He had it all: looks, personality and most of all, magic. Something Cyrus believed was that the only true essence ladies went for and which was the very thing he had none of; however, if he were to hang around Jake long enough, the one the world knew unequivocally was his brother, he'd pick it up.

"You're kidding me!" Jake blurted as he rose over Cyrus. "You like her too."

Cyrus smiled broadly and nodded his head, ". . . but I ain't no competition for my brother, and don't care ta be. She's pretty an' all, and I like watchin' her, but she's more a pullet for you."

"I already told ya I ain't so easy with girls . . . they scare me, Pudge. Don't know why but I get all confused and wobbly when I get 'round ones I like. Now put me 'round Pritchett's sisters an' I'm easy as rain off the roof, jus' kinda struggle when I see Cheyenne comin' my way. What's it you like 'bout her?"

Cyrus giggled uncomfortably, "Well, I like her skin kinda", he began, watching Jake's expression. "I like how soft it looks, and when I get close enough, she smells real good."

Jake smiled and agreed. Both were shy about admitting these things and it was particularly difficult for Cyrus since this was truly the first he'd ever considered about feeling for a girl much less talking about it.

The inevitable question hung in the air thicker than the occasional backwash from the fire and Cyrus was dead pan in asking it: "You ever kissed before?" Jake looked at him with raised brows, turned a nice shade of pink and timidly shook his head.

"Naw, never had the chance come up."

"Neither have I. Don't rightly know I could without makin' a fool."

Jake fumbled with the quilt and Cyrus stared at the fire, both seemingly with yet another question that wouldn't be as easy as the last but much more critical if not taboo.

"What?" Jake asked.

"Whatdaya mean what?"

"I daknow, thought you said something."

"No."

They stared at each other for a spell and Jake edged over to Cyrus, his face close to his.

"Are you thinkin'-a kissin' me?", Cyrus laughed.

"Ya-know, I was wonderin . . . just ta see what it was like. It wouldn't be serious."

"Would you think ill of me if I said I didn't care? I really don't. I mean I chewed yur gum before, drank pop after you, what would be the difference?" Cyrus asked.

"Why would I?"

"'Cause probably it would a-bit strange, I guess."

"Strange to who? Who's here?"

Jake leaned into his face slowly and lightly kissed a laughing Cyrus who just as quickly stopped and stared.

"Now we know and don't have to be made a fool." Jake whispered.

They fell to sleep next to each other and what had transpired that evening was never spoke of again.

CHAPTER TWELVE

"Hey, you gunna go to the Halloween thing at school?" Jake asked while kicking a sardine can. "Your Grandma's makin' a cake for the walk."

"My Grandma? Geminnie, she dotes on you more than her blood . . . but then you are my blood", Cyrus smiled.

Jake had become so a part of the Buckman household that his overnight on school nights seemed more a rule than a pleasure. From every angle it was a positive thing though: Mr Thompson's dream of a mother's influence; Grandpa Cyrus' view of Jake and how much he wanted Cyrus to emulate him, and his Grandma Mattie's contentment at seeing her Grandson grow out of his private world. All of this without mention of what they did for each other in just plain learning to live life. It was too easy to fall in love with Jake. They watched him bring Cyrus out of his private world of banged up wooden ponies and imaginary Indians to their world of real problems and heartaches. Nearly ten and still much a boy, his reflection of Jake, the world, and how it all fit in this giant cauldron became both their magic wonder.

"Oh, I guess soooo", Cyrus answered slowly, lost in thought.

"What's with you there, Pudge. Any slower and you'd be backin' up", Jake laughed.

"Naw, I am goin'; we're goin' together—right?" Cyrus said.

"Yeah, you can make a run after that lil' chicken", Jake mused.

"She likes you, Bruiser. She don't cotton to me. Dang you are a stubborn cuss."

"Me!" Jake blurted.

The indelible marks the "Pritchett Affair" made upon his timid soul had seemingly disappeared—even Pritchett, on a few occasions, found it in his darkness to acknowledge them when they crossed paths. Jake never responded, but Cyrus, the soft-hearted and caring individual he was, forever believed they would all become bosom buddies someday. Jake, however, was the more pragmatic and knew to his bones that Pritchett was still on the prowl for a chink in their armor; some crack in their veneer overlooked in the planning phases of the Farley Thompson showdown. Cyrus smiled at Pritchett when they passed him on the bus and much to Jake's chagrin.

"Will you quit that crap!" Jake whispered loudly.

"What?"

"He will never be your friend, Cyrus, or mine; he's a snake in the grass, and all he's waiting for is a chance to strike when he can get away with it."

"Hey, he waves sometimes. Maybe he really wants to be friends?"

They sat to their respective crates.

"Look, if you think for a second that Pritchett is gunna forgive being embarrassed by my cousin, yur crazier than a crap house rat. The Pritchett's are all spiteful folk, Cy. They work to find where yur weak, then . . ."

Cyrus interrupted: "Wait, how is it you know all *the Pritchett's*?"

Jake leaned to the canvas flap and motioned for Cyrus to come closer.

"My Pa an' Mr Pritchett bought in on a passel-a hogs together 'bout three, four years back: sows an' boars. Pritchett already had a bunch-a paddocks that would be strong enough ta hold four and five hundred pounders. My Pa's part was to build a farrowing barn where the sows could farrow their litters an' all. Everything went pretty well until Pa finished the barn; then, everything began to go south. Whole litters at a time showed up missing. Sow would go in, come out weeks later with no piglets. When Pa tried to find out what was happening, Pritchett locked him out of the property and called the law. The law eventually sided with Pritchett since the pigs were on his property and most of the bills of sale were in his name alone. Only when Pa was actually there did his name get on the paper. Even though we lost a lot, Pa was smart enough not to gamble everything."

"Geez", Cyrus muttered.

"Pa ain't never said a word to anyone about what happened", Jake concluded.

Jake's portrayal of the Pritchett left him to wonder just how clueless he actually was about life, its affairs and the people in it. After all, Jake had brought him from his earthen den into the sunlight of the Spirit; the world of living, breathing, feeling spirits who reflected what his private world did not.

After chores they milled about the Buckman barn trying to figure how they were going to be costumed for the big carnival. Grandma Mattie suggested they show up as father and baby time, with reasoning that it wouldn't be too difficult to suit out and definitely original. That wasn't going to happen though. Grandpa didn't have any suggestions, nor did Mr Thompson, which pretty much melded with the men's thinking on Halloween. It wasn't a day the men felt worthy of recognition, worthy of anything.

It was obvious to the boys, who stood slouched against the foyer wall with raised brows and staring at Grandma, that the only creative juices there were being sloshed in a Mason jar just behind them.

"Why don't you boys see what the Thompson barn will yield?" Grandma queried.

"Hey", Jake muttered. "Let's see what S.T. might have."

S.T. had been with the Thompson clan since Jake's seventh birthday. They met in Pearl, Mississippi when FDR was in his first term and folks were still looking just to make it one day to the next. The streets stayed full of folks even in small towns since every able-bodied soul looked for work. Those from the farm fared better than town folk since staples came better with decent weather and some luck. S.T, Sterling and Jake came together out of need; Jake was too young for the field, his father couldn't watch both and S.T. needed work. So, they found each other.

They stormed the barn entrance in a race that was shoulder to shoulder and they didn't quite make it through. Both of them rolled around on the dirt floor moaning while S.T. appeared from the other end toting water and chuckling at what he knew happened.

"Whats ever ya here fo, better make it quick cuz I gots lots ta do!" S.T. said.

They explained their dilemma which didn't bring more than a vague smile. S.T. smoothed his hand over his bald head in a state of concentration, occasionally looking over at the boys, scrunching his lips up to a pucker and then back down.

"I thinks I gots the perfect line fo you tadpoles." And that he did.

All three joined in on a scavenger hunt of sorts after S.T. shared his intention for their costume and identified what was needed.

"How we gunna get corks, S.T?" Jake asked.

"You jus' leaves that to me. You all fetch a red saddle blanket, those low-quarter black shoes we use fo stall cleanin' and in ma room next the bed is a tube-a white salve—then we be in business."

S.T. worked on the boys for about an hour before the carnival opened. They liked what they saw, but how were the big folks going to view this? Both made it to the Buckman front porch in slow steps so as not to sweat overly and cause their faces to streak. Facing each other it was difficult to keep from falling apart with laughter. If they weren't kicked out of the carnival there were sure to win best costume.

"Whatdaya think, Pudgy? Think they're gunna twist off?" Jake whispered.

"Da-know. Grandma won't give a twitch, but Grandpa an' yur Pa may go over the falls in a flat bottom boat. Really 'pends on how many times they filled that fruit jar."

Jake entered first with Cyrus glued to his back. From the kitchen there came bits of laughter that were easily attached to their inebriated fathers. Grandma could be seen in the sitting room, her snow white hair barely topping the rocker while she darned socks and hummed hymns in concert to the buzz of the cicadas. They sneaked in behind her and Cyrus whispered: "Gran'ma!" When she turned her mouth fell open wide.

"Lord-a mercy, children!" she startled. "Oh, this is richer than eatin' a pecan pie at a sittin'. Jus' wait til your Pa and Gramps see this."

When they entered the kitchen neither knew what to expect; both boys stood motionless at the edge of the table between the men. Grandpa Cyrus leaned forward around Cyrus and Mr Thompson forward towards Jake.

"Mr Thompson?" Grandpa Cyrus slurred.

"Yes, Mr Buckman."

"Are you seein' two Negroes a-holdin' lamps in front of us?"

"I do believe so, Mr Buckman", Mr Thompson answered in the same diminutive stumble as he leaned into his son's face. "Yep, this-un's a negro alright—bit scrawny too, and something is a smidgen familiar 'bout him."

"It's me, Pa", Jake answered tersely.

The men bellowed in laughter that came like a gunshot, slapping their knees and acting like fools they were. Neither Jake or Cyrus said a word.

"Grandma, wouldja give us ride to the school?" Cyrus asked.

"Yep, and we'll just let them . . . well, I almost forgot the cake."

"I got it", Jake trumpeted.

As they rode down the dirt road, Jake stared back to the house in thought about what life was to be like for them later; were they bound to be like their caregivers, like their fathers? Is this what it's all about? He looked over to Cyrus, who at the moment was concerned with his bottom against the hard truck bed and the associated potholes his grandmother seemed to go out of her way to hit, and he smiled.

"What?" Cyrus yelled over the road roar.

"Our folks—back there", Jake pointed behind. "They won't recall us even bein' there will they?"

They jumped from the truck bed before it was on school property and Grandma honked her disapproval, but they felt their costume's to be a hit and wanted to enter in stealth.

"Think anyone's gunna guess us out?" Cyrus queried.

"I da-know, kinda only care about getting a cake."

"How much your Pa spring for?" Cyrus asked.

"You mean how much did I earn . . . two bits, and I plan on spending it all for a cake. You?"

"Eighteen cents, I think. What happens if ya pop a no-hitter and don't get chose? I'd at least hold back half so I could buy one from a no-account who'd just as soon have the money. "

This was about the only tiny, minuscule, ever-so-invisible character defect he witnessed in Cyrus that pissed him off to no end: his consistent practice and near worship of the glass half-empty thing, and never failing to rub some of it off on Jake as he prepared to do something like WIN a cake!

"If you weren't such a friend I'd throw you to the pavement!" Jake blasted.

"What? Why so mad?"

"Tired of yur negative thinking, Cy? I got so much negative 'round me that I'm drownin' in it and nobody even knows . . . so tired Cy", he finished in a whisper.

"Why you like this?"

"I'm gunna walk around a bit—I need to think some."

Cyrus set his lantern on a hay bale that was stacked with a number of others for seating around a canopy. He lay down and stared up at the sky, the full moon and all the stars that surrounded it. This was his escape and it never failed him: the night sky, the fall breeze inculcated with the smell of swamp moisture, a distant train whistle, one star, one thought, all equaled his dream. It's how it came to him from his window box, everything at his summons: the pecan tree's wave, the cicada's hypnotic buzz, the cloud's drift that soothed him as the arms of his mother's embrace and the face of the soul who loved him—features he could not see but knew. It was real because he felt it; it held him without touching, it was there and they knew each other so well.

"Hey you!" came a soft voice from inside the darkness; these voices with absolutely no respect or consideration for privacy, he thought.

"What! . . . ", Cyrus yelled. "You just scare the freckles off someone . . ."

"Sorry Cyrus. Hey, that near rhymes."

"Cheyenne?" he muttered nervously.

"Uh huh", she answered stepping closer. "What are you doing way out here—by yourself? Wow, that costume is to die for!"

"Jake went for a walk an' should be comin' round the corner—as we we sing", Cyrus laughed uneasily. "You know, the nursery rhyme . . . the song?"

"Jake?"

"Well . . . yeah, ah, your lookin' for him ain't ya?"

She chuckled uncomfortably and asked if she could sit with him.

"Sure", he began, standing to give her a seat. "I promise I won't bore ya. I won't even talk."

"No silly, I want you to talk, and you can sit right here", she said, patting the hay bale

"You do", he laughed, "Okay, Whatdaya wanna hear? Ah . . . why are ya staring at me?"

She smiled the prettiest smile he had ever seen. A small gust brought her smell to swirl about him—there wasn't a description he could grasp. Her skin of alabaster (if he knew what that was) looked as soft as a week old kid goat's. An image he thought better pressed unsaid. She edged close to him and he was uncomfortable.

"What?" Cyrus uttered.

"You're scared to death of me, Cyrus Buckman."

"Ah, I . . . well, I ain't . . . I think *scared* is a bit strong. You might could say I was *runnin' amuck.*"

"Running amuck?"

"Sounds a bit like something scourin' don't it?" Cyrus explained genuinely.

"Scourin'?"

"Yeah, well, when I heard Grandma yellin' it, Chelsea, our Guernsey, was just so happenin' to be scourin' something fierce— so I kinda put it together, ya know."

"So, you're *scourin'*?"

"Oh no, not me. What I was meanin' was that I'd rather be running amuck than deemed scared of ya."

"Cyrus . . . I ain't here about scours or running amuck, or anything else except just to sit with you."

"How old are you?" Cyrus asked.

"Ah, I'll be eleven in January—I started a little late."

"Yeah, hmm, **you** are just 'bout as old as, guess who . . . Jake! Ya know we're brothers?"

"Cyrus, Jake's nice an' all . . . but I'm kinda wanting to be around you", she said. "If that's okay with you."

"Why?" Cyrus answered dumbfounded.

"Because . . . I da-know", she fumbled. "I like the way you smile, the way you say things--the way you walk."

"The way I walk? Whoa, he's really gunna be mad."

"Who? Jake? What is it with Jake?"

"You gotta be kidding, right? Everything."

She stood from the bale and adjusted herself to facing him and instructed him to do likewise, which he did.

"Gimme your hand", she said.

"Which?"

"Either", she chuckled. "Turn it so I can see your palm."

Holding his one hand, she combed his palm in a massaging way that halted his world on its axis. Even though her skin was softer than he could have ever imagined and her attention to him more mesmerizing than any magician could command, it was her maternity that brought his train to take a dirt road. Feelings and thoughts welled inside that were as foreign to him as the universe: the stars and the heavens that held them; this place he recognized from his dreams.

She inched close to his once boyish face that was now chalked in foot salve and burnt cork; the image in itself enough to cause recoil as from a hot flame, he imagined, yet she kept coming, her breath against his.

"Are you scared?" she whispered. He did not answer. Their lips touched and he could not move.

"Hey y'all", Jake blurted, stepping to their midst and sitting behind Cyrus, his hand on his shoulder.

Cheyenne stood back and watched them, "Ah, I gotta meet my Ma at the cake walk. I'll see you Monday Cyrus J—and you too Jake."

"Hey, how'd she know?" Cyrus muttered.

"Know what?" Jake asked.

"That I was called Cyrus J."

"Maybe she's an *imagine* too", Jake laughed.

She disappeared from the moonlight when she past the canopy, but not out of mind. It had been a big night for the both of them: Cyrus' kiss and Jake's revelation that his younger protégé was growing up.

"Was you made a fool?" Jake asked.

"Naw", he smiled.

CHAPTER THIRTEEN

The carnival had become his life's zenith to that point. When he began daydreaming about his new buddy, Cheyenne, who was exactly that and no more, his feelings became muddled and blushingly unexplainable. Even though Jake was totally responsible for his new outlook on life and would forever be his image, Cheyenne seemed to place a whole new perspective on recess. Though they spoke little and only when moments presented themselves, he orchestrated those he could without being overly awkward—moments between happenstance and contrived, that is. Either way, the instances came out awkward and Jake loved gigging him about it.

"Hey goose, you don't have to corral her every chance you get", Jake scolded. "She ain't cattle, ya know."

"I ain't corralin'—am I?"

There was a tenderness mixed with some jealousy since Jake juggled affection for her as well; something that was confusing to him because he was typically the one the girls fluttered about and gave all the attention. He set it aside though as a tribute for Cyrus, not to mention the enjoyment of watching his *little* brother stumble about trying to make flight.

At recess Cyrus saw Pritchett with several of his toadies staring his way, something he hadn't seen lately. Why Pritchett could not find it to leave him alone, that old and familiar coldness of fear nipped at him again. The image of getting *pants'd* in front of Cheyenne was unthinkable. It would be like zipping yourself up and having your first grade teacher unzip you—well, somewhat like it. He looked for Jake who was yards from him and talking with others. He threw a handful of gravel at him.

"What?" Jake mouthed with a shrug of annoyance as he ambled over. "What?"

"Pritchett. He's over there and keeps lookin' at me."

"Pudger, he ain't gunna do nothin' in the open; Farley's standin' just over there."

Jake shadowed his forehead with his hand and stared at Pritchett until they locked eyes. He then nodded towards Farley, who in turn winked at Pritchett.

"See Pudgie, just like Ms Fugate learned us—checks and balances", Jake mused. "Hey, let's do a tent-out this weekend?" he asked.

"Yeah, okay."

"You reckon, ah? You reckon I could bring someone . . .?" Jake asked.

"Who?" Cyrus interrupted.

"Pritchett?"

"You ain't funny. That ain't funny."

"Just joshin', but it would be fun if we had someone else see our place. It's like havin' a race horse pinned in a paddock you won't let anyone see."

"I ain't too sure I'd really want anyone else in our place, Jake. Main reason is they would tell and then more would know. Before you know it, it wouldn't be ours no more—it'd be the feed store with a bunch-a old hackers sittin' around playin' dominoes and tellin' lies. Think about it."

For the first time he could recall his little protégé made a poignant, rational point. Jake smiled and ran his fingers up Cyrus' forehead and through his hair somewhat like a puppy's.

"Sometimes you set me back, Pudger."

Pritchett had something brewing and Jake sensed it, but didn't let on to Cyrus. It had little to do with him in the first place, and then, just about everything. Pritchett, like everyone, knew what Cyrus meant to Jake and it seemed his gunning for him was for that reason solely. The throw-down that nearly occurred between their father's came so close to happening that it still gave Jake troubled thoughts.

He was on the porch behind the wood box one night when Mr Pritchett came over to worm a signature out of his father on some papers of ownership. Mr Thompson agreed to it if he had proof there was anything there he owned. Jake heard the threats exchanged and knew both of them to be credible enough to follow through.

The Constable and county moonshiner, who shared more than legitimate business dealings with Mr Pritchett, was part and parcel to how the hog operation went down. Jake knew more than his father gave him credit. Even though his father let on to him that this "deal" was over and done with, there were still embers glowing that bled over into their children's lives.

None of this truly had a thing to do with Cyrus except to create more tension, which made Pritchett more the bur under his saddle. In fact, Jake's eye over Cyrus had now become more protective than loving because of this thing between the families. It was difficult for Jake to keep the bridges separate.

The things that transpired on the school grounds, like with Cheyenne, was the loving part. Even though his heartstrings for her was plucked a time or two, he knew without doubt that

Cheyenne's favor lay with Cyrus and there was no way he would attempt to rock that boat.

He came to be this way because of his father, who the towns folk came to know in like regard. Just like everybody though, there were character flaws that small town hood-winkers would shred an individual over, like a more than occasional nip at the bottle; but, the general consensus was to overlook them in light of specific trials endured. It was like that in the day, to dismiss character blemishes that were, for the most part, intolerable unless there was a reason: lose a wife to a slow, debilitating disease, it was acceptable to become a drinker.

His father's drinking was noticeable during his mother's illness but worsened during his dealings with the Pritchett's. Like most children, especially the ones as bright as Jake, he knew where his father hid his mash and would stay hidden for hours in the barn watching him finish a bottle. Mr Thompson would sit propped on a hay pile next to the tack room, swigging and muttering circumstances; acting the times of being with his mother and in a fashion as though she were sitting right there in a conversation. It was through these moments he came to know his mother and the kind of woman she was. It was also the time he came to miss her near as much as his father.

CHAPTER FOURTEEN

"I don't know why you gotta act like the butt end of a mule, Jake!" Cyrus said incensed "All my days I ain't never seen a person work as hard as you makin' someone mad 'ceptin my Grandpa."

"And I don't know why you're so wadded up about nothin'", Jake mumbled. "It really has nothin' to do with you. Well, it does and it doesn't—kinda funny that way", he chuckled to himself.

It was now six in the eve and they were only halfway to the fort because Jake and his father had been ensnared in a conversation of sorts that shouldn't have been: Jake refused to understand why his Pa would not acknowledge Cyrus as his brother, which was the foolishness in itself because he wasn't, but then he was—or is. Can you see the craziness? It all depended upon how it was viewed. Jake's contention was that blood had not a thing to do with some-one being kin, it was the heart that did. It was the only place that couldn't be muddled by the outside world. It was the place that was real, truly real. "Cyrus is closer than *any* kin could ever be!" he said.

"I told you, that's what came to mind when you and my Pa showed up in the barn all of a sudden", Jake stated. "I was getting somethin' when you surprised me, that's all."

"What?"

"Some-thing. You'll know soon enough."

Their contention over the controversial embattlement of *how* Cyrus was his brother without like mothers continued through their scurry to the fort.

There were rituals observed when they arrived: Jake straightened up, checked for varmints and other trash while Cyrus combed the gulch for firewood and set the bedding. Supper was anything scavenged from the kitchen that wouldn't smell or spoil and was easy to hide. S.T. had known what was happening for a time and usually left something out that was good and wholesome, like corn fritters fried in goo grease balled up in molasses with chunks of pork and chicken. To any extent, they were here without the monitoring of adults, their hollow squabble, their rule restrictions and their smell.

It wasn't so much the thrill of overnighting in the wild, unshackled by mindless questions and plastic concerns, that made these moments so enriching; or even the time spent acting they were on their own, sitting in front of their campfire, spitting and picking their nose in between stories shadowed by the folklore of those heard at the feed store. It was because they were together, unveiled, unfettered and unobstructed. They were both free to be what they were in spirit that was without condemnation.

"Sorry 'bout my fit", Jake whispered, sitting candles upright and dusting the ledge.

"Don't matter none. Why was you so wadded up anyways?"

"--a surprise", Jake smiled broadly.

"I'm guessin' my Gran'pa finally got to your Pa and now he dislikes me too, huh?" Cyrus asked.

He jeered at Cyrus with a look of disdain as he sat back against the rolled bedding behind him, reaching inside and pulling out a Government-issue Colt .45. Cyrus glanced to it and rolled his eyes with a vague grin camouflaging concern.

"Whataya think there, Pudgie?", Jake mused. "Why do you feed on those kind-a thoughts?" he questioned nonchalantly, setting the pistol in his lap and watching Cyrus' bewilderment. "My Pa thinks fine of you, he just don't understand *us*."

"What's there to understand? His prize winning rooster hobbled by a spotted chicken—and is that real?" Cyrus said, nodding to the pistol he couldn't take his eyes from.

"Ya know, I just as soon bash your head in than be *hobbled* by you; but, I want to be around you, every time I am around you—get it! You make me feel poorly when you banter that way, like I should be from the same mud or something, and I ain't—and neither are you, Cyrus J."

"I guess I watch how everyone is around you, and then I see how they are 'round me; the rest is simple math."

". . . and you ain't ever been good at it, so quit. Take it as it is, not as you see it. Nothing is as it seems, Cyrus!"

"Ain't known any other way, Bruiser; everything has always been the way it seems. If I feel I'm gunna get hit, I usually do."

"Yeah, it's real—the gun. Found it hidden in the kitchen and guess he don't know it's gone."

"Can I hold it?"

Jake handed it to him. Cyrus seemed more amazed by the weight than its presence, "Is it loaded?"

"Yeah."

"Ever shot it?" Cyrus asked, pointing up at their silhouettes against the cave wall.

"No."

"Then how you know it's loaded?"

"I undressed it a dozen times—scared to fire it off though. S.T. would tell Pa for sure."

"Wow", Cyrus muttered when he handed it back.

Jake brought a deck of cards to show Cyrus the game of rummy. The cards and learning a new game were as unimportant as Ms Fugate's history of electricity, but in a manner of speaking, was a horse their attention could ride awhile until the more important issues of life could be addressed, some of which Jake still had hidden. Jake was queer about talking seriously, even when alone during campfire fodder, but Cyrus? Well, he was freer than a range rooster on discussing faults and weaknesses, especially with Jake. A fire to Cyrus was somewhat like a bottle to grown men: it made words come easier; and then, Cyrus never shirked ways to lighten his load and talking was the cheapest route, at least cheaper than the roads Jake took.

"You didn't answer me", Cyrus said, picking cards into his hand.

"What?"

"Why you brought that thing?"

"Dang Pudger, you gunna wet-nelly this thing or act the part?"

"No, I'm just askin'."

"Well, there's sometin' I wanna show you a time after dark; that's if you wanna play a bit-a fun on Pritchett?"

"I reckon I might" Cyrus answered uneasily. Anything that came after the word "Pritchett" honed his attention to such a point that it brought a discomfort, enough at times to make him ill at his stomach.

"I got somethin' planned that'll be *real* fun", Jake added with a smile.

"Like . . ."

"Like, you'll see when I'm ready."

They shared a fritter and a crème soda while Cyrus studied rummy with little attention. Spades and hearts were their usual game, but Jake was the soothsayer and Cyrus didn't buck it. They spoke a bit on Cheyenne but the topic was too hot, mostly for Jake. His feelings for her were deep and Cyrus knew it, which was enough not to bring her up. Trying to get a handle on these out-of-nowhere feelings for her was as difficult as getting the stripes off of a Zebra and Jake was the only life scientist that he knew.

"What do you think Pritchett's really like—underneath all that ugly?" Jake laughed, taking a sip from a fruit jar he had hidden under his arm. "Dang that stings!"

"What!—you brought a gun and that?" Cyrus said angrily.

"Now what!" Jake said.

"If I wanna be like my grandfather, that's all I need", Cyrus said pointing.

"Back up, brother. There ain't more than two fingers here, and you don't have to if you don't want."

Now in the full regalia of manhood they snickered back and forth in boyish whispers, laughing and cajoling each other on salient points, like those of mothers and fathers and why they were born. What the whiskey afforded was amazing and wonderful. Cyrus mentioned only once about the day after, the being ill and such, but that conversation came and went as unattended as a church fart.

"Well, I jus' so happen to know where S.T. has his traps", Jake garbled.

"What traps?"

"The ones he catches varmints with, idiot."

"I didn't know."

"The burden of what you don't know would bust the sides of a corn crib", Jake said.

"Okay, consider 'em busted—now what about the traps?"

"You know where Miller's Pass is, just behind . . ."

Cyrus interrupted, "Yeah, yeah I know."

"Okay—where?"

They busted into laughter loud and hard, rolling into the dirt, into the fire and back until they were completely without breath. It wasn't from anything more than Jake, his impeccable timing and the fact that they knew each other better than God—and the whiskey.

"Okay, okay—Miller's about a mile and a-half from here, but if we walk it in the creek bed it'll take less time and we won't risk bein' shot at" Jake said.

"Sot at!—I mean, shot at!" Cyrus laughed.

"Oh yeah, anybody porch settin' is gunna have a gun and will pop you after dark."

"Maybe this ain't such a cream idea", Cyrus contended.

"Take your dress off, lil'brother; you're a horse and you can't *ever* run with mules again!"

A good hour after their typical lights out they were ready to head to Miller's Pass. Light-headed and a bit disoriented, Cyrus gave little more thought to their task at hand because he was with Jake, even though there was a question or two.

"Jake, what are we gunna do exactly?" he asked as they stumbled down the side of the creek bed.

"We're gunna see if S.T.'s trap has a varmint, and if it does, we'll stick it in this here tow sack, haul it over to Pritchett's and let it lose—in the house", Jake laughed.

The night was dimly lit by the half-moon so the creek was dark. At turns it was even darker, near enough you couldn't see more than a couple of feet, but Jake never slowed a bit and Cyrus followed closely. They stopped a moment.

"Right over there, if we weren't down so far you could see, is Pritchett's. 'Bout another quarter mile is the traps."

"How far's a quarter mile, Bruiser?"

"From yur house to Burle Barn."

Cyrus loved being with Jake because he knew everything and he was safe. The one thing—the only thing—Cyrus had plenty of that Jake didn't, was fear.

They reached the edge of a clearing that was knee high in Bahia grass and the scant moonlight caused it to look like a giant gentle stream, their seed tops rowing back and forth in concert with the wind like a conductor's baton that mesmerized him. Cyrus forgot their mission being transfixed on the beauty he was walking through, his hands gliding over the tops feeling their softness and timing, his stride to the rhythm of their sway—until he ran into his mentor.

"Pudger!" Jake began angrily. "Get with the program here."

"Sorry. Hey, what's the gun for?"

"It's", Jake chuckled. "It's for in case we don't want what's in the trap—or if I get bored with *you!*"

"I gotta pee", Cyrus muttered.

"Then pee, I ain't yur Gran'ma", Jake answered, walking ahead.

"My Gran'ma? What's my Gran'ma have to do with peein'?" he replied.

Jake kept walking ahead and was about twenty feet in front when Cyrus asked, "What are you throwin' at me?" Just at that moment Jake heard the distant pops.

"Cyrus! Get down!"

"Get down? Whatdaya mean—get down?" This time they both heard the whistle of something coming over the seed tops and hitting the ground, then the distant report that followed.

"What the world?" Cyrus muttered as he swayed in the wind trying not to wet himself.

"Someone's shootin' at you, Cyrus!—You're bein' shot at! Get down, damn you!"

Cyrus just stood there holding himself and looking back at the dim porch light that shown several hundred yards back, the silhouette of a porch-sitter standing with something in his hands.

"Why?"

"They think you're a coyote or something", Jake said, running towards him. Now the whistles were coming every few seconds with the lagging pops in metric rhythm, until one stopped short of them and Jake disappeared into the grass. Cyrus knelt down until only his head shown above the seed tops.

"Jake! Are they really thinkin' a coyote can stand up?"

"I'm here, over here", Jake hollered back. "I think I got shot."

"Keep talking, Jake, so's I can find ya!"

Jake kept shouting out while Cyrus ran serpentine until he found him.

"They quit I guess", Jake said as he stood. "Either they got me or I got bit by somethin', it sure burns. It's on the back of my leg."

"Can't see squat in this mess", Cyrus muttered. "Let's get out to the creek."

Jake had his arm over Cyrus' shoulder and they ambled to the creek's edge where the moonlight shown enough for Cyrus to see.

"There's a tear in yur britches leg, just a bitty one", Cyrus mumbled squinting. Jake took his pants down and the wound could be seen. It didn't seem more than a scratch.

"What's it look like?" Jake asked.

"Not much I reckon; can't rightly see good enough, but it don't look like it's a bleeder--yet. Can you walk on it?"

He pulled his pants back and started off without saying anything else. Cyrus followed as they walked a spell in utter silence and it gnawed at him fiercely. The silent treatment never bothered him from anyone but Jake. As always, in any circumstance where contention was apparent, Cyrus' mind placed the blame on himself. Each scenario that crossed his thoughts left him with the same bottom-line—it was his fault.

"Jake, you mad at me?" he asked sheepishly.

"Why would I be?"

"Well—I was peein' back there and you told me to get down, and I didn't—you see, I couldn't right then cuz I was still goin'—and."

"Stop!" Jake interrupted gruffly. He held Cyrus by the shoulders and looked him in the face. "You gotta quit thinkin' every bad thing that happens is because of you. This world don't give one hoot-in-hell about Cyrus Buckman and his ability to make twisters, or floods or cause someone to fall over dead! Because you don't, Cyrus—things just happen sometimes all without your help."

"Well—alright. I wasn't the one at the end of the rifle, but . . . okay, I see what you're sayin', Jake Thompson." Jake thought no more of the subject as they continued to the traps and Cyrus though of nothing but.

When they reached the trestle, what Miller's pass was named for, Cyrus remembered back when they had just arrived in Alabama. They were unloading their possibles when a group of locals came up on horseback. The men and Grandpa spoke off the porch a spell and Cyrus listened with his Grandmother from the living room window. The men spoke of a neighboring farmer who had lost a Negro about a week back, one they thought had taken to the creek and was living off stolen chickens and such. As it came to pass, they found him hanging from the trestle and were wondering if Grandpa Cyrus wouldn't mind using his truck to fetch him down.

"Fella's, we just pulled in and I don't much cotton to gettin' involved with a dead man—Negro or not. Why not just put him under where he is?"

It was the first exposure Alabama had of the Buckman's and vice versa; but, every new town they moved was like that, folks "tire kickin'" as Grandpa called it.

Jake and Cyrus stood gawking at the ominous structure; its giant iron beams shadowed the dimly lit sky while its snake like girth bent and turned as though burrowing into its hole and disappearing into the darkness. They stood just off the right-of-way as Cyrus peered down into the wash—into the black. Next to his parents, this was the closest he'd been to death.

"What?" Jake asked.

"Oh, nothing."

"You been here before?" Jake queried.

"No, just heard about it. It's so hard to see, Jake. How we gunna find anything in this?"

"See that Elm that sticks out from between the top of the trestle?"

"Yeah, barely."

"There, right there. There's a stream that cuts to the creek and I seen at least a couple traps there before; never got up close enough though."

"How'd ya know it was S.T. who put 'em here?"

"Cuz I followed him one afternoon—he'd always cut out just after Pa went to town and I was figurin' he was—well, I wasn't sure. Just thought I'd follow to see what he was doin'."

They walked under the trestle to where a faint glistening of the stream began, and there was something there alright because they could see movement and hear a whimper.

"What is it?" Cyrus asked.

"Now if you can't tell, how am I? It sounds a bit like a dog or somethin' akin."

"Dang, I hope it ain't no dog", Cyrus muttered. "I'm kinda head-scratchin' here, Jake, what are we gunna do if we can't get the varmint into the tow sack?"

It wasn't difficult to get put out with Cyrus since all he could see was the bad in every situation, even the ones that began with fun in mind. Jake's leg was throbbing and he could feel the gooey, cold of blood hardening on the inside of his boot that made it stick to his skin. The marvel of the corn mash had long since faded too, which only served to make the pain worse along with his temperament.

"You wanna do this or not?" Jake said.

"Yeah", Cyrus whined.

They eased up to the trap and the animal lay still. It had shanked itself around the tree base and each time it moved they could hear the rattle of the chain and then a whimper.

"Ahhh, dang", Jake muttered. "It's Pritchett's dog, Bear."

"Pritchett—", Cyrus began laughing. "Oh-my-god; the very critter we came to get and surprise Pritchett with is just gunna get a free ride back home. How funny is that?"

Jake pulled the pistol out from the tow sack and Cyrus saw it, "NO Jake, you're not gunna shoot his dog!"

"His leg's pert near tore off and he's hurtin' bad—we'll be doin' him a favor", Jake said, raising the gun.

"No!" Cyrus yelled, stepping in front of him. "No! Jake Thompson! I ain't gunna let you."

"Let me? I got the gun Pudger, and when have you ever *let* me do anything?"

There was a standoff until Jake began to laugh, but Cyrus stood firm.

"Pudger. I can't believe it. You stood up for something all on your own and in front of a gun, no doubt! I weren't gunna shoot him."

Cyrus put down his arms and turned towards the dog which began to growl at him. It had circled the chain around the base of the Elm and was all the way against the trunk. The teeth of the trap were all the way to the top of its rear leg and there didn't seem much room to work. Cyrus turned back towards Jake.

"I don't reckon . . . "

There was a tremendous flash and a deafening sound that came feet from Cyrus. It lit the entire gulch for a split second and left a print in his eyes like a photograph of everything around him. He couldn't hear a thing except a shrill ringing as though his head had been suddenly jammed into a grain can while someone beat on it with a ball peen. He stood rubbing his eyes and an image began to materialize. It was the image of Jake, who had his hands against his shoulders and was shouting at him but he couldn't hear. Geez, he was laughing. Cyrus was dazed and couldn't put together what just happened. He turned towards the dog that was now facing the opposite direction and lying on its side.

"What the hell happened?" he screamed, only to feel the vibration of his words.

Jake stood there bowing up and down in laughter, pointing and laughing again and again. Cyrus stepped closer to the tree and the dog that lay mostly covered by the dark. He poked its backside with his foot and it didn't respond, so he pulled it towards him by the back leg and into the moonlight. Its head was completely gone. Jake had shot it. That's what it was. An anger of a proportion he had never experienced welled inside and became confusingly blended with the sorrow he'd known since forever and neither made sense. He knelt to one knee and touched the dog's side and it jiggled like a Jell-o mold. All he could imagine was what would come to Pritchett when he found out; as he remembered when his own sidekick was jumped by a pack of river dogs in Nebraska. There was nothing he or his grandfather could do but watch while the pack tore his friend limb from limb.

With the shrill sound still ringing in his ears and the bright spot of the flash fixed in the middle of his vision, he could barely see Jake's silhouette just feet from him. He wanted to kill him. He had never held such contempt for another like this. Not even for his grandfather after an undeserved beating; not even Pritchett after he had *pants'd* him in front of the entire elementary school. Cyrus stumbled over to a felled tree and sat down. Jake sat next to him and they were there in silence for what seemed forever.

"You mad at me, Pudger?"

Cyrus did not answer. The evening came noticeably cool, or maybe it had before and he just didn't notice because of all the walking—and perhaps the booze. Why did he do this? Cyrus was in conflict with every element of his thought and character. When he didn't want to do something, when he knew he didn't want to deep within, why did he? He didn't really want to drink the corn whiskey, but he did. He didn't really want to take this trek to the traps, but he did. He didn't even want to leave the fort, but he did. For the first time in his young life he was questioning his actions. Why? Was it because he was so weak and afraid of what might happen, or was it that he might be unacceptable to Jake? Maybe it would be he'd find out he was unacceptable to everyone—to the whole world, that he was truly a mistake of nature. After all, that would explain why his parents were taken so quickly after his arrival, to spare them the agony of being saddled with such an error. What was God thinking when he penciled out this form? He had sneaked by the natural order somehow. No. It couldn't be that simple, he thought.

"Hey! You gunna answer me?" Jake shouted. "Or just set there like a frog on a log?"

"Reckon I'll set for a spell—as a frog or whatever."

"So you are mad—bein' a smart-ass and all", Jake muttered. "He was gunna die anyways. I just helped it be sooner than not."

"We're all gunna die, Jake, just depends who reckons how fast it needs to be, huh?"

His vision and hearing were coming back, enough that he started back to the fort on his own. There was something different he could not quite pin down. Something inside that brought him to a different thinking about himself, the world and his part in it. For the first time in his short tenure he began to feel in control; but in control of what was the larger question, yet that didn't matter right now because he was still basking in the new—the new something.

Jake followed him. Nothing was said since Miller's Pass, even when Cyrus heard him stumble and fall, bemoaning to the stars how much his leg hurt, but he didn't as much stop or turn to look.

When they got back to the fort, Cyrus put a few more twigs and kindling on the fire and sat down next to it warming his hands, ignoring Jake. While in thought about everything that transpired, the largest part of him worried how he was going to handle Jake. He couldn't just forget it and he would never forsake their bond for the death of a river mutt, but the whole incident was too shocking. What he witnessed was nothing he believed Jake to be and the image of his mentor was untenable. It was tantamount to the shock of finding out about Santa: the sleigh, the elves, the deer—everything. This conflict scared him, but he let it alone; another approach he had never attempted.

He picked some rocks out from under his bed roll, smoothed it down and lay back against a pile of dirt he raised for a pillow. All the while he could feel the tenseness in the air and Jake's incessant stare that begged for conversation and perhaps forgiveness, of which he would not extend.

"Cyrus—I'm sorry for what happened. I'm really, really sorry."

Cyrus turned onto his side away from him, curled his legs with his arms between them and watched the fire.

CHAPTER FIFTEEN

Cyrus hadn't slept much that night so when he woke to find Jake sitting alone outside the fort, he wondered if he had had the same restless evening. If he had, he deserved it. It was unusually cool and Jake was in nothing but his underwear.

"What are you doing?" Cyrus asked perplexed.

"Nothing much. Just watchin' a Yellow-tail hawk", Jake muttered.

The same tenseness remained from the night and Cyrus was adamant for it to stay that way; he had no intention of apologizing. He hadn't done any wrong. Jake said he was sorry but that wasn't enough in his book—so what was? This was new territory for him: this 'standing your ground' thing. He would not let the picture back into his head. The image of that dog, whose name kept bouncing about in his head, the name Pritchett would be calling incessantly to no avail, made him feel cold inside. Maybe he wouldn't miss it, he thought. Maybe it was one of the countless river dogs that hung around their shack because pickin's were easy and no one ran him off. Maybe . . .

"Cyrus!" Jake called. "My leg's in a bad way here."

"Whatdaya mean?" he asked, crawling from his bed sack.

"I daknow, look at it, it's all swollen-up."

It was swollen twice its size from the ankle to the back of his knee, and red all about the wound that oozed a cheesy, sebaceous substance that resembled . . .

"What are we gunna say happened—and where?" Jake asked.

"You cut it in the barn playin'?"

Jake shrugged his shoulders and shook his head, "Pa ain't gunna believe that, and I bet your Gran'pa won't neither, not as bad as this is. They know something has been up with us for a spell, just hadn't said nothin' since we ain't done no bad."

"Til now, I reckon. I don't care to take no strappin', Jake. Let's say what I said."

"Funny, you bein' the one to bend a story", Jake mused.

"Why?"

"Just from you; Mr do-right."

"I ain't neither; you just ain't been strapped by Cyrus Buckman, the First."

It had only been half hour since sun up, but it was safe to assume that both parents had been up for a while. This meant they would have to sneak in whichever house they were supposed to be and that was going to be difficult. They typically came in as though they had been doing chores so making noise wouldn't have been a problem, but this go-round would be tight. Back a time they actually forgot whose house they were to be staying, so their story then was they had just come from the others looking for—a book. A bit stupid sounding, but it worked. Their charade had been a pretty neat deal, this thing they concocted for tenting out, but the air seemed to be pointing towards a change and it wasn't much in their favor.

His Grandpa was out in the barn and Grandma was in the kitchen clanging pans and humming hymns, so they opted for through the front passed Grandma. Cyrus listened at the kitchen window from the porch while Jake went in. He hadn't made it to the first step when Grandma Mattie met him coming out of the kitchen.

"Well mornin' Mr Thompson, you and Cyrus been chorin'?" Grandma asked.

"Ah, well—we."

Cyrus rushed in behind Jake who was standing there with one foot on the step and looking like a chicken eyed by the fox.

"Hey Gran'ma, Jake's got somethin' wrong with his leg and we need you to look at it", Cyrus said quickly.

He was an expert at applying salve on a story before his Grandfather had his turn at it. The secret lay with his Grandma because whatever the story's rendition was supposed to be, she never got it right from the start when she told it back to Grandpa. In fact, she'd get it so discombobulated that Grandpa would end throwing his arms in the air and be done with it, rather than try to untangle it. Reason enough Cyrus would never let her ease into the situation and jumped in with both feet before she had as much as an eye-blink to think.

"Well let's looky here", she said as she bent over his leg. "Oh child! That wound is plum infected to the bone and needs a poultice yesterday! Has Mr Sterling seen this?"

"No mam, I did it—last night", Jake mumbled looking at Cyrus. "We were cattin' round in the barn and I hung it cross a nail, or something."

"I thought you boys were to stay at the Thompson's last night?"

"Well, you know how things get—we got to messin' round", Jake stuttered, grimacing at Cyrus.

About that moment Grandpa could be heard coming up the porch front, each step hammering the pine-slat flooring like John Henry driving railroad spikes with a twenty pound maul. Just the sound of his approach was disconcerting enough. Both looked at each other with that unspoken question--"will he believe it?" The door opened while he banged the side of each brogan against the facing, knocking pieces of barnyard here and there and evoking a disgruntled sigh from Grandma.

"Whats-you hay seeds been up to besides no good?"

"Pa, look at Jake's leg. It is infected to the bone, I tell ya", Grandma said.

Grandpa ambled over like a loaded brick truck on an upgrade, squinting his eyes, favoring the wound with a touch from his finger.

"Damn—."

"Pa!" she interrupted.

"Well, it is mighty juiced up. How'd you say that came about, boy?"

"He ain't said—yet", Cyrus interrupted. "He scratched—or, caught a nail in the . . ."

"Weren't no nail that made that gouge—no sirree bob, that there's a bullet wound", his grandfather pronounced with unequivocal precision. "Right there's where in came on, and right there's where it left—see how it put in a nice little trench. That's 'cause it was hot and it burned the hide closed as it passed."

They all stood with their mouths wide open, staring at Jake's leg then Grandpa, back and forth. The jig was up but how? How did his grandfather nip this bud before it was as much a seedling? Cyrus looked his grandfather straight in the eyes with utter amazement—and fear. This was big time; as big a thing he'd ever attempted. The worst of it was that he was covering a long time crime with a lie to cover another lie. Can you see how this cake was layered? What popped into his head as suddenly as his grandfather's fortuitous discovery was his grandmother's saying he'd heard so often before when she'd catch him in a twist, something about a spider and getting tangled in the web because of a lie. He couldn't rightly remember it word for word but the message sure hit home.

"You wanna tell me what really happened?" his Grandfather murmured. It came like that before the storm; his speech tight and taut would be like water pressured through a crack, his lips barely open. The moment was so tense and thick that it seemed to fog up right there in the foyer. Jake turned to Grandpa and began the litany of confession.

"Mr Cyrus, we been crawfishin' y'all for a spell—me and Cyrus J", he began. He told him, he told both of them; told them everything they had done since the beginning of school, everything that pertained to tenting out: the tomfoolery between their houses; the pistol he sneaked out with; the trek along the creek and where they were shot at (this is where Grandma nearly fell down) and that it was all his idea to keep it a secret. He said nothing about Pritchett's dog or the whiskey and was something Cyrus held his breath for. That would have been the proverbial straw. Cyrus would never have been seen again, and no telling what would have happened to Jake, who was now swaying like a wet willow and white as chalk.

"Child!" Grandma hollered. He fainted just as Grandpa caught him.

Grandpa toted him into the living room and set him to the couch, while Grandma fetched a cold cloth from the kitchen.

"Cyrus, go fetch his Pa", his Grandfather ordered.

It was a long and arduous journey that Cyrus didn't want to end. The thought of what he might say and what Mr Thompson would do didn't come together in his head, and he ran through every possible scenario. This was something he could not command; that realm completely outside his world he was unable to configure. This something was the people in his life; the needful thing he could not change or remove, which would be the easiest and best solution. Would he have to get rid of everyone though, even Jake? Yeah, if it meant it being back the way it was. There were things about his old life that didn't make sense either, but at least there wasn't this anguish about turning corners to find a surprise. He was either confronted with a handshake or a brick in the face and he was quickly becoming desensitized to both. Is this life, he thought? Is this what everybody makes such a roar over about being so wondrous and beautiful? It stinks! It's nothing but a bag of horse dung that someone said, "Here, hold this for a while."

These were the thoughts that brought pain and would pull his plane into a flat spin if he dwelt long enough on it. It was these times that Jake would shake him to wake him, to yell and fit until he came back to the world of challenge and discomfort; but, when Jake wasn't there these paths in his head led him straight to his hole. Strangely there was a sort of comfort there, though dark and obscure where things and people were vague silhouettes, where you weren't called to touch or care or be a part of anything and nothing interrupted you. That is the way it should be, he thought. Perfect.

"What is it, Cyrus?" Mr Thompson asked him. "Where's your sidekick?"

"Ah—well he's back at the house and we need you to come get him."

"Come get him! What's the problem?" he asked, dropping the long handle shovel.

"Nothin' real bad, he just cut his leg and Gran'ma thinks it might be infected."

They loaded into Mr Thompson's truck and sped back to Cyrus' house. He could hear Mr Thompson speaking but the words weren't audible, they came as hollow squawks like a horn on a distant ship at sea, so Cyrus would shrug his shoulders and shake his head as though he were really listening and Mr Thompson might not hit him. It was here he was concentrating mostly on not crying. He wanted to be alone and the only one he wanted talk to about it was canvassed in his own world of fear—his Grandpa.

When they arrived at the house, Mr Thompson was on the porch and the truck was still moving. Cyrus was in no hurry to face the inevitable so it took him a bit longer. They were all in the living room crouched over Jake like a banker over gold when he came in. He could hear Jake muttering to his father and only once did his Grandpa look back at him. He scowled at him like rabid dog chained to a tree might. Avarice overcame him for a second at the thought that he was going to take all the blame for this incident, as with everything else, and Jake was going to come out smelling like a rose when it was him who should be getting the attention. That's just the way things were in life: Cyrus was the kid who did things that looked good, and Jake was the guy who did things that were good. They didn't know though. They hadn't a clue what really happened—who brought the whiskey; who shot the dog; whose idea it was in the first place to go out into the creek to Miller's Pass? Nothing. All this will end up on him.

"Cyrus, thank you for being with Jake", his father said. "You are his best friend in the world."

Wow! That should teach his grandparents a thing. That should teach everyone. Once out of a thousand times was he recognized for something that wasn't bad.

"You and me are to have a visit when this done", his grandfather said.

Jake sat up and got sick to his stomach. The men jumped back and Grandma lunged forward with her apron out like a basket. There wasn't much in him but some fritter left from last night. His father scooped him up and mumbled something about Doc Wash as they made it to the front door. As Cyrus watched Jake loaded into the truck and disappear down the dirt road, they were left there with nothing but themselves and silence; silence that evoked what had become his signature.

"Well, I'll meet you in the barn", his grandfather said.

"Pa, let it be for now", Grandma said quietly. "There's been enough for this day."

"No. Ain't proper to let somethin' like this stew."

He went out to the barn and waited in what seemed an eternity. His strapping's were closure to beatings than anyone could imagine unless. they had ever been at the receiving end. His heart began to pound when he heard the porch screen door open and close. His fate was moments away. The seconds before were worse than the incident it seemed. The part he feared the greatest was that his grandfather's hatred for him would overcome and he would beat him to death, or worse yet, into a disability. The belt he used wasn't even a belt—not a belt for humans. It was the back cinch from a saddle that weighed better than two pounds. And why would he use something like that if he wasn't intending to do maximum harm? There wasn't anything he learned from this except fear. Mistakes weren't doing bad; doing bad was something you did with intention. This wasn't his deal, it was Jake's and he just went along. He was never allowed to explain the situation, ever. It was this, then that. God, how he hated this place—the rules were completely turned around and justice was rarely served. The good intending were always the ones who got the bullet while the real culprits stood on the sidelines and laughed. Jake never did though. Jake was the diamond in the ruff; his gift from God, even though there were times, like this one, where things became all "bass-ackwards", Jake would still straighten it all out before the storm. He couldn't put Jake into that pond with the other riff-raft. He saved him more often than not, and this particular incident was way out of typical. If Jake hadn't been puny he would have stood up for him more than he had. In fact, this might have even got to this point if he hadn't been so ill. He was going to take this medicine for Jake.

His grandfather came into the barn and stood at the door. He motioned his head to the saddle rack Cyrus would bend over, and he did without a word or a whine. It was the worst he had ever been beaten.

CHAPTER SIXTEEN

He was walking home from school solo and doing what he always did when his thoughts were not forcibly someplace else—ponder Jake. He'd been sick for three days now, at moments seeming to get better, but then lapsing back into sweats and high fever. His leg looked like a splinter of wood next to the other and Doc Wash had said several times that he could lose it; lose it before the infection overtook his body. The thought of losing him was beyond unbearable. He posed the loss of his father with the loss of Jake and imagined how his Grandfather might have felt. It was the first time he seemed to understand him.

"Hey Cyrus, wait up!" Cheyenne called from behind. She was some distance back and it was warming to hear her voice. He usually waited for her after school for the walk home, but since Jake had been down he worried she'd work the conversation into what happened. Everyone seemed preoccupied with this thing and it was none of their business, he felt.

"Hey Cheyenne, sorry 'bout not waitin' but I wanted to see Jake before my chores and all."

"That's okay, I was kinda wanting to see him with you—if you think it would be okay with him."

"Ah—hmm."

"You think it might bother him if I came along?"

"Well, he might be taken back a smidgen—seein' he'll be laid up in bed and all."

"I won't go if you think I ought not."

He wanted her to go and he didn't. Everything about her and the feelings she stirred in him were more confusing than Ms Fugate's rendition of the Civil War, not to mention the feelings he knew good and well that Jake had for her; but, this was that self-ishness he disliked so about himself and what Jake had labored to change. He had been in his private world so long that this way of thought was as comfortable as a porch sit on a morning rain, and Jake knew it to be his greatest impediment: "Pudger, yur in the world of skin and bone when yur with me; it's okay to cotton to *Imagines* once in a while, but not 'round the clock." This thought made him smile.

"What?" she asked somberly.

"Nothing I reckon—Jake. I was just thinkin' what Jake would say."

"And . . ."

"He'd like it; he'd like you to come", Cyrus nodded.

They walked the way to Jake's and spoke mostly about school and folks outside his world; the ones he only knew of. Cheyenne was as temperate as they came because she accepted him with bag and baggage. He considered her as beautiful inside as she was out, but couldn't lay claim to that observation since his Grandma pointed it out at least once a week. The thought brought a blush and her occasional question of why because it gave him a reason to talk about something he knew a lot of: his world. You see, just as aloof as he was of the others common to their lives, she watched his with a salience an artist might a sunset or a field of flowers and was enamored of it. It was this obscure magic about him that mystified her, and too was the thing about her he loved: her Jake-like nature to circumstance without concern for the outcome. Both of them had no fear, and he was nothing but.

He could feel her incessant stare and it made him blush again. There were many things he wanted to say but dared not because he wasn't sure how to couch them. There are some things, his Grandmother would say, which aren't meant to be said and he took that to mean everything about feelings.

"Cyrus J, why are you always ridden with smiles 'round me? Is it because of something I say—the way I talk or something?"

"No mam . . ."

"No mam!" she interrupted quickly.

"Ah Cheyenne! You know I trip o'er myself when I get 'round you."

"Why is that, Mr Buckman?" she answered and both of them laughed.

"I daknow, I reckon it's . . . I daknow."

"Cyrus Buckman! How's anyone to know you if you won't let them? You have so many nice things about your character."

"Character?"

"You know what I mean."

"Not really", he muttered with a chuckle. "Okay, name one—no, two."

"You care a lot about people but you're afraid to let them care for you . . ."

". . . and that's a good thing?" he interrupted.

"If you'll allow me to finish", she instructed. "Carin' for folk is a good thing, but not lettin' them care for you is not so good."

"That ain't all together right, Miss Hold. I care 'bout Jake probably more than his Pa does—and he's someone. And—I let him care about me."

"Yeah, but what about me?"

He had tossed a soft clod her way and she returned with a horse apple. It was like that for him; he had such difficulty on the field of life and Cheyenne had no qualms in jumping in with both feet just like Jake. He almost stopped walking and was just as suddenly thankful he hadn't, but he had to process this and he couldn't while he was moving. How was he to entertain this question without making a dismal fool of himself? This thought was way too far from home; it was about feelings. And then again maybe this was one of those times Jake spoke of; the ones where he should chance and step outside himself to risk being accepted for who he is—or rejected, which was the part he expected and typically got: "Pudger, nobody is liked by everyone; you gotta find the distance between the plates where you won't get tagged", Jake would say so eloquently. "It ain't the losin' you worry about so much; it's how you fend the play."

"Ah—I, geminnie Cheyenne, you gotta know I think yur the cat's meow—heck, yur the whole cat. Ain't no girl in school who can feed calves, throw hay, clean stalls and still smell as nice as you—ne'er look as pretty, neither."

"Cyrus J, that's the sweetest thing ever said to me."

"It is?" he fumbled. "You mean I made the play?"

"What?"

"Nothin'."

They were just up the walkway to the Thompson house when Mr Thompson came from the side and up the front steps to the porch swing, occasionally looking back at them with a vacant stare that told Cyrus he wasn't himself. It wasn't so difficult if you were used to it, but became so when you were with those who didn't know.

"Mr Thompson must be really sad", she mumbled to Cyrus.

"Yeah."

"Doesn't he look sad to you?"

"Sad as can be—but he'll better."

"Well, well, well, Mr Buckman and a pretty gal. Who might you be, one of Jake's girlfriends?" Mr Thompson said casually from the swing.

"Well, I am a girl and I am Jake's friend—my name is Cheyenne Hold, sir", she said, extending her hand as might a dignitary.

"I meant, his girl-*friend*. He's been known to have one or two."

"I'm Cyrus' girl-*friend*" she replied emphatically.

"It's a pleasure there, hon. And nice to see you there, Pudger", Mr Thompson chuckled. "Yur lookin' fit n' fiddle—course Jake's a bit under the weather, but then you know about that."

"Uhm, we was wonderin' if we could see him, Mr Thompson?" Cyrus asked tensely.

"You know where his room is", he added with a wave towards the house.

They went inside. Cheyenne kept muttering questions to Cyrus but he wasn't paying any attention. Mr Thompson's demeanor hung in his head and it brought him to feel weak-legged. The tone and what he said took his breath away and left a sadness to stifle his kinship that meant the whole world to him. Mr Thompson's look of contempt and malice hurt to the bone, especially in Cheyenne's presence. What was she to think? What was Jake to be like?

He nudged Jake's door open just wide enough to push his head through, while he had his hand against Cheyenne's stomach that kept her from coming in before he could apprise Jake; and, because it gave him reason and thus full permission to touch her.

"Hey there, Pudger", Jake whispered.

He lay there covered to his neck with a quilt made of ponies and cowboys while the only thing showing was his head and an arm. Both were pale and his eyes looked different. Everything looked different. Even the room was different as if something unseen was there taking up the light and air. There was a translucence that covered him as though you were looking at him through a glass and dimly, vague streaks of an image with the only color from the quilt that wasn't from this world.

"What's that smell, Bruiser?" he asked.

"Cyrus!" she scorned.

"What? He don't mind. Jakie knows me better than anyone."

"Hey is that Cheyenne?" Jake said. "Com' on in."

Cyrus was acting the sentinel, keeping his hand against Cheyenne's stomach, refusing her to breach his position and authority until she demanded it, which she did. She was bigger than he was all the way around so she boldly walked forward past him, but with grace and dignity.

"Cyrus, he said for us to come in."

"Yeah", he replied with a surrendering whisper.

Their presence brought life into the room that made Jake smile as though it were his birthday and long awaited family had surprised him. Jake wouldn't stop staring at Cheyenne and they both kept walking over each other's questions. Cyrus tried to interject at each point there might have been a pause, but soon realized this wasn't a normal conversation. It wasn't a conversation at all. It began as one, then melded into a match as might two in a political debate, one having something more important than the other to say and neither addressing the one before.

"Hey!" Cyrus yelled. "Geminnie cricket, this is a sick room."

"Oh hush up, you", Jake teased. "Hadn't seen Cheyenne in an age, and I see you every day."`

Funny enough that Jake didn't see it, but she did. As only a lady could, Cheyenne put her hand on the back of Cyrus' head and smiled at him. He blushed tremendously and not from the effect but the cause and everyone in the room knew it, and they were okay with it because of that very thing: they knew it. That was their beauty.

They spoke between each other as might a sewing circle, Cyrus on one side of the bed and Cheyenne on the other. Cyrus filled him in on the scuttle-butt from the men's point of view and Cheyenne on what really happened. They ended spending the better part of an hour together with what seemed only a handful of minutes. It was in these moments that life became what it was meant to be, and oddly, only recognized when it was over. The unbridled affection and joy these young souls traded were a mystery because it happened without a plan. A very small snippet of this menagerie Cyrus held to himself; that *something* he felt the others had but never spoke of was the *something* you had to acquire on your own.

"Hey Cheyenne, I was wonderin' if I could say somethin' to Jake", Cyrus added as he stood away from the bed.

"Sure", she answered.

"Well, you gunna go?" he asked perturbed.

"Oh alright", she mused with a wink. "You get better, Bruiser, you're missed."

"Hey, that's my name for him", Cyrus said.

She left and Cyrus waited for her to shut the door, but she didn't. He stuck his head out and told her he'd meet her on the porch and then pushed it to.

"Might heavy handed with her ain't ya?" Jake commented. "Dang lil' brother, she thinks higher of you than rain might a cloud."

"You gettin' better, ain't ya?" he asked, sitting down again.

"Did you hear me?"

"Yes. Did you hear me?" Cyrus replied. "Lemme see yur leg."

Cyrus pulled back the quilt to view an awful sight; it was now only a leg in the academic sense: it was a bone attached to the hip in the place it was supposed to be with little more. Now that Cheyenne had left, the temporary facade disappeared and Cyrus was alone with reality. The coldness of that thing before came again and he became uncomfortable. Cyrus put his hand on Jake's chest and stared at him.

"You ain't gunna turnabout and kiss me are ya?" Jake mused.

"That ain't funny, Jacob."

"Wow, why'd you call me that?" he asked excitedly. "You know that's my Christian name. No one has ever called me that."

"Really, that's yur name, your real name? That is so neat. It just came out."

"I only found out about it when I seen it on a piece of paper and Pa told me; said it was the name my Ma gave and he didn't cotton to it."

"What if I was to call you Jacob?"

"Naw, that would only serve to bring trouble about. Everyone is used to callin' me Jake anyways."

"I will in my prayers; no one can call me on that."

"You is a stubborn cuss, you know", Jake muttered. "But yur the best cuss."

Cyrus put his arms around Jake. Jake put his hand on Cyrus' head and patted him.

"Pudgie, yur the best friend I'll ever have."

Cyrus looked up with a perplexed look, "Best what?"

"Brother", Jake added. "I was wonderin' if you was to catch that."

"I bes' get before Cheyenne turns sour." Cyrus stopped a moment and turned.

"What, you?" Jake smiled.

"I'll never love anyone like I love you, Jacob, will I? I mean, I will never trust anyone like I do you."

"Yes you will. I promise."

"Cyrus, don't lose eye of her. She thinks mighty strong on you, and she'll end up bein' the best friend you'll ever have."

"Ain't no one takin' yur place, Jacob."

"I knew I should-a never said anything to you about that."

Cyrus met Cheyenne on the porch and they set out. She lived another half mile past Cyrus and he obliged to walk her home, but she refused.

"You know Cyrus J, you and Jake are like two pieces of magic that when both of you are in the same room the angels dance. I had more fun just watchin' you two cat with each other—he's your hair, Cyrus."

"My what? My hair?"

"Don't you know the story about Samson and Delilah? The story in the bible silly? You do read the bible?"

"Well, not like my Gran'ma, but I have. Didn't recollect no story 'bout hair."

"It's not a story about hair, it's about a man chosen of God and his strength came from his hair. The longer it grew the stronger he became."

"Wow! Guess I should grow mine out."

"That's not the point—I'll tell you about it sometime."

They reached the edge of Cyrus' farm and he hemmed and hawed if he was doing right by not walking her home. He asked her twice and she said no for the reason before. He came to the turn row that was some ways up to the farmhouse. He stopped behind an oak tree that left him hidden so he could watch what was left of her walk away. Loneliness overtook him. This thought along with those of Jake brought an ache to his chest that stuck in his throat. His blood turned cold and a shiver covered him for a second as he leaned against the giant live oak and watched her disappear.

Five-thirty came without cause—again; he lay in his feather bed balled up in his quilts just staring out his window at that huge pecan tree and thinking of nothing at all. Its branches connected to the mammoth trunk were silhouetted from the full moon behind it and made him think of how small he was. If God were all the things everyone says he is, up to and including Pastor Higgins, then why is life this way? Why did what happened to Jake happen? Why wasn't it him? That way everyone and everything would be back to normal and the good, strong and beautiful people of the world would be whistling away the day and doing what they do. Sure, Grandma would be sad for a while and Grandpa might even have missed him for minute or two, especially at chore time, but on the whole, everything would be back to normal: Cheyenne would be sneak-peaking and giggling with her friends, eyeing Jake (her true love), and Jake would be tossing Pritchett and his toadies around on his lonesome. Yeah, that's the way it would be. And him? Well, he would be somewhere the defective parts were put, staring at something in the sky and waiting for himself to be re—re-manufactured, that's it, into something good, strong and beautiful.

He could lie there all morning thinking of what and how things ought to be and it wouldn't feed and water Dud, or the goats, or clean up the barn and he'd end up having to deal with his Grandfather's breath and demeanor. He reached behind and felt what was left of his strapping four days ago. That back cinch laid a ridge across the top of his butt just at the small of his back; it was a stray that wandered past its target and near sent him unconscious, but he didn't cry or rise up.

Monotony was really his middle name, even though he couldn't spell it or for sure knew what it meant; it was something that ruled his world when Pritchett was on his prowl and Jake wasn't convalescing. Even the thought of conjuring Many Moons had lost its appeal. Life was just plain dreary. He did his chores and had a biscuit for breakfast, all without provocation or mishap in between. Although his Grandfather made a feeble attempt at conversation, he did what he could to stay away from him and thus keep his attitude further from the dark. The prospect that Jake would be better, better enough to come to school brought his demeanor to higher state—even made him smile.

"Cyrus J, you bes' skedaddle on to school without botherin' Jake this morning. His Pa said he be taking him into town early to have Doc Wash clean out his leg", his Grandma said. She gave out her daily instructions and rebukes from the stove front; dressed in her apron, she'd wave her spatula about like a conductor's baton, accenting where punctuation was to be placed.

"Takin' him to Doc Wash?"

"Yes, that's what he said."

"Me and Cheyenne saw him after school and he was lookin' just dandy."

"Child, he hasn't been lookin *dandy* since your episode. That boy is plumb ate up with the infection."

"Ate up! Gran'ma, his leg was just a might red when we seen him—he's gunna be okay."

His Grandmother set her spatula to the stove, removed her apron and sat down next to him; a posture she'd occasionally take when what he was about to have an intersession with his Grandfather.

"Cyrus, he could very well lose his leg, and that ain't the only problem; the infection is all about him—he's sick, child."

"What are you sayin', Gran'ma?"

"Well, I'm sayin' that this ain't no small thing."

"I ain't meanin' this as a sass, but you're sure taking the long way around the barn, Gran'ma."

"You recall the times after church when we chatted 'bout God and prayer and such, that it was hard for you to understand why folks did—I think you said, 'where's the good come in talkin' to the clouds like there's someone there when you can't see them?' Well this be one of those times, child, and the fact you can't see 'em is more the reason."

"So yur sayin' Jake might lose his leg and prayin' to something I don't *know* for sure is there just might bring him to keepin' it?"

"I'm sayin' this is one of those times grown folk ain't got an answer, and God just might be willin' to help you understand if you was willin' to ask."

"Gran'ma, I'm still lookin' for you to throw the ball; is Jake gunna—stay sick?" he asked deliberately. "Is there something you ain't tellin' me?" "Cyrus, I'm tryin' as hard to tell you I don't know but there is someone who does; whether He chooses to bring you to the table here can only be known if you was to ask."

They sat staring at each other in the quiet while nothing more than Jake was in his head. His Grandmother reached out for his hand and he smiled, but there was no consolation. Nothing took away the pain.

"Sure, Gran'ma", he said quietly. "Can't hurt, and maybe could help—right?"

It was a long and lonely walk down Burle Road, and became even more so when he reached the Thompson Farm and no one was there. The truck, usually parked in front, was gone and probably on its way to town toting his wounded brother. He thought for a second of Cheyenne and how nice it would be for her conversation. She and Jake were the only ones around who could change his thoughts at the drop of a hat. It wasn't so much what she said but how; her quiet, melodious voice would slow everything down until there was nothing in his head but—well, nothing. It was so unlike his relationship with Jake, where he was not able to communicate his feelings in a way Jake might consider acceptable.

He most assuredly did not choose this path, it just happened. If he had his true druthers he'd definitely be Jake, or least someone with similar traits: strong, up standing, good-looking, worldly, good-looking, smart, lots of friends, good-looking. His thought became hung in a loop—he wasn't Jake, and constantly thinking that way did little more than push him further into his darkness. Okay, then how was this to change? Should he believe them: Cheyenne and Jake? Or should he stay with the ones who *brought him to this dance* like his Grandpa; they were older and definitely knew more? No, his Grandpa didn't seem to have anything more going for him than what came from that bottle. Jake and Cheyenne lived in his world, knew his world, and in many ways knew him better than his own blood. Yep, they were the ones who cared the most.

In no time had he arrived as the school just popped into view. Cheyenne was standing outside with a couple of girlfriends. Just as soon as he saw her she saw him and it was too late to change course. He didn't mind seeing her, it was the others he cared not to have conversation with.

"Hey Cyrus", they all hollered. "How's Jake doing?" Molly Pritchett asked, blood kin to "The" Pritchett, and much more tolerable. She was somewhere in between the Pritchett clan of eight, and he wasn't sure if she was on the top or below the scoundrel. Tad Pritchett, somewhere around the oldest, was shaving by third grade and was bigger than the Principal.

"Cyrus just happened to be there Molly, that's all", Cheyenne interceded. "Yes, he sees him every day but he doesn't know everything."

"Well, his Pa did take him to town this mornin' so Doc Wash could clean out his leg", Cyrus added.

"We saw him yesterday, me and Cyrus did, and he was doing just cherry", Cheyenne nodded at Cyrus.

"Yeah, pert as a ruttin' buck."

The balance of the day fared about as well as the morning: a question here a question there, a nod, a wave and constant thoughts in between. Only once, when he was in the outhouse, did he catch himself talking alone and it brought him to wonder how many times he was doing that and didn't catch it. How many times were folks watching him with a high brow wondering who on earth he was talking to? Didn't matter in the grand scheme, he thought, he was already on the outside looking in so nothing was truly bizarre here. Oh, his grandparents probably take a ribbing when they go to town: "So, how's that boy-a yours doin'? Understand he's been havein' some trouble fittin' in out there—kids will be kids, huh Cyrus?"

Didn't at all matter to him what pressures his grandpa succumbed to or as much had to face, it was his grandmother that concerned him. She thought highly of him even though she didn't have call to and he worried that someday she too would tire of living under the onus of his image. These preponderances of himself bothered him to the extent he couldn't stop them, or wouldn't. That bothered him more. It was a vicious cycle. Those he loved seemed to truly like him: Cheyenne and Jake. They were everything to him and if he lost that he would simply vanish, he thought. Why would they, or anyone for that fact, pretend to like someone and force themselves to be around that which they didn't like? That would be insane. It just wouldn't happen. Well, maybe for a while like they were acting out something Preacher Timbers said they ought do, but like everything Preacher Timbers would command, it would last until around sundown Monday and then back to normal. No, what he had with Jake and Cheyenne was as real and sturdy as his pecan.

Cheyenne waited for him outside the school house just off the turn from Chicken Ranch road, where she typically waited and since Jake had been down. This was a milestone in his thoughts about her and Jake and him, while all the time he believed she waited for Jake it was really for him.

"Hey Cyrus, my Ma's gunna take me in to town; you wanna ride home with us?"

"Ya-know Chey', I'm gunna beg out this time. I wanna stop by and see my brother."

"We can give you a ride there; it's just off the trail a measure, Ma won't mind."

"Naw, I 'preciate it but I wanna walk it."

It was a good solo walk home; the thoughts were good ones, even when his Grandfather worked his way in to them, he'd laugh at his effort and shut the door. His private world was orderly this day; nothing to go into the record book, just a decent day—a

Pritchett-less day. He came to the front gate of the Thompson farm, placed his arms across the fence top and rested his chin. The truck wasn't in the drive and nothing was stirring so he walked the long dirt drive to the front door and knocked. Nothing. The door wasn't locked, as nothing in that day was, so he went inside.

"Bruiser, you in bed still!"

He walked up the squeaky staircase and into Jake's room only to find an empty bed. The room was different than his; it had things on the wall and across his dresser. Things that a boy their age would: cane poles in the corner, a lever-action 30-06 (Jake would not allow him to handle) which he picked up and pointed to the ceiling and around the room, making a firing sound with his mouth. The room smelled of Jake and he drew it in with a long breath. It was kind of like lemons or something of a tangy nature and he smiled—it was Jake. Strange, he thought, everyone's house had a smell that was them. Jake's bed was messed up. The quilt was pulled back to where he had been with his pillows bunched at the head and one at the side like it was him when they had sleep overs. When he woke, Jake would be holding him like a bunched up pillow, his arms and legs around him in a way that made him feel more secure than he'd ever known—he loved it. He lay down in his spot and smelled the pillow, half-draped himself with the quilt and stared at the ceiling until he began to feel tired and all too comfortable. A very strange and distant feeling came over him and it brought a quick shiver. His body went flush for a second as though his blood left and made him gasp for air. He sat up quickly, near dizzy when his breath jumped back in him. "What the . . ."

He wasn't sure he hadn't fallen to sleep; he had no idea what time it was and how far behind the clock he was from chores. He ran out of house and down the drive to the road. There seemed a good amount of daylight left so it couldn't be too late. He ran half-stagger for a time until he could see the Buckman wind vain on the barn.

"Child, where have you been?" his Grandma Mattie questioned. She was sitting on the porch swinging, humming hymns and shelling purple peas into a bowl on her lap—"Where has my little boy been?" she asked deliberately.

"I been at school, Gran'ma—and I stopped by Jake's for a spell."

"And how's he doin'?"

"Don't rightly know, no one was there—reckon they're still in town or somethin'."

"You bes' get your chores done; I'll have supper at the usual."

"Okay, but ain't got much; I got the goat and some barn straightenin'."

"Shelby's gunna lamb here any day now, so you'll be milkin' her in between her young'un."

Shelby was the goat. They acquired her a couple years back at a county fair somewhere in Tennessee because Grandma loved making goat cheese. Grandpa would roll his eyes every time she'd call to it, explaining what an embarrassment it was and forbid her to speak of it when visitors were about, especially when it became painfully obvious it was pregnant. This was the way of the Buckman household that was a scourge to young Cyrus' heart and thought: his grandparents' way, namely his grandfather, they placed more emphasis on what things *looked* like rather than the way things truly were. So much wasted on whitewash because they were too poor to paint and everything in between became meaningless—because it was. Jake was where the rubber met the road, and in a strong sense, so was Mr Thompson; at least that's the way Cyrus saw it. He examined the way Mr Thompson and Jake were to each other like a doctor would a wound with an eyeglass. Every nuance, every touch, and every gesture he would file away in his memory and call upon it when he was with his grandfather.

Nothing was close, not even remotely similar, except one was a boy and the other a man.

"Did you wash up?" his Grandma asked as he entered the kitchen.

"Yes'am."

"Where's yur Gran'pa?"

"Don't know; truck ain't out there."

Just as soon as Cyrus answered did his grandfather pull up the drive. The kitchen had a large bay window that was left of the stove and the table sat in front of so it was easy to see who was at the house without having to get up. Cyrus put his hands between his legs and yawned while his grandmother began setting dishes to the table.

"How's everyone?" his Grandfather bellowed through a sigh.

"Just fine I 'spose; where you been?" she asked.

"Oh, been in town talkin' to some folk at the feed store; how you doin'?" his Grandfather asked him pointedly, which was bizarre. He never asked anything of him that concerned his well-being—ever.

"Okay, I reckon", he shrugged.

"I was just wonderin'—with what's gone on and all."

"Whatdaya mean?" Cyrus asked

His grandfather stared at him blankly for several seconds and Cyrus looked back with the same strangeness.

"Well", his Grandfather began, glancing to his wife. "You all ain't heard, I take it?"

"Heard what?" Grandma asked.

His grandfather pushed back from the table and kept glancing back and forth to the both of them, crossing his arms then uncrossing them as though he was about to ask Cyrus who had been in the hay bin.

"Yur buddy", he said to Cyrus.

"My buddy, what?"

"Jake."

"What about him?"

"He's gone, son."

"I know, he went to town; he went to Doc Wash's."

"No Cyrus—he's gone."

It was a bit like time stopped. The earth's spin. Everything just stopped, even his thought—gone.

"Oh my!" his grandmother whispered. "Oh Cyrus, honey."

"What? What are you all sayin'? I'm tellin' you his Pa took him to town to Doc Wash—I seen him yesterday, me and Cheyenne and he is fine."

Cyrus stood from the table and his Grandmother kept trying to put her arms on him but he kept knocking them away. His grandfather told him to sit down.

"No! I'm sick of you! You drunk bastard!"

"What did you say!"

His grandfather lunged for him but Cyrus was as quick as a badger from a striking snake. The table and everything on it hit the floor with a crash as Cyrus dodged each of his grandfather's lunges. He ran to the front door, outside and towards the corn. The sunlight was all but history, a silhouette of the horizon. He just kept running in blindness—crying uncontrollably and screaming for his brother.

He saw a flash, then nothing.

"Be still and know your Papa is coming."

"Who are you?" he uttered faintly.

CHAPTER SEVENTEEN

It was the third day before he came around fully: busted his head wide open, his grandfather reported to the feed store brethren. It throbbed so that he would lose where he was for moments until his Grandmother came into the room. He could recall bits and pieces of the kitchen episode, but his balance was hazy like being twirled in a feed sack and told to stand straight.

"How are you this day?" she asked.

"Don't rightly know, 'ceptin I hurt—where's Gran'pa?"

Her mood turned maudlin and her face tensed making the wrinkles at the corners of her mouth like a spider's web. They hadn't spoken of "the incident" because it neither fit nor had cause; the one topic thick in the air like a wet wool blanket was Jake. No one knew how to talk about it; it just hung there like a portrait.

"Yur Gran'pa is in the barn—he's lookin' the corn over. It's about time for croppin', you know."

"What happened, Gran'ma?"

"Well child, he was real sick . . ."

"No Gran'ma, to me", he interrupted.

"Yur Gran'pa was tellin' you about Jake . . ."

"Grandmother! I know that—I won't ever forget that. What happened to me?" he said pointing to his head.

"You ran into the corn, it was dark out and I reckon you couldn't see—you ran into one of yur Gran'pa's scarecrows."

"One of his scarecrows? When'd he put up scarecrows?"

"Couldn't say."

"That ain't all Gran'ma. There was someone there. I heard 'em."

"Where child? In our corn? At dark? No."

The moments he was completely alone brought a pain he'd never known but felt oddly familiar. The unfinished chapter torn from his book left him completely barren without explanation: Jake was gone and it didn't figure. The question bounced in his head like a ball in a tumbling box.

The only time he felt better was when Cheyenne had come to see him, and for the spell that wasn't interrupted by his Grandmother with impeccable consistency, he felt near normal.

In moments, and when he wasn't with Jake in thought, the few moments he could consciously recall in that corn patch were beyond mystery; those seconds just prior to his Grandpa scooping him up was where he was stuck. It was those vague but audible words he heard; the words he so plainly felt came from his Grandpa, who wouldn't own up to it.

"I haven't one smidgen of a clue what you are referrin' to there, Cyrus. It took near an hour to find you in that dark mess, and when I came on you I just picked you up—I never said a word.".

All of it gnawed at him so that it became an obsession: his wanting to get back to the spot where he ended and the voice began, if not for anything else but to see it in the day's light. But, the problem was downstairs. How was he to get past the sentries, and if caught by his Grandfather the days of sandbagging would be over? Grandma would fuss a measure but the consequences would be negligible. The true mountain was recalling where he ran into this thing; how far out and where it was he couldn't remember. The whole situation was such a puzzle: his finding out about Jake, his run from the house, the field, and where this mysterious voice fit in was all scattered from hell to breakfast, as his grandfather would say.

As best he could remember they had just set to the table when his Grandpa entered so it had to be dark out. He definitely remembered what his Grandfather said, but after that was a mystery.

The fence along the front paddock was a good six feet high, but dropped a measure from the gate and was likely where he entered the patch. Yes, the point he entered the field had to have been where the fence was lowest; but, where to from there? She would remember.

"Grandma", he began, while she fluffed his pillow. "Can you recall where you and Gran'pa got me that night in the patch?"

She studied the question as she always did, stare at the ceiling and count off on her boney fingers, like the answer would come from above: "Well child, I believe . . ." she began. "I reckon from the time you skedaddled to when your Gramps fetched ya was somewhere 'round thirty minutes, give 'er take. We had to trail you in circles; I held the lamp."

"Yes 'am, you figure Gran'pa would recollect?"

"'Course he would child, but so do I; I ain't that slight-a mind. I say that, it was so dark in that mess-a stalk, but I know where the scarecrow's is posted anyways", she smiled. "One thing 'bout your Gramps is he ain't n'er changed a lick in anything he does, from layin' out scarecrows to puttin' on his long-Johns." She paced out directions with her finger on his quilt and Cyrus knew exactly where it was.

"Gran'ma", he began. "When you and Gramps found me, did you hear anything before, like folks talking or maybe Grandpa sayin' something?

"Like what? You thinkin' other folks were out an' about in the patch?"

"I ain't sure, I just recall hearin' someone say something . . . I can't be for sure, but it seemed like it was saying, *Your Grandfather is coming.*"

"Well, I don't recollect any talkin' out there, 'ceptin your Gramps hollerin' for more light and to keep up."

"You sure he didn't say nothin' when he found me?"

"He said a trifle about all the blood you'd run out, and for me to make sure it was covered up so the varmints wouldn't catch scent . . . don't recollect nothin' about *gettin' ya.* What's all this bother have to do with; you still thinkin' on Jake?"

"I think about him a lot, Gran'ma. I think about him an awful lot. Sometimes it hurts more than I can stand", his lips quivered. "I occasion to be with him I miss him so much!"

"I know child. I miss him myself", she said patting his head. "Life ain't at all fair at times. No sir, not fair at all for some, but you can't go thinkin' like that Cy; only the Lord can take."

"Gran'ma it don't make a lick a sense to take someone like Jake and leave the Pritchett's. I don't wish harm on anyone, but it just don't make sense to do what He did and not leave a reason behind or somethin' sayin' why."

"Child, it don't work that way and I'd give an eye-tooth to have an answer for ya, even a wrong one ifin' it would settle you. When He took your Ma and Pa I thought I couldn't draw another breath when the sheriff brought news. It just didn't make a lick-a sense neither—takin' your folks when you was still a yearling'. I cried for days; hours and hours on end."

"Don't He know that some folk are needed down here?"

"You know Cyrus J, and this is just a thought that came a time after your folks were taken. The thought of it was a-kin to a reason I pretended true and it made me feel better—I couldn't truly say how I came up with it, but it was like I had to *put* a reason to that crash and this was my answer: God, in all of His glory, might and power, made the heavens and earth and all the angels who worship Him. Now, the way I'm seein' it was in all His place, everything around Him had ne'er a choice to be in His presence because He made 'em for that reason. Now, like us folk down here, we really didn't conjure none to be here neither, we just were; but, and this is what sets us from the angels: we have a choice to know, love and believe in Him or not. When we choose to believe in Him, without ever seein' Him, just on faith that He is real, that makes us the most special thing He's ever made. I reckon that sounds crazier than a barn owl full-a corn squeezin's, but it made me feel better thinkin' the Lord took my boy because He could hardly wait to see the expression on his face."

Cyrus lay in his Grandmother's arms about to fall asleep when his grandfather could be heard clumping up the porch stairs.

"Want me to ask your Grandpa to come up and have a chat with ya? Maybe he can iron out any questions 'bout the scarecrow."

"Ah, no mam. I reckon you cleared it up."

Cyrus piddled about his room until he heard the front door shut. When he heard the second door slam and the truck start, he put on his overalls and boots and set out.

His head throbbed as he began to serpentine through the cornstalks that were about three feet over his head. It wasn't as simple as he thought because the stalk's height and density confused his bearings. For a moment he thought how it would be getting lost in this maze for a second time. Geez, the beating that would come from that.

There it was. An invariable statue. It could have been made of stone and likened to something you would worship it was so big. What was his grandfather's thought for placing this monstrosity so close to the house? It must have been ten feet into the air and a good four feet over the corn. What was he looking to scare—buzzards? He circled it several times, pushing down the stalks around it, touching it on passes almost caressing it. He squeezed the legs that dangled from each side of the four by four that ran through its backside as a spine, up and through the cross member for its shoulders and its head that was made from a pillow sack. Yep, it was a pair of his grandpa's long-handles alright and it even resembled him to an element. He pushed the corn down around it so he could gander at this thing on a stick.

"What in the name?" he muttered.

Just a few feet back were small splotches of blood his grandmother had missed, some indentations that were the size and shape of his grandpa's brogans and then corn again. He stood over the spot he laid, all the while staring up at this thing in bewilderment and whispering: "Was it you who was talking?" God, how stupid is this, he thought?

"You'd be one heck of an *Imagine* there buddy ifin' you could talk", he whispered as he walked about it. "Yep, ifin' you had said somethin' then Grandma or Grandpa woulda heard ya."

"Why would it be so difficult to believe?" a voice came.

He froze.

"What is the problem, Master Cyrus?" this voice inquired.

He kept looking around himself, squinting through the corn, not at all able to pinpoint where the voice was coming.

"Ah . . . I . . . ah, is that you Grandpa? I can explain what I'm doin' here. You see, I lost . . well, I . ."

"I don't believe your grandfather is here", the voice interrupted. "In fact, I don't think there is anyone beyond *us*."

"Then can I ask who you are?"

"*May I*", the voice began. "And yes, but I cannot say."

"Why?" Cyrus asked, stepping closer to the scarecrow.

"I do not know that either."

"Well then, here's somethin' pretty simple—how's it you know me?"

"That is another good question; I only wish I had an appropriate answer."

"Appropriate? What's that?"

"A sound, meaningful answer to your sound question."

"Okay, you know words I ain't ever heard before but you don't know yur name?"

"Yes, I know a lot of things."

"Okay . . . okay, you say you ain't my Grandpa, and you don't sound like him so I'll run with that. You say you know lots of things . . .", Cyrus continued while peering through the corn. "What's say I ask you questions and you answer them, but not with what you been answerin', like *I don't know* or *I can't say*. If you ain't got the answer . . ."

". . . *If you **don't** have the answer*", the voice interrupted.

"Huh? If I *don't* have the answer? What's that mean?"

"That is the correct conjunction, in fact, word. There is no such word, ***ain't***."

Cyrus muttered to himself, "Oh my god, there's a teacher lost in my corn."

"Alright. Can—may I finish?" Cyrus added sheepishly.

"Certainly."

"If you **don't** have the answer you can at least say why; one or the other."

"I will do my best."

"The only thing—the only people—out here are you and me, right?"

"I suppose."

"Good. Now, are you a scarecrow?"

There was silence for several seconds and Cyrus asked the question again.

"I think I am. That is to say, I think I see you though dimly; you are below me."

"Well, at least yur thinking", Cyrus answered, walking to the base of the scarecrow and staring upwards to its face. "Talk again and I'll watch for yur mouth to move."

"What would you care for me to say?"

"Ha! It didn't move, so someone is out there crawfishin' me and doin' a great job! I'm on to ya! You can come out!" he shouted into the corn.

"Master Cyrus, there are no others here. I am able to feel for miles."

"My name ain't Master, and it don't begin with such neither."

"It's **isn't** and **doesn't**, and I am aware of that. Are you not the oldest male child of the Buckman household?"

"I'm the *only* child of the Buckman household and my fanny will prove it."

"Your fanny?"

"Yeah, it's somethin' hooked to me that ain't—isn't made of straw and stings when a chunk-a leather straps it."

"My."

"No, mine. Listen, are you for real? I've conjured *Imagines* before but most are scary, and I'm just wantin' to know if you are . . . are real this go-round. I've had some *Imagines* run me about before, chase me with arrows and knives and such, but none ever worked up a fret on my words."

"I think I am."

"Ya know, this *I think* garbage is really gettin' old; if I shoot straight pool with you then I expect the same back. Don't know where you come from but you obviously went to school, somethin' I'll try not to hold agin ya, but if you care to be friends yur gunna have to try harder. I just lost my brother, my best friend—the only thing that meant anything to me in this stinkin' place and I ain't— **don't**—care to dally."

"I thought you only lost Jake?"

Cyrus fell back from the scarecrow and stared at him while his eyes began filling with tears. In some bizarre, distant note of familiarity he thought he knew this voice. The nuance was so familiar—the diction, the sass, even the condescending tone—it was all JAKE! He lunged forward and grabbed the scarecrow about his legs and hugged as much as he could hold.

"Jake! Jake!"

"No Master Cyrus! I am not Jake."

"But you just got through saying you don't know who you are. How do you know you ain't Jake?"

"Because what I know of him is enough to know that I am not him. Master Cyrus, in all candor, I do not know who I am, I only know who you are."

He let go of the scarecrow in silent sorrow and bewilderment. He stood back a measure and again stared up at the triangular face that resembled his Grandfather. He wiped his face and eyes and found himself back at the beginning with a handful of answers to silos of questions. With his foot he scooted a pile of snapped stalks to a heap and sat down. Though it was humid in this southern tundra he smiled upwards, squinting at the sun's rays through the corn tops that illuminated his spot and brought it to seem an altar of sorts: dust particles and small insects floated and danced in an iridescence of holiness that showered and bathed him with a comfort that things were to be okay. It came to him funny, this thought of being forever alone and yet comforted by an *Imagine* after his world had been completely demolished. Only then did *Imagines* appear, when reality was ever so difficult to handle—Jake would climb him about that. "Pudger! When you gunna grab-a-holt?" he'd scold. Cyrus laughed aloud for a moment and then again came that pain—the reality. He was never going to see his brother ever, ever again. All this struggle just to get past standing up to Pritchett and the rest like him to come; was it so for naught? This, just to teach him how to love someone and then the daunting pain of losing them? Why, why would God—if there was one—bring his Jake into this life and just as quickly take him for no damn good reason, he thought. God was supposed to be love, at least that's what Pastor Higgins cajoled. Maybe that's why Grandpa never churched because he knew it was all a waste of time: Praying and such to no one you could see or feel; standing and singing hymns you could just as well do sitting. Or maybe, just maybe he was to see Jake again. Maybe it would be in a place where *Imagines* were real and pain was not, and all this down here was just a test to see how well you weathered storms. All he had to do was be tough and weather it. Yeah.

"Hey, Scarecrow! Candor? What the world is *candor*?"

"It means, to be frank, to speak in honesty", the voice replied.

"Hmm, why wouldn't you do that anyway?"

Again there was a stream of silence as he sat waiting patiently for the scarecrow to reply—

"What?" Cyrus inquired. "Is this the way this friendship is going to be; me asking simple, plain questions and you just hangin' there?"

"No, Master Cyrus, and I apologize. I just did not expect—well, think that you would be so inquisitive or insightful. And yes to your question; folks—ah, people should be honest in what they say."

"Then wouldn't it just be a waste-a words to say that, lessin' someone was expectin' a lie right off, and ifin' they were, there wouldn't be much point in listenin' to that *folk* in the first place. Grown *folk* are more a mess than us smaller ones, aren't they?"

"Yes sir, I *reckon* they are."

"Now there ya go Mr. Cornfield, you're comin' round—hey! Mr Cornfield! That's gotta be yur name. It fits perfect. Now all we gotta come up with is your first one."

"Hmm, does seem to fit, doesn't it? Especially when considering my position."

"How's 'bout . . . no, that wouldn't do", Cyrus queried himself in a murmur. "Hey! I think I got one—John, you know, for long *John*?"

"I'm not too sure, Master Cyrus--."

Cyrus interrupted: "Mr Cornfield, we gotta have some ground rules up front here. First, you gotta pitch that *Master* garbage; not only it don't—doesn't fit, it makes me feel like I should be wearin' something gamey like ankle shoes with starched socks. Next, let's both talk the way we want. Does that sound okay for starters?"

"Well, I will concede the first *ground rule* but have a bit of difficulty with the second. It should be in any man's interest to want to better himself, and the first representation of one's self, apart from the visual, is in one's ability to communicate; would you not agree?"

"I didn't understand much of what you said but it damn sure sounded good."

"Mas—Cyrus, cursing is another suit you should rarely, if ever, put on. It's the impression you make."

"You mean, cussin' keeps *one* at home plate?"

"Exactly."

"Mr. Cornfield, even though I'm not sure who *one* is, I'm gunna do my damnedest to do what you say because I really think . . . hey! I got it again. Argie. You love to argue—Argie Cornfield. It just came to me like you did, outta nowhere."

"Argie Cornfield . . . oh yes, that has a definite ring. Fine, Argie Cornfield it shall be."

"Can—may I call you Argie? I mean, since you did come to me and I gave you your name and all."

"Why yes, of course."

"Good. Listen, you been to school and all, that's a cinch, you reckon you can help me with Ms Fugate's work?"

"I reckon, but know that *help* is all I will extend. School is for you to learn."

"I gotcha, I don't plan on making you do my work, just askin' if you'll help like Jake did. Argie, I have to be gettin' back before my grandparents do, so can I guess you will be here when I come back?"

"Yes."

"You promise?"

"I don't see I have much of a choice, you think? Besides, I want to be here—with you."

He began his trek back through the maze all the while in wonderment of what he had found, or had found him. The farther he came away from Argie the more he questioned his existence and the soundness of his own mind. The many times before he had come to rely on these *Imagines*, they disappeared as quickly when they were shared. If he kept Argie a secret then all would remain right with the world. That was it. That was the chain link that snapped in every incident—he told someone else and everything changed. Well, not this go-round. Argie was his and his only and no one, not his grandparents, not school friends, not even Pastor Higgins would get wind of Argie. He was his diamond in the ruff; his pig in the poke—his friend.

By the time he reached the porch front he was completely tapped and soaked with sweat. He made it to the swing and collapsed. The cool but humid breeze was inviting as clips of Jake brushed through his mind with his incessant banter concerning Argie:

"Pudger! Here ya go again and with what this time, a damn scarecrow? Okay, okay, *Many Moons* was a nice conjure, 'cause you could play cowboys and Indians with him and all, but a scarecrow! Dressed in yur Grandpa's long-handles?"

"You don't understand, Bruiser, this time is different; Argie ain't like any of the others, he's like *you*. He ain't scary, he don't—doesn't have a knife or arrows or noth—or anything, and he's smarter than Ms Fugate and Mr Burnside put together."

"And another thing, he's callin' ya on the way ya talk? That ain't right, Pudgie."

"***Isn't,*** and 'course it is. I wanna be respectable and make a good *represent*. You know, one . . ."

"Pudgie!" Jake interrupted. "I heard all the *one* stuff I care to. You really like him don't you?"

"Yeah, but he isn't you Jake. No one will ever be you. Where are you?"

"Right here. I'm right next to you."

"Don't leave", Cyrus whispered.

CHAPTER EIGHTEEN

His eyes opened to the morning that came through his pecan tree; radiant beams flashed over his eyes with the wind's
gust as though a dozen photographers were couched in its limbs.
He lay there and daydreamed. Several days had passed since the
discovery of his *Imagine* and the conversation that ensued (one-sid-
ed, of course) concerning his being found late that morning "unconscious" on the porch swing. He was only enjoying the outside
air, he argued, and had fallen to sleep, but his Grandmother was
fit-to-be-tied and Grandpa, who only cared whether he was ready
for duty or not, shrugged it off as a misfire in judgment.

"Cyrus! Cyrus J, are you awake?" his Grandmother hollered
from downstairs.

"No mam!" he hollered back, laughing at his mischievousness.
He could only play with his Grandmother in that fashion.

She stepped to his door and knocked quietly with her coon like
hand, saying as she stuck her head through, "There's a friend here
to say, hey, are you covered?"

That salutation meant it was Cheyenne because no one but Mr Thompson and Doc Wash had paid him a visit, and his being covered was never an issue.

"Ah—just a second, Gran'ma."

He scurried to straighten what he could at arm's length, pasted his hair down with a spitball, fluffed his pillow and set it vertical so just his torso was exposed and he could sit upright like a baseball player might resting from an injury.

"Gran'ma, would you come in for a second—alone?"

"What is it, child?"

"Ah, would you please put those over there under my bed, and . . ."

"Under yur bed?" she interrupted. "Yur britches and such?"

"Gran'ma, please."

"Cyrus, it's Cheyenne."

"I know who it is", he whispered tensely. "It's a mess in here and my clothes smell of pork renderings."

Cheyenne stuck her head through the doorway and stared at Cyrus, who was busier instructing his Grandmother about than who was watching. When he realized he froze in embarrassment.

"Hey you", she whispered.

"Hey, Cheyenne", he stuttered. "What ya doing this way?"

"Just thought I'd come by to see how you were doing."

Grandma Mattie stood there gawking back and forth at each utterance between them, all the while holding a pair of Cyrus' soiled underwear.

"Grandma! Please!"

"Okay, Cy", she smiled.

It was tensely silent for a moment as Cheyenne milled about, ambling towards the bedside in a soothing manner. It was difficult not to pay attention. She was so . . . well, he hadn't been around long enough to spoon up the proper adjective, but whatever she exuded was perfect. She was just opening her mouth when he interjected, "Whatdaya think of my pecan tree? Gran'pa says it's probably over a hundred years old."

"Wow."

She wore bib overalls that were well worn with a long sleeve flannel shirt of blue and red stripes, and lace up boots like a farm hand and not someone as dainty as Cheyenne, but she wasn't that way at all; dainty, that is, and it was the most alluring feature of her character: that element of androgyny many girls of the day labored to hide but was so becoming. It proved she had little fear and her beauty was enhanced by that.

"So, when you thinkin' on coming back to school, or are you just gunna lay here through Christmas and rot?" she giggled.

"Oh, I gotta get back in the saddle soon enough. I reckon I'll be there tomorrow."

"May I?" she asked, pointing to the bed's edge.

"Oh—yeah, sure", he answered, scooting over.

"Cyrus", she said, looking out his window.

"What's wrong?"

"Nothing really—I guess. Pritchett is running his mouth a lot", she blurted.

"What's new? So what's he saying?"

"Nobody can stand him, Cyrus. Everyone but his toadies and they're just as bad. He keeps saying things about Jake and all, since he isn't here anymore, and you--."

"What about me?"

"Nothing particular, just that your *bodyguard* ain't around any-more and that you'll have to fend for yourself."

What she said cut him to the core: the coldness of the truth and having it come from her was numbing. It took everything to look at her and smile nonchalantly.

"I guess I'll have to prove it wrong, won't I?"

"I reckon you don't have to prove a thing, Cyrus Buckman."

"'Course I do. Jake was with me cuz we was brothers, and he'd expect nothing less of me to stand for myself."

"Cyrus, Pritchett doesn't stand for anything let alone himself; he has a passel of hedgehogs that do it for him and everyone knows it. You don't have call to stand against all that."

"Yeah, but Jake would. He taught me more than anyone in this place, with the main thing not to take guff from anyone", he said with assertion.

She smiled at him while she blushed with that thing that made young boys feel strong and appropriate.

"Cyrus J—I like that name for you. I know it belongs to your Gran'ma, but you think I could use it too?"

"Course, silly girl", he answered with his red face. "Know you be the only one though."

She kissed her forefinger, touched it to his nose and smiled again. She had this smile that would make a train take a dirt road. Cheyenne Christian Hold was her name and of German derivation, which was written all over her. A bit larger than Cyrus, she was big-boned and walked with a gate of assurance yet poised; a flat-footed gate that was graced by an ever so soft pigeon-toe. Her eyes were the same color as his but deep blue, somewhat like clouds set in lids that had been hand-traced from an Elm leaf and near impossible not to get lost in. All this centered with a button nose on a beautiful round face of alabaster and long blonde hair, which she wore in a bunch with a stick through it, but when she was with him she wore it down, bound to a ponytail with short strands left to float in what Cyrus kidded as *reins*. They were so young and what they shared so innocent. They were the best of friends.

Cheyenne left with his Grandparents to hitch a ride. Before they were out the house door he already had on his coveralls and socks. He was completely ready when the truck started. There wasn't much time to get in and out of the patch because he didn't know the schedule now—Cheyenne, although he was glad to see

152

her, had thrown an uncalculated variable into the mix by taking the ride home.

"Argie!" he hollered, coming into the arena of flattened stalks. "Argie! Mr Cornfield."

"Yes, Cyrus."

"You awake?"

"No", Argie chuckled.

"Funny. Do you just *know* everything?"

"No, I don't think so. For whatever reason, I just seem to *know* the things that concern you."

"Then you know about Cheyenne?"

"Well—in as much as she has to do with you, I suppose. She is quite a beautiful person."

"Yeah, I know. She's got great hair that smells good, and I believe she could whomp anyone at school", Cyrus muttered matter-of-factly.

"Whomp? I don't think I would associate such a verb with Miss Hold—."

"Oooohh, Argie! Rail the sentence correction stuff an' just talk to me!"

"My apology. What is it you care to talk about?"

"Some things—everything!"

"You're worried about going back to school?" Argie asked.

"Yeah. I got problems with a guy, which is stupid to say since you probably know 'bout it anyways."

"Mr Pritchett?"

"Yep, that's the guy—and all his gang. I know they wanna *pants* me, and I know they'll do it in front of Cheyenne. Even though I know it's pretty much gunna happen, I don't think Cheyenne will pay any attention or think ill of me when it does."

"I think your summation is correct—concerning Miss Cheyenne, that is; couldn't say either way for the other."

"What's that mean?"

"I mean, I cannot say about what is to come."

"I thought you knew everything."

"No sir, not like that."

"Then how do you know 'bout Cheyenne, and *knew* 'bout Jake? Oh my god, I'm bantering with a straw-stuffed scarecrow in long-handles!"

"Yes, but they speak well. Very important to heed your under garments, straw-stuffed or not."

"You wouldn't look at me as a loon if you were down here, would ya? Ifin' you were a person and all?"

"No. I feel you are the sanest of the lot, in a term familiar to you—."

Cyrus sat down on the heap of dried stalks and stared up at Argie in thought. Confusion seemed to be his *lot* in life, as with fear and trepidation; they came as a package deal. Loneliness was running a close third quickly and would overtake him if he allowed the thoughts of Jake to lounge in his head for any time. There were so many emotions he was feeling and so afraid to put them to words. Who would hear them much less understand them if he could? Hey, what about Argie, he thought? What would be the risk there? I mean, he never gets to town or school so who would gossip with him; and even if he did, who on earth would take anything serious from a pair of long-handles with a pillow sack head? He wouldn't do that kind of talking anyway.

"Hey Argie", he began sheepishly. "You reckon if I was to . . . if I was to just talk to you 'bout things that ain't—aren't, right?"

"Yes sir."

". . . things that *aren't* right in my head, that you could *just* be my friend like that?"

"I would love to be your friend *just* like that, Cyrus. I will be your friend anyway that you need me to be."

The morning light was fresh in its autumn twist as it edged its way through the stalks and against his damp cheeks. These were not the usual tears, the footprints from emotions he could not escape, but the ones of hope he had yet to understand. They were like the ones he knew when he was with his brother.

"Argie, what am I going to do about this thing at school?"

"Tell me what this *thing* is about and we will discuss it."

"Well, for no reason I can come up with, this guy named Pritchett has been rankin' me out ever since I came to this school. When Jake was here, he was kind-a my . . . guard—my brother, and he stood in front when trouble came. I've never been 'round anyone who made me so . . . so quiet and still. Now, it's like it's always been again. I'm just plain yellow when it comes to standin' up. I'm so small and wimpy that I just as soon have a sign on that says, 'kick me, I won't do nothin'."

"*Anything*, and of course you do something, just not what you feel you should", Argie answered politely. "Cyrus, all the things you have in your head about what you *should* be are not lining up with what you are: you feel you should be like Jake, but you are stuck with Cyrus. Herein lay the dilemma . . ."

". . . the what?" Cyrus interrupted.

"Excuse me, the *problem*. When you compare yourself with another you will **always** find traits you wish you had that are near impossible to gain. One, you have wanted to be as big as Jake, as strong as Jake, as assertive as Jake; but, you see yourself as small, weak and timid Cyrus who has nothing to put into this huge pot of stew. Two, all that you are dismissing of yourself, more often than not, is more important than what you think you should be."

"Boy Argie, I didn't cipher much what you said but it sounded better than anything Ms Fugate could come up with, and she's the smartest person I know", Cyrus said in astonishment. "What I'm hearin' Mr Cornfield is, I'm just as good as Jake but ain't seein' it?"

"Yes my child, and in many senses—better. You have been spending too much time in your head on thoughts of grandeur—excuse me—thoughts of greatness you believe you should have, and swept under the rug all the beautiful things you truly *are!*"

"Okay, name just one great thing I *am.*"

"You are *discerning*", Argie answered with a chuckle.

"I'm *di-what?*"

"*Discerning*", he answered. "It means, sensitive to perceptions only you can see, and in many cases feel. Things are *always* as they appear to you, Cyrus."

"Now I know yur off the rail 'cause Jake taught me, if he taught me anything, *nothing* is like it appears!"

"For him Cyrus, not for you", Argie replied. "Are you hearing me now?"

They were silent while he thought of what Argie had said. He remained stuck for a moment on the idea that he was anything like his brother, much more, better than, regardless of how big the word to describe it came. He rocked back and forth with his arms about his legs and pondered these notions.

"So what are you saying, Argie? That I'm somethin' I don't know I am?"

"In some ways, yes; but in more ways you are something you have yet to recognize—You are a diamond in the ruff, my child, and probably enough that you do not recognize it, for at least now."

"Ruff . . . and diamonds? That doesn't help where I am, Argie. What about Pritchett?"

"Okay, what about him? What do you see about Mr Pritchett, Mr Buckman?"

"Huh", Cyrus chuckled through a whisper. "He's one giant pain in my—fanny is what I see."

"Go past that."

"Past what, Argie?" he answered incensed. "What are you giggin' me about? What is it yur fishin' for?"

"I would like for you to look past what is easily seen—look to your heart, what it sees."

"My heart? I don't quite understand ya. What I *feel*?"

"Think of Jake. What did you see in him? What was it in him that made you a kindred spirit?"

"I guess that he liked me."

"Why?"

"That he liked me for me?" he laughed. "Oh—is that it?"

"You're on the track,"

"Argie! I'm still holdin' an empty sack here! What am I going to do when they front me?"

"Think of you. Think of Jake. Then think of how you came together. It will be difficult, as all beautiful things are, but you must see it for yourself. Face it without fear, Cyrus."

"Unbelievable!" Cyrus yelled, throwing his arms to the air. "Only I would cotton to an *Imagine* that argues, speaks nonsense while he corrects *me* and then leaves me with face it! Face what—Pritchett?"

"The music", Argie mused. "I'm very tired, and your parents are on their way."

"*Grandparents*, and what music?"

"You will know what to do when it arrives."

"How is it you're tired when all you have to do is *hang* there?' Cyrus muttered, making his way towards the house. "I'll kiss a fat man's bear ass before I heed a yappin' pillow sack."

Coming over the fence at its usual spot and still muttering disgruntlement, he could hear the sputter of his Grandpa's truck at Burle Barn near a quarter mile away. He was home free, but just stood there with his hands clasped behind his head, gawking down the road in disbelief.

"My god, that sack-a hay is real", he whispered.

CHAPTER NINETEEN

The weather drifted into something of a cold, greasy southern slop; the kind of winter only known in the south where waking to an open window left you damp and feeling like a grungy sock. To Cyrus though, it was a welcome respite from the summers that stayed strong in his memory, yet with exception for the bugs and swamp stench it was still Alabama.

A week had lapsed since Jake's funeral, and like the weather, absolutely nothing had changed. Strangely, he expected something from the ordinary that wouldn't give: a sign from God, an answer for His actions; an apology from his Grandfather—there was no answer. The only piece that brought color and depth to this dismal mosaic was utterly gone. It was all so turned around, he felt.

His Grandfather's voice came like pistol fire that made him run for cover in his thought. His muscles tensed and his blood turned cold for a split second. His only resolution was to get back into the game and away from this. His daydreaming of Cheyenne brought him comfort that it would soon be better, but it was only a thought that just as quickly became empty space.

"Cyrus J", his Grandmother called from the kitchen. "Are you to try school this day?"

"Yes 'am", he replied.

His Grandfather added something but he didn't pay it any mind; a dangerous position he traded for sanity. His attitude towards Grandpa Cyrus audaciously wandered into apathy, and any retribution that might befall him was without consequence anymore.

He sat on the bed's edge with everything on but one boot. Staring out at his pecan tree, he could not escape the question: why wasn't he allowed at Jake's funeral? It was partly explained by his Grandfather until interrupted:

"They can't keep him cold long enough . . . "

"Gran'pa!" she interrupted forcefully. "Cyrus honey, you can visit him anytime, but it bes' they handle the services now and Doc Wash just don't feel you're up to it."

He was learning that "candor" was only a casual expression in the adult world most likely used only between them. There wasn't much in life that occurred without smoke and mirrors. While Mr Cornfield had said it was a gift, that enabled him to see people for what they truly were, it now seemed more a curse. His only attachment to this world anymore was Cheyenne, and the occasional thought of her leaving gripped him with an unspeakable emptiness.

He finished with his attire and went downstairs to eat before chores.

"Cyrus J, Miss Cheyenne said she would be happenin' by on her way to school—maybe you could take a ride with her."

"Yeah!" he said elated.

"I thought that would bring you up."

His Grandfather sat in his usual place, chewing on his pipe and peering at Cyrus sideways as though he were thinking of something, anything, to bring him back down.

"Cyrus, since you be back to speed an' all, I want the loft cleaned out this afternoon", his Grandpa commanded.

"Gran'pa, I don't want him high up for a spell", she contended from the stove.

"I don't . . ."

"Enough Cyrus!" she interrupted. "He cannot, will not be up high until he's right. There is nothing that loft can't wait for. That is all I'm gunna hear of it." Her opposition was strong and especially on an issue that concerned her grandson, but not yet strong enough to face him in a soliloquy; she never turned from the stove with intention. Cyrus smiled quietly as he glanced at his grandfather.

He ran through his chores with a modicum of effort because his thought was on Cheyenne. His feeling for her was consuming at times. The only one he felt comfortable talking about her with was Argie, and that was strange enough since he was no more than a sack of hay. When his grandmother spoke of her it made him blush and only served to compound the confusion. Most of what he truly felt he kept to himself.

He heard Mr Hold's truck at the front turn row a ways from the house and everything in his head disappeared. By the time he'd jumped the paddock fence his whole persona took an entire twist: he was bigger, stronger, assertive—whatever. He was some-one else, at least that's what his grandmother saw.

"Hey ya Chey", he cheered, and gavotte to the passenger window.

Mr Hold was near as big as Grandpa Cyrus, but without the gut or disposition. He was a quiet man and commanded a presence because of that fact, with the funny thing that no one knew him; he wasn't much on standing idle about the feed store which the bulk of the townsmen did as right-of-passage, but Mr Hold had nothing of it: "Those men would lose a crop before givin' up that time of day", he'd say.

His daughter was a lot like him in that regard. It was easy to see where her character came from. Mr Hold had the exact same golden hair, blue eyes and big bones. Everything was evenly placed in Amish style and his gait was so plainly *Cheyenne* that it made Cyrus laugh aloud the first time he saw him.

"What?" she asked him.

"Nothin'", Cyrus giggled. "Ah, your Pa; he's just like you, or you're like him—ain't reckoned which."

Cyrus hadn't been at the truck a second before his grandfather was coming off the porch steps, the only thing that would distract him from his girl.

"Mr Buckman, how do ya?" Mr Hold said as he stepped from the truck.

"Fair to midland."

They stepped away from the truck for local banter. Cheyenne put her arm on top of Cyrus' that was draped over the passenger window and he smiled sheepishly.

"You always blush when I come 'round, Cyrus J."

"Don't neither—I just hold my breath."

"That makes no sense a-tall, goofy boy" she said grinning.

"You reckon I could hitch a ride to school with y'all?" Cyrus asked.

"No room."

He stared at her with a slight smile that disappeared when her expression didn't change.

"Really?" he said.

"You are as gullible as a porch puppy, Cyrus J! Why on earth would we have just happened by—to see your Gran'pa?"

"I didn't know", he cowed.

She got out to let him in. He squatted to his knees, straddling the gear shift in a boyish manner and it was fine to be there. It was at the moment she closed the door that he could hear his Grandfather and Mr Hold's conversation and he heard Jake's name. He giggled smartly when his Grandfather looked to him for a second as though he hadn't an idea of their conversation. Cheyenne was oblivious to the men and kept distracting Cyrus, which he juggled well.

"Sterling ain't doin' well at all, and some of the men are planning a get together to help him crop out", Mr Hold said. "He was a mess at the funeral, but can you blame him?"

"I know. I was there."

"You know I don't pay much mind to the feed store folk, on account I ain't got time; but, I heard Bounce Teal say that if he had got Jake in to Doc Wash before he did they might not have lost him" Mr Hold mumbled matter-of-factly. "What I heard, anyways."

"Huh. Well, you can count on me and my plow horse."

Even with Cheyenne next to him, with all her attention and kid affection, he and his thoughts left the truck. Pictures of his buddy shadowed in front of him. Her being next to him was in a way permission for him to let go, but he couldn't. It was unexplainable. All of it was in his chest. In that moment her youth disappeared as she put her arm around his waist and her hand against his face.

"He left me, Chey", he barely uttered.

"I know, but not on purpose."

The men spoke for a minute or two longer and Cyrus wiped his face clear of the moment. She kept squeezing him every so often and it made him stronger. He had never been sure what love was, but if it had anything to do with that very second, he was hooked.

They arrived at the school in silence, surprised by the feelings they had just experienced without instruction. Each day they found something new about each other.

"Cheyenne, you wanna come see somethin' with me this afternoon?" Cyrus posed.

"Sure", she smiled. "What?"

"Somethin' you might or might not see."

"I don't mind crazy."

Just as she finished, her face changed as he turned and ran into Pritchett.

"Hey, lookie-lookie, it's little Cyrus Buckman and his girl, curds an' whey", Pritchett said, surrounded by his toadies.

Fear and embarrassment came over him and it was difficult to tell which was worse or came first. He could think of little more than where he could hide or who was in sight that could rescue him. Where was an adult when you needed one?

"Pritchett, why don't you find the rock you came from under and go back?" she said.

"First, he has Jake; now he has a girl front for him."

"At least he has a girl", she muttered.

Those in ear shot cooed, and it seemed to take the wind right out of Pritchett, just as it took the wind out of Cyrus. It would have been better if it had come from him, but danged if she didn't have a quicker draw.

"Buckman, yur day is just 'round the corner—and whoosh", he said, making a downward motion with his hands about his waist.

Cyrus, just as everyone else in that little caucus, knew exactly what that meant except Cheyenne. None of the girls really knew what being *pants* meant, but the boys did and they all laughed aloud.

"Cyrus J, I'll see you later", Cheyenne added, turning with her girlfriends.

"Yeah, you certainly will", Pritchett laughed, patting Cyrus on the head.

Oddly, he didn't think on Pritchett the entire day because Cheyenne kept interrupting his thoughts. The incident embarrassed him a little, but he was almost finding himself trying to be afraid and it wasn't happening. What kept coming into thought was what Argie had asked him about how he felt about Pritchett.

He didn't think anything of him, certainly not like he did about Jake.

"Think of you. Think of Jake. Think of Pritchett", he remembered Argie saying and it was just as disconcerting now as it was then. "What did I see in Jake and Jake see in me", he muttered to himself. Sitting on the cottonwood stump just yards from his protective classroom window, he took another bite of johnnycake and pondered that very thing.

Final bell, and everyone shuffled outside where again the weather had turned. It was about ten degrees colder. Cyrus stood on the edge of Chicken Ranch road waiting for his walking mate when he caught a glimpse of Pritchett, who was busy torturing innocent's with his enclave some distance away. The thought of what lay in store wasn't a bother anymore. What he kept thinking of was that feeling he had when Cheyenne put her arm around him and whispered in his ear. It was nothing he had known. This is to say, he liked her, that was a given, but after that moment in the truck, he had a feeling about her that went far beyond the kid goat thing. It was tingly, and her hair smelled so good, and—nothing made sense!

"Hey, hey Cyrus J", she said from behind him.

God, she was beautiful. What did she just say?

"Hey, hey Miss Chey."

"Cyrus J and Miss Chey!" she said and they both laughed.

They started off towards home and she didn't stop talking, which was plenty fine with him because he wasn't listening. What he was caught up in was her expressions; whenever she was making the point he couldn't hear, she would pop her head forward and bring her golden hair to flow back and forth over her cheeks. Her skin was so smooth and silky that the kid goat thing came around a second or two then disappeared when he caught a glimpse of her nose as she smiled; it would . . .

"Cyrus!" she hollered. "Are you listenin'?"

"Yeah!" he answered with a hard swallow.

They were coming to the Burle Barn. Cheyenne quit talking and began watching Cyrus who was eyeing the barn peculiar.

"What?" she asked.

"I daknow", he shrugged.

As they came closer he realized there weren't any birds chirping and there weren't any crows sitting on the hayloft doorway to pitch stones at. He stopped in the middle of the road and stared at the barn. Several yards off the road between them and the barn was a mammoth Oak that had a trunk wide enough to shadow a truck.

"Is what you wanted to show me here?"

"No."

Behind them was a patch of careless weeds that was as tall as it was thick and had been home to a feral sow and her piglets that spring, but everything was eerily silent now. Cyrus stepped forward with Cheyenne murmuring incessantly behind him. Pritchett stepped from the giant tree's shadow; his buddies emerged one by one from different places, even some from behind in the turn-row of weeds. Cheyenne went silent until there was a complete circle around them.

"Pritchett", she shouted with hands on her hips. "What is it with you? Why . . ."

"Quit", Cyrus interrupted.

"Well, at least he ain't gunna let a girl wear his britches", Pritchett said, shuffling towards Cyrus who was in the road on the other side of the fence. Pritchett climbed through the barbed wire. Something was odd about that moment and, he hadn't thought of it until Argie crossed his mind—he wasn't afraid. Pritchett stood near nose to nose with him and he didn't flinch.

"What?" Cyrus whispered. "Why is it you hate me so—tell me what I've done and I'll make it right."

There were murmurs and giggles that echoed around them from the group.

"I can't stand little boys who are really little girls."

"Is that what it is, really? Ifin' I was to show you, you'd leave me be?"

"Whatdaya mean, show me?"

"Ifin' I was to show you I ain't no girl."

There was a long silence, even from the crowd as they stood staring at each other. It was as though Cyrus had stepped from his body and was standing there watching all of them.

"Think of you and Jake, Cyrus", he remembered Argie saying. "You'll know what to do when you come to it." "Face it without fear."

"Face what, Argie?"

"Think of why you and Jake came together—think of Jake and think of you . . . and WHY."

"Oh!" Cyrus muttered as he began to unbuckle his trousers.

"Oh, what? And what are you doin'?" Pritchett questioned.

"I'm givin' you what you want—you wanna *pants* me, don't ya? Well, I'm givin' 'em to you so I won't get skinned up."

"Stop, idiot!" Pritchett yelled. "You lost yur basket? That ain't what I want."

"Let him go on, Pritchett! He's an idiot! Let him *pants* himself in front of his girl", one of the toadies hollered.

Cyrus had his pants to his ankles while Pritchett stopped his hands from going further.

"Pritchett, you gotta let me shed my brogans because my britches won't go over 'em."

Pritchett grabbed Cyrus by the shoulders and shook him until he stopped talking.

"Put yur britches back up!" he barked. He looked to the onlookers and they were quiet, even Cheyenne was mum. Cyrus pulled his pants up and Pritchett turned away and started down the road.

His followers ambled after him, muttering and pointing, occasionally looking back at Cyrus who stood there with his mouth open.

"Oh my Lord, Cyrus Buckman!" Cheyenne said. "You just— you just whomped him without even, without doing nothin'."

He finished buckling his trousers as he watched the entourage become smaller and smaller in the distance. He wasn't afraid. Not once did he feel fear and he was never without that. He said nothing and Cheyenne wouldn't shut up. He just smiled while she kept bantering, until she grabbed him.

"Cyrus Buckman, you tell me what's got into you. Tell me what just happened!"

He shrugged the shoulders she had hold of, "I ain't sure. Well, I might have some sure, but you'd think I was more off than Pritchett does", he laughed.

He took her hands from his shoulders and placed them to her side deliberately.

"It has something to do with what you wanna show me, don't it?"

He began walking towards home and she sheepishly followed, clearing her throat occasionally and feverishly working to getting his attention without avail. He couldn't get away from the thought of what just transpired. My God, a pair of long-handles on a stick told him what to do, he followed it and it worked. Would he dare introduce his *Imagine* to Cheyenne? It was a promise he made to himself a time back, that he wasn't going to share Argie with anyone, but this was Cheyenne he was talking about. Argie already knew about her so it wasn't like a huge breach of promise; but, then every time he brought a confidant into the picture all hell would break loose.

"Cyrus!"

"What?"

"Will you pay attention for longer than a hummingbird's wing bat?"

"Chey, I got a lot to think on. I wanna tell you what I *think*, but ain't too sure that what I *think* ain't really what *is*."

"What in the world you babbling' about? You just stood to Pritchett and his gang without as much as a blink—it was like Jake standin' there!"

"Yeah", he sighed. "I was a bit like Jake."

They stood in the middle of Chicken Ranch road, one waiting on the other.

"Chey, there is something I have to show you but I gotta think it through first. It's really hard to explain without coming across like a loon, but I have to see on some things."

"Like what?"

"You're gunna have to trust me here, even though you got no call."

"Why wouldn't I have call, Cyrus J? I will. You tend to what you need and I'll wait."

Little more was said until they separated at Cyrus' gate and he kept an eye on her until she was out of sight. He set off on his way to Argie like a bat from a burning stump. He could hardly wait to tell him what he most likely already knew.

"Argie! Argie! Wake up."

"I'm not asleep."

"You won't believe what happened today; well, knowin' you—I finally stood up to Pritchett."

"Really", Argie answered blandly. "And what did that entail?"

"What did that, *what*?"

"What did that have to do with . . .?"

"What?"

"Exactly."

"Will you STOP!" Cyrus screamed. "This is probably the most important thing in my life: I stood up for myself."

"That is wonderful, and my question was how?"

"Oh, Pritchett and his toadies were gunna *pants* me at the Burle Barn, in front of Cheyenne and everything, but I didn't let him."

"And that was it?"

"Yeah, that was pretty much it; he walked away and I still had my pants."

"Oh. What did you do, growl at him? Pull a gun? Flex your muscle?" Argie asked facetiously.

"What is it with you, Mr Cornfield? Something really good happens and you fun me."

"I'm sorry, Cyrus, but I want you to reflect on what happened and why, not that you just walked away with your pants."

"Okay, what would you like me to *reflect*? That Pritchett and his toads jumped me and Cheyenne; that he stared me down and I stared right back, that he . . . wait a minute, why did he give up?"

He sat down on the dried pile of stalks and put his arms around his legs. He was going to hand over his britches without a fight, maybe that was it; Pritchett wanted to fight him in front of his girl because he liked Cheyenne, and what better way to . . . no, that was all too complicated.

"Argie, why is it your job to be a stick in my spokes? This was all plain and simple until I told you."

"Oh contraire my little one, it is you who loves complication."

"Oh, *what*? When you go to talkin' trick I knows I got a preachin' comin'."

"The only thing I hope to do with you is incite thought, nothing else."

"Okay, I'm thinking here and I feel like I gotta ton of bricks on my head; a ton more than I had when I came into this patch."

"Do you truly believe that Mr Pritchett's game with you concerned Miss Cheyenne?"

"How the world . . . ?"

"Let's not mince thoughts here, Cyrus. Answer my question."

"Well I might have thought that for a quick spell, but it didn't come right. I mean, if Pritchett was gamin' for Cheyenne he'd-a handled me in front of the whole school. No, it's gotta be somethin' else."

"Then what?"

Cyrus put his hands behind his head and lay back on the dry stubble while he contemplated this conundrum.

"Can you gimme a hand here, Mr Cornfield? Just a tiny nudge."

"What did you do when Mr Pritchett confronted you?"

"You mean when he came out from behind the tree? I was a might nervous, but wasn't really afraid. I don't rightly recall exactly. When he looked me in the eye I saw somethin' though, or maybe it was that I felt it. I did recollect what you said, what you said about me and Jake."

"And what was that?"

"About what me and Jake saw in each other."

"And where was that?"

"At the water cistern, you know that. He came up to me."

"Why?"

"I daknow, maybe because—oh wow", Cyrus smiled.

"What?" Argie asked.

There was a long silence while Cyrus stood from the corn stubble and began walking around the scarecrow. He'd stop and shake his head, begin to say something then start walking about again. Neither said a word for some time.

"Mr Buckman, what are you thinking?'

He stopped and stared up at the giant on a stick and smiled, "Why is it you do this to me, Mr Cornfield; you know what I'm thinking probably before I'm thinkin' it, then ask me what I'm thinkin'?"

"I reckon cuz I'm stuck up here on this stick all the day long and I just need some funnin'."

"You beat all. I know why Pritchett has been doggin' me all this time—I think. It's gunna sound crazy but it's what came to me: he really wants to be friends. Is that plum out of the tree?"

"No sir, and how did you come to surmise this?"

"I know you meant to say, 'how'd I tally this', so I'll tell ya; I thought about Jake and why he came to me. He knew I needed somebody—a friend. Why or how he knew, I couldn't say; he just did."

"How does this sit with you?'

"Heavens Mr Cornfield, everybody wants to be liked, I just can't really see why Pritchett would want someone like me when he has all those others. That's the reason I think this is outta the tree."

"Cyrus, I think you are spot on."

"But Argie, Jake and me loved like brothers. I can't see anything in Pritchett like I seen in Jake."

"This is the impasse where most others stand, Cyrus; the one beautiful and genuine difference in you that sets you apart, yet is painful: your desire to see with your heart, to look past the exterior. So many desire to do that but are so afraid of what they will find."

"Afraid? Afraid of what?"

"Afraid of their humanity. Afraid the world will see them weak and vulnerable. Your virtue Cyrus is that you do not care how you are seen because you are strong in yourself; regardless what you think, you are strong and others are drawn to that."

"So yur sayin' Pritchett really wants to be friends, and all his rankin' on me for months is for that reason? Argie, that makes as much sense as a dog and cat joshin' because they really want to be runnin' buddies."

"You've past the hard part here, Mr Buckman. Mr Pritchett has seen your colors, and you have seen his."

"So, what? I've *faced* the music and now I have to face colors?"

"It's been a long day and I'm very tired, Cyrus."

"Please! How is it yur tired when all you do is hang there?"

"I think I've done a bit more than hang here; I've handled a big piece of you today."

"Well", Cyrus shrugged. "I guess. Argie, before you nod off would you mind if I bring Cheyenne over to say hey?"

"Say, hey?"

"Yeah, I want her to meet you."

"You may want to consider that long and hard. You recall your covenant to yourself?"

"Yeah, but this is Cheyenne."

"It's up to you, but know there are no guarantees she will hear me."

Cyrus stood at the base of the huge monolith, looking up and smiling. So much had been proven to him this day but there was still a lingering, nagging, incessant thought that he was crazy like a rabid dog; a quiet threat no one knew of because it was secretly in a corn patch. It had to be real, though. Nothing this good could be from crazy. In the midst of his loneliness there appeared from nowhere this sack of hay that took away his sorrow and replaced it with purpose. Cyrus squeezed its legs for flesh and bone.

"Argie", he whispered.

"Yes."

"How long will you stay with me?"

"Until the end of time."

CHAPTER TWENTY

He tied Cid off to the low branch of the smelly-ass sweet gum, and eased himself under his belly with the barrel of his Henry Repeater against his cheek and one hand on the ground. They hadn't heard him because he could still see the lookout high in the birch not a hundred yards from him and he hadn't signaled. Very unlike the Kiowa, who weren't as savage as the Pawnee or Comanche, to be so easily surprised and it made him leery being that close. Cid was his eyes and ears in these situations; he'd signal with his hoof against the ground, once for . . . —what?, he blurted.

"Mister Buckman!" the teacher hollered. "Where are you, child?"

The class giggled and stared at him with distant eyes like he had just materialized.

"Uhm", he shrugged. "I'm here now."

They laughed again which was foreign to him, since it usually happened after he'd lost his pants or was looking up from the burn barrel. This time they were laughing with him. He glanced to Cheyenne to make sure she approved, or at least wasn't frowning.

She was his barometer on just about everything that happened at school now, which was okay with him since she filled that bill nicely.

Ms Fugate stood at the front and scolded him with her look, but he was rarely in contentious situations so she just shook her head and smiled with a point of her ruler. Cheyenne sat there staring with a funeral smile which told him nothing.

"What?" he whispered to her.

"What are you doing?" she whispered back.

He shrugged his shoulders again and shook his head with a cat-like grin, "Just dreamin'."

After school he waited out at the front of the building on top of the drainage pipe in the bar ditch. Most everyone walked home save for the handful whose parents had little more to do; the wealth ones. With his mind wandering as usual, he glanced to a side and caught Pritchett staring at him. Only one of his toadies was there with him. They looked at each other intently for a handful of seconds then Cyrus turned away. His thought was that he had been given a nice present that day at the Burle Barn and he didn't feel like upsetting that water unnecessarily. Almost everyone was gone and he hadn't seen Cheyenne. He waited until no one else was left and then looked in the front door of the school. He saw Mr Burnside and another teacher chatting in the foyer, but no Cheyenne. It was strange, but not enough to worry. A part of him looked forward to the walk solo.

Coming up to the infamous Burle Barn he slowed to grab a handful of stones for the crows. He put a measure in each pocket and edged quietly towards the barn entrance, staying in the shadow of the giant oak and peering around its edge to glimpse at the loft's eve. If he surprised them just at the moment he got a rock off he could generally hit one in flight, they were bunched so tight. They were about the size of Alma Bainbridge's porch beagles and made the same hollow thud when hit with a stone, except the crows left with a magnificent puff of feathers and no sound. The beagles on the other hand yelped loud enough to call Caribou, as well as Alma.

Oddly, only two crows were perched on that eve and they skedaddled before he was even in eye-shot. There was an uneasy air about him so he put the stones back in his pocket and turned around.

"Hey Pritchett, Whatdaya doin'?" Cyrus mumbled.

He was standing just inside the barn, out of the light. Cyrus moved to the door, looking to either side with caution but no fear.

"It's Marshall", he said.

"What?"

"My name—it's Marshall."

"Oh, yur first name—everyone calls you Pritchett, so I just . . ."

Cyrus' reaction came knee jerk; what he always did when he was surprised—alone. He looked around in hopes they were alone. If the toadies came present the undeniable was bound to follow and the thought of being found naked on Chicken Ranch road was so disheartening—but he wasn't afraid.

"Yeah, that's what they call all us cuz we're so many; no one remembers our name."

Cyrus was tense and somewhat bewildered. Maybe Pritchett and Cheyenne had figured this thing out together and all this was planned from the get-go, but why he thought? There came over him a special uneasiness he had felt most of his life when he was the center of a scheme; one of betrayal and circumspection; one where the loss came deeper than the cut, where he was the last to know.

They stood a distance from each other and it was difficult to see Pritchett's face; most of him was silhouetted in the half-light of the barn that came from the loft door above, sporadically broken by the fallen beams and joist and made both of them more opaque by the lingering dust that bellowed with each of their moves.

"What are you doing here?" Cyrus questioned. "Where's everyone else?"

"I'm by myself."

"Why?"

"I daknow, why are you?"

"Cuz there wasn't anyone to walk with me", he answered quickly. "I was gunna stone some crows."

Pritchett moved about uneasily, rubbing his hand over the top of a tack rail, gathering the dust into small piles then in to large ones—they said nothing for a long while.

"Did you think I was really gunna *pants* you the other day?" Marshall asked.

"I wasn't sure; I kinda did when I looked at Cheyenne—I thought, what a good time to do it."

"Was you really gunna shed 'em yourself?" Marshall asked.

"Yeah, I was tired of fightin' and thought it just as well", Cyrus replied with a slight chuckle. "Is your name really Marshall?"

"Yep."

"Is that what you want me to call ya?"

"No matter, you'll be the only one ceptin' my sister" he laughed.

Cyrus moved closer to his nemesis while Pritchett stayed with his immediate chore of fingering the dust into piles, occasionally looking up at Cyrus.

"So you know Cheyenne?" Cyrus asked.

"Course. Who don't? She's been to our farm before with her Pa—they do some business, I guess."

"So you talked to her?"

"Whatdaya mean? Yeah I talk to her. I say hey and all."

"Pri . . . Marshall, what is it you hate about me so, or is it just me altogether?"

He left the dust alone and stared into the dark away from the both of them as though he were looking for someone. Cyrus moved within several feet from him and stood still.

"You waitin' for someone?" Cyrus questioned again.

"I don't", Marshall answered.

"You *don't*, what?"

"Hate you . . . and yeah, I was kinda waitin' for somebody?"

"Who?" Cyrus asked openly.

"Why did you and Jake—I mean, how did you and Jake become pals?"

Cyrus walked over to a hay bale and sat down. Marshall tested the strength of the tack rail then pulled himself up.

"Not real sure, he came up to me one day when I was sittin' out at the water cistern and asked what I was doin'."

"What were you doin'?"

Cyrus sighed heavily, "Hidin' from you."

"Me? I wouldn't-of done no harm. Might-of scared you some, but never woulda brought no harm."

"Well, *pantsin'* me woulda been a smidgen of harm—embarrass the hell outta me!"

"I wouldn't done such to someone I liked."

"Liked?" Cyrus queried. "We on the same page here? We even in the same book?"

"I wanted to be pals with you like Jake."

"Me! Are you crawfishin'? What the world would you wanna be pals with me for?"

"I daknow exactly. I figured you nice to be pals with—to do stuff with and all."

"You got half the school pal'd-up; I ain't got no one before or after Jake."

"Those ain't *pals*, those are hang-ons who like everyone to think ill of 'em so they'll fear 'em and such—they don't care a lick about me. You and Jake were pals."

"Yeah, you could say that."

"What did y'all do together?"

Cyrus blushed a moment when he recalled the headless dog, the pistol, the whiskey and the fact that the former belonged to Marshall.

"Uhm, we tented a lot."

"Tented? Where, in the creek?"

"Yeah, how'd you know? Well not actually, we made kinda a fort."

"Really."

"Yeah, I can show ya, maybe we can even camp sometime."

"That'd be the berries!" he smiled.

The air became thick again as both realized the other and what they were doing. Cyrus sat looking at his foot moving the straw around the floor and Marshall went back to pushing dust. It was like a new pair of shoes, tight and confining but looked nice.

"You miss him, don't ya?" Marshall asked.

"Yeah", he replied awkwardly. "He was everything—he was my *brother*."

"Funny, I have four of 'em and they ain't nothing."

"Yur Pa? What's yur Pa like", Cyrus asked. "I mean, you close with him?"

"My Pa? Yur kidding", Marshall burst out loud. "You don't know much of the Pritchett's then do ya?"

"I heard stuff, but no. I don't know many folk about. I ain't ever stayed long enough in any spot to make solid pals. This—I mean Jake is the first pal I've really ever had."

"Where's yur Ma and Pa?"

"They was killed in a crash before my first birthday. Been with my grandparents since and it ain't ne'er been a party neither. Grandpa hates my guts and livers, and I'm guessin' it's because I remind him of my Pa—his son. Now my Gran'ma thinks kindly of me and fends me when Gran'pa finds a hot spot, but mostly I stay outta sight."

"Maybe yur Gran'pa and my kin ought to take up porch sittin' together", Marshall mumbled. "You said that Jake was yur *brother*; what does that mean? You weren't blood kin, was ya?"

"No", he answered uneasily. "I reckon it's hard to say; it's a bit like he knew me and I knew him better than anybody could ever know another. Does that make sense?"

"Kinda, I guess. I thought you was payin' him or somethin' to fend for ya."

"Payin' him? I ain't got no money—and even if I did I wouldn't have. Shoot, payin' someone to be yur buddy?"

"I'd a paid him", he muttered.

So much of this puzzle seemed to come together in a picture Cyrus could have never imagined: one, speaking friendly with the town bully, and two, his speaking back—friendly like. This certainly wasn't meshing with Argie's theory of "everything is as it appears."

"Cyrus, were you crawfishin' when you said you wanted to tent out?"

"Not in a measure. We can go to the fort Friday and you can decide whether you want to."

"I ain't gotta see it. Let's just say we're gunna do it."

"I gotta figure how I'm gunna pass it with my folk, and I'm gussin' you the same with yur Pa."

"My Pa; by Friday noon he'll be oiled. I won't have to pass nothin' with him."

"Okay then", Cyrus said, holding out his hand. He was doing everything contrary to his nature and nothing that he had ever done and before, without concern for the outcome. He wasn't thinking of what was next, which in itself was exhilarating because he was in it. For the first time he was living in the present and clueless; life was happening and he wasn't writing the script.

"Okay then", Marshall added. "So we're Pals?"

"I reckon. You ain't greenin' are ya?"

"Nah."

They separated; Marshall towards his home and Cyrus the opposite direction. It was different this walk alone. His new friendship wasn't the same as his and Jake's. The way he saw Jake was different than the way he viewed Pritchett; well, Marshall. Jake was someone unattainable, a character who began as the hero and ended such; Marshall was the villain and still stood that ground in a way, but there was another light about him now. Was what he just experienced real or a dream? This was where he seemed to always trip up. People. They were so unpredictable. How much easier things would be if they were like the weather and you could tell what was coming. Take Jake, for instance: Cyrus knew where Jake was in his thoughts and attitude most all the time, and whether it was a storm or calm Cyrus would adjust accordingly. It was simple. Maybe that's what made being with him so special.

Now Marshall was going to be a whole new ball game. New rules. New everything which would inevitably mean having to scrap the entire board; but, it would be interesting, he thought. Maybe that was it. What someone—like Argie—was working to teach him?

He found himself completely oblivious and in the middle of the corn patch walking to his mentor's hanging place.

"Argie! Wake up."

"I'm not asleep."

"Something is happening and I ain't sure what it is."

"Oh?"

"Are you kidding? You are kidding, right? Of all the times you act like you don't know what's going on!"

"Well . . . "

"No Argie", Cyrus interrupted. "I'm serious now; I don't need a lesson."

"Okay, I'm all corn."

"What?"

"Ears! All ears."

"You know Pritchett. Well, his name is Marshall and that's what he wants me to call him now. Get it?"

"Yes, his name is what he wants you to call him."

"Yes. And he wants to be friends! He wants *me* to be his runnin' buddy. All those other guys, you know, the toadies, well, he doesn't even consider 'em pals; he said he liked me! Can you believe that! And I wasn't even afraid when I saw him in the barn—the crows weren't there like they usually were, and . . . "

"Slow down, Master Cyrus! I am having a time catching your drift—if you catch mine."

"Huh? Okay. Marshall Pritchett, the guy who has hated me all these days, really likes me and wants to be my friend. People. I don't get 'em. Now Jake wasn't *people* like everybody else, no. Jake didn't care about making somethin' outta nothin'—that's what was so nice about Jake Thompson, he either liked you or he didn't and you knew exactly where you stood—no sugar, no mud! Just plain grit—and he gets taken. I don't get it Argie!"

"Cyrus, my little gift. You had a good day and you are beside yourself."

"What? Did you hear what I am saying?"

"How could I not have? A bit garbled in the sense, but yes, I heard you. Take a deep breath and look me square in my pillow."

"You are a sight, Mr Cornfield. How is it you always run the wheel off the wagon that ain't even yours?"

"I need you to settle a-mite so we can have an intelligent conversation about, what appears to be at this point, one of your finest days."

"Finest days?"

"Most certainly one of your better ones considering the recent, wouldn't you say?"

"How so?"

"Heavens child! It seems you have, how is that said, killed two crows with one stone, or in this case, perhaps an albatross and a crow: to any extent, you've successfully surrendered a foe in exchange for a friend, and you did it without firing a shot or losing your pants", Argie said matter-of-factly.

"What the world are you babblin' about crows and Alba's and such? I'm tryin' to tell you that Pritchett is no longer Pritchett, or my enemy—he's my friend, whose name is Marshall."

"Yes, and that entire diatribe at your arrival meant what?"

"You mean my babble about folk?"

"Uh huh."

Cyrus sat down on the damp stubble and began to smile uncontrollably as he pondered further the intrinsic marvel of this day. In between the thoughts of why and how were what happened. It was the truth and not a fable because it actually, physically happened. There were no *Imagines*, no conjectures, no whispers or innuendos; just plain life. It was strange how loneliness had brought these two unknowns into play.

"I think I can say with *candor* that all this would not have happened if it hadn't been for Jake Thompson—and you of course."

"Really—in all *candor* you can say that?"

"I sure can! Do you think this would have happened without you guys; even Cheyenne."

"Huh. I don't know." Argie muttered.

"What's buzzin' in your pillow sack there Mr Cornfield? You beat all—you absolutely beat all; I'm havin' the best day of my life and you have to completely run off a wheel!"

"No doubt it is your best day, and well deserved, but what amazes me is how it came about."

"What part?"

"All of it, child!"

"What ain't clear?"

"Who, why and how?"

"I told you."

"What I heard was something about everyone who wasn't there."

The patch came stone quiet as Cyrus walked to and fro and around the base of the scarecrow. He'd stop for a second, begin to say something, then walked about again. He knelt down against the back of his legs, on his knees, and swirled his hand in the corn stubble.

"You mean—me?"

"Yeah."

"What about me, Argie? You think this short, fat no-account had much to do with . . . "

"Yes!" Argie yelled emphatically. "Who else was there?"

"Wow, why are you so mad? . . . "

"I'm not mad, I'm confused a bit. I've been biting my tongue for a while—it so difficult to be serious hanging in your underwear—anyway; do you seriously not see your input here?"

"My input?"

"Alright, let's back up a tad: why is it you think Pritchett, who had you in the perfect place and time to pants you, decided not to take your pants?"

"Jake."

"Jake! He isn't here."

"Marshall said he always wanted Jake and me to be his pal, but Jake ain't here now and there's just me. Simple math Mr Cornfield."

"So now math is involved. What you are saying is that Marshall would not want to be your friend if Jake hadn't been here first to make him want to be your friend—you and Jake were a package deal, and now Pritchett has to settle for you?"

"Pretty much."

"You are too confusing my little friend, but I'm crazy about ya", Argie mumbled.

"Which makes me want to ask—why?" Cyrus quizzed.

"Why am I crazy about you?"

"Yeah. I'm nothin' special Mr Cornfield. I ain't big or tall, or fast nor a looker; in fact, I'm all the opposite."

"I do not see with eyes, my young one, like you and everyone else. I see—no, I feel the heart, which is where the true person lives. All of your perceived flaws are limitations from others you have accepted. There will always be folks different than you, and you are allowing that difference to make you separate. Do you think there would be a fat if there wasn't a thin; a short if there wasn't a tall? And what would that have to do with anything more than space? No, the shape and size of a container hasn't a thing to do with its content—that isn't you."

"Gee Argie, I didn't think of it that way."

"I know. I'm just spitballin' here, but I think Mr Pritchett sees more than a short, fat kid."

"Then what the world do you reckon he sees?"

"A friend."

CHAPTER TWENTY ONE

I t was nearing the weekend and the shine from his new friendship, or as it was termed, had not only worn off, had all but disappeared. Where he made himself noticeable, Marshall paid no
attention. Cheyenne warned him that Marshall's new demeanor
was likely some kind of ploy for a better position, but he couldn't
believe that what he experienced at Burle barn was mere smoke
and mirrors. These thoughts were so troublesome and what made
it all the more so was he had no one to talk to but Cheyenne; a
distant second from Jake, the formidable soul he only trusted completely, and whose opinion always fit the situation like a glove.

Even as Jake's stand-in, Cheyenne's lackluster reaction to
his mysterious rendezvous and handshake with the school bully brought his morale to a new low. This thing with Marshall
had been just enough to rekindle a fire for life that had all
but burned out; his faith that there just might be a purpose
to his up-til-now worthless existence tottered between the im-
pressions of a beautiful farm girl and a bag of hay nailed to a
four by four. All this, combined with the weather and a distant

relationship with his grandfather, brought tears on his walk to school down Chicken Ranch road. It wasn't shocking dismay, this feeling of darkness he couldn't finds words to describe, it was the fact that the only one he could describe it to was dead and gone. He pulled in a deep breath that stopped him from falling completely to pieces. Cyrus began to think about Argie and how warming it was to have him around, even if he was an *Imagine*. A thought came over him at that moment of how badly he wanted to be touched; a touch that wasn't painful. Was that such a mammoth request?

He was suddenly wrenched back into the present and Chicken Ranch road by the truck pulling up next to him; his eyes in such disarray that he did a double-take. It was Cheyenne, someone he did not want to be with for reasons that were painfully obvious.

"Hey, hey Cyrus J; you wanna lift—what's wrong?" her demeanor changed. "Pa I'm gunna walk the rest of the way." Her father stopped.

They walked a spell in uncomfortable silence which was perfectly okay with him. As if totally out of the blue, Cheyenne started in with some weather talk, and then what was happening between her girlfriends, and finally up to the inevitable—"So what's going on with you?"

"Nothin' to rattle about."

"Com' on Cyrus J, it's all over your face; somethin' is goin' on and I bet I know what."

Where was it written that he was perpetually a student and everyone else a teacher? He was so exhausted by lessons from folk who had no more experience at his game than himself.

"Chey, I ain't much for cussin' or discussin' this day. There are some days that, for no reason atoll, are just bad days."

"Yeah, you may well be right, but if you go to the beginning they typically got something that made 'em start out that way—you reminiscing on Jake, are ya?"

He took a breath and let out a long, tiresome sigh, "Some—but mostly about me, why I'm here and the rest just on plain, *why.*"

"You know you have someone to talk to, Cyrus."

He laughed a loud and caught himself quickly, "Yes—yes, I do."

"What was so funny about that?"

"Ah, nothing." He paused with the overwhelming urge to tell her, "Well—Chey, there's kinda something I been wantin' to tell you but its way out there. In fact, so far out you'll think my load is short a bale."

"Try me."

"It ain't somethin' you try—it's a bit more . . . well, it's something you'd have to be a part of, kinda. It's impossible to explain."

"Does this have anything to do with what you wanted to show me before Pritchett snagged us?"

"Yeah it is. I forgot about that. Yeah, I guess I could show you, if you wanted. I have to check on somethin' before though."

"Is this somethin' that'll bring trouble?"

"No. It's has to do with havin' someone to talk to, like you were saying, but it's real hard to explain. It's about someone you don't really see . . . it's."

"Like God, or something?"

"Well yeah, but I don't think he's god."

"So it is someone?"

"I'll just have to show you. It's better if you see some of what I'm talkin' about."

They walked the balance of the way with some talk about Argie, but with Cyrus shooting all around the target and not coming up with anything specific than, "You'll just have to see." Much of his thought during the day was surrounded by this *thing* he allowed out of the bag; some of it comforting and the rest extremely scary: Comforting that he was ready to bring another into his world with Argie, and scary that it wouldn't work—that Argie would remain just what he was, an *Imagine,* which would put him in a more precarious position with the world. This was huge. Not only might Argie possibly disappear, but so would Cheyenne after she found out he was a certified loon. Who'd want to be around anyone who not only spoke to a scarecrow but who swore it spoke back? It was becoming a tight place in his head and the only way to ease this tension was to pose it to Argie the minute he got home. The one sure thing about Argie was that he was either hot or cold, no in between.

He saw Marshall and company in the schoolyard just as Cheyenne was running off to be with her girlfriends. It was the first time since the barn incident that Marshall had as much made eye contact and all he did was trade a faint smile—it was something though. Cyrus kept a mild distance and a watchful eye on him. It wasn't spying, in the true sense of the word, it was caution, and maybe a bit of curiosity. His thoughts commingled with Cheyenne's and he kept doing the 'good guy, bad guy' thing in his head. What was Marshall's intent? Was he really working to get another position on him; or, was he like him, in search of a friend—a real one?

Jake had rubbed off on him in many ways, but the one way that gave him courage was being bold and aggressive in situations regardless of the outcome. That was where Cyrus always tripped up, projecting the outcome before he'd ever step to the plate. Jake taught him that no one but God knew the outcome of anything, so wondering about it was not only a waste of time but the second of hesitation could make you fall. It was good to think about alternatives and weigh them against each other, but when at bat, you go with your gut. Just at recess, Cyrus saw Marshall without his entourage and a chance to talk to him unfettered.

"Hey Marshall."

Marshall looked at him for a second and then around to see who else was gazing, "Hey Buckman, what are you doin'?"

"No thing", Cyrus smiled genteelly. "When we goin' to the fort?"

"Ah, don't know. Sometime though—hey, maybe Dale Worth can come with us?"

This was an uncomfortable queue, but not now he stood his ground, "Naw, reckon not. I'd go with you solo, not with any of your other buddies though." He couldn't believe his ears. In fact, it was Jake talking and it made him smile.

"What?" Marshall asked.

Cyrus shook his head and almost felt Jake standing right next to him. It was on the tip of his tongue to say something, to tell Pritchett what was happening, but it was too personal and if he told him, too odd. In his heart, at that very moment, Cyrus realized who Marshall truly was. It was so strange. It was ethereal but real. The realist thing he had ever felt. Suddenly and with all the force of a storm, Cyrus saw the essence of Marshall in his most naked form—scared, alone, bewildered. It was him. Marshall was exactly like him!

"What's wrong with you, Buckman?"

"Ah, nothin'. I was just thinking about somethin'. Hey, we'll talk about this later if you want", Cyrus said as he turned off toward the water cistern. "We'll do the fort thing soon, if you want."

Almost everyone was out of the building and milling around the grounds, except him, who was off in solitude at the cistern. In the very spot where Jake first roused him, he sat and stared down Chicken Ranch road, but this time he was smiling. Pritchett, the infamous bulldog of Alabama, was exactly like him. They were peas in a pod, corn on a cob, hay bales adjoining—maybe everyone is the same, just in different suits, he thought. This was a revelation beyond Edison's light bulb. "That means I ain't that strange", he said out loud. "Okay, so I am pudgy and short, but that ain't who I am—it's just what I am seen as."

This knowledge overcame him: First, Cheyenne coming to him at the exact time he needed her, and now his vision of himself through his old nemesis? Life's answers all neatly bound in one package! Hold your horses, he thought. Remember how things come—the calm before the storm. No! "I ain't gunna look ahead", he shouted.

"What?" a voice came from behind.

It was Polly Bainbridge, one of Cheyenne's runnin' buddies and Alma's granddaughter, the lady with the beagles he'd pelt with stones on cloudy days.

"Hey, I was thinkin' out loud and you happened to be there."

"What were you thinkin'?" she asked, sitting down next to him. "Oh, is this okay?"

"Sure. I weren't thinkin' of much."

"You like it out here? It's quiet isn't it?"

"Pretty much", he answered uncomfortably. "What, was you lookin' for some quiet too?"

"Oh no, I was just walkin' about when I saw you over here. Thought I'd say hey."

"Hey", he murmured.

"Yeah, hey", she laughed. "Cheyenne sure likes you", she said uneasily.

"That heavy on your mind, was it?" Cyrus smiled.

She laughed, "No, didn't mean to just drop that like a hot potato. It's just that she's my best friend and all, and if you was to not like her back—I mean, it's your business, I just didn't want her to feel . . ."

"Did you come here of your own makin'?" he quipped.

"Oh yeah, if she was to get wind of this she'd be madder than a swat hornet."

Cyrus smiled broadly and uncontrollably while he hid his face between his knees, but she knew and it brought her giggly. It was as though this secret, which never was one, was now openly not one, if that makes sense.

"What, Cyrus Buckman? Everybody knows."

"Knows what?"

"That she likes you; they just don't know if you like her."

"But they will, huh?" he laughed. "She knew I liked her a long time back."

"You don't let many folk know anything about you, Cyrus."

"Is that the way everyone thinks?"

"That's the way it is", she said pointedly. "I gotta get back before bell. I'll see ya."

He had to get back too, but he had to have a minute to swallow this. What a day: First Cheyenne, then Marshall, then Cheyenne again with little bits and pieces of Jake and Argie along the way. If the rest of life was going to be like this he was sorry he'd ever been disdainful about it. The uncertainty of it was still scary, that tightness in his stomach that came with the darkness and worry of when the other shoe would drop; that moment when maybe, just maybe, he'd find out someone else died or they were moving again—or both. That's the way it was. The higher you got only meant the further you fell, and was the part of himself he could not speak about to anyone, not even Argie. It was a good day he was laboring to ruin. It was utterly impossible for him to accept happiness.

"Hey Cyrus J, you wanna go do this *thing* real quick?" Cheyenne said outside the school. Her girlfriends were hovering around her like sugar ants on a picnic pie and it not only made him uncomfortable, but a bit mad; she seemed to be making this thing of theirs an open forum.

"No! I told you Cheyenne", he said tensely, motioning her from the group. "Are you spoutin' off that I'm gunna show you somethin'?"

"Of course not, I've haven't said a word to anyone. Cyrus, this is about you and me, and I wouldn't say anything to anybody about *you* and *me*. You gotta know that you are a special friend—real special", she added, reaching out to his hand and squeezing it tightly. It was the touch he thought about this morning and it was worth all the stars in the sky. There was something so strange about his feeling for her and every time he felt he was getting a handle on it the damn thing would slip into the shadows again. One minute it was exactly like what he had for Jake, but more, and then it disappeared completely. It was one of those questions he posed to Argie that was swept under that rug, "You'll find out on your own in due time."

He left the grounds running on and off all the way home. He'd begin walking quickly and then into a run when he began thinking that Argie knew what was happening, and as soon as he'd get there Argie would be gone. Nothing, he thought, would run an *Imagine* off quicker than bringing someone else into the picture. It made him worry something fierce that he had betrayed someone—his letting on to Cheyenne about Argie; but, he hadn't actually done so. He never said anything as of yet. She didn't even know where the *thing* he was to show her was so how would Argie be upset? He slowed to a quick walk again.

Yeah, but what if she and her friends were following him? What if she had already told them what was going on? What if she had told Marshall, then the cat would really be out of the bag? He broke into a run again.

"Well it's my little friend, Cyrus J", Argie bellowed.

Cyrus collapsed at the base of the scarecrow, writhing back and forth trying to catch his breath and speak at the same time. His worst thoughts were quelled at the first word, "well." He was still here and his tone wasn't upset—in fact, he seemed in good spirit.

"Argie, I was really scared you took off."

"Took off, why?"

"It's hard to say."

"No it's not, you've been doing so well for a while—open your mouth and just let a word come forth."

"You don't understand, I was worried you'd be mad at me for almost letting you outta the bag."

"I'm confused, almost; and what bag was I in to be let out of?"

"Argie, you can be such a pain for someone who's been to school!"

"Haven't ever been to school—not sure how I know what I do."

"So you don't know 'bout Cheyenne?"

"Course I know her."

"No, *about* her—what I have been thinking *about* her—and you?"

"I know that you have wanted to bring her here, and I told you to think about that since it has brought you trouble before."

"I know, but I want her to *know* you."

"Is that why?"

"Well *dawgone-it*, it's kinda why", Cyrus continued, stomping about and kicking stubble. He sat down on a pile at the base of the scarecrow, put his arms about his knees and his head between them.

"Is this pouting? I've heard about it, but never actually felt it. Why is this so important to you?"

"Because."

"That's not an answer, it's a conjunction."

"Because—I want her to know that I'm not crazy."

"You?"

"Yes sir."

"Do you seriously think that?"

"I don't know Argie, you tell me; here I am in a corn field talking to a scarecrow—not only talking to a one, but listening to him which means he's talkin' back. I'm a fat, dumpy little kid who has one friend he can trust and another he ain't so sure won't knock him in the head because he used to be, a couple of days ago, his worst enemy; oh, and I forgot, he's bein' raised by his grandparents cuz his parents got to go home seven months after he was born."

"Not too sure much of that has anything to do with crazy— sounds more like lonely, which is fairly normal. Cyrus, what is truly on your mind, or should I say, heart?"

If the corn were still growing you could hear it. Cyrus fumbled with the stubble like usual and pondered deeply what was on his heart. Here in the corn was a safe harbor. The place where nothing mattered, but truly it all did and he was comfortable with it— the truth.

"Hum", he sighed. "What truly is on my heart? I wanna go home, Argie."

"Home? Are you not there already?"

"No playing, Argie. I wanna be with Jake, and my Ma and Pa. I hate it here. Nothin' makes any sense whatsoever; I hate the rules; I don't like the folks—I ain't made for this place!"

"Hum", Argie sighed. "Home? That's a big one. I do understand, believe me; but, I'm not so sure you do. I mean, you've had a total of ten years to assemble what? Nothing, because, how is it said, 'you ain't knee high to a piss ant yet'. You place everything on your appearance, which isn't remotely complete, and absolutely nothing on what you can do, not to mention what you have done!"

"Done?" Cyrus yelled. "What have I *done?*"

There was silence again for several moments.

"Argie."

"Yes."

"What have I done?"

"I think it in good order that you bring Miss Cheyenne here."

"Will you show her you are real?"

"That is up to her, Cyrus—it will be her belief, not mine. She is strong in character and heart and is a true friend to you."

"Argie, what have I done?"

". . . Wonderful things, Mr Buckman, with more to come if you will just be patient."

"Name one."

"No."

"Why are you being such a pain?"

"Because you are being a petulant child, which is a characteristic far beneath you, one, and two, I am not here as your fortune teller. You know what you have done because you were the one who did it, you just have to assemble the puzzle—which is to say, you have the pieces."

"Are you going to act this way in front of Cheyenne?"

"I'll act any way a bag of straw may decide to, which I feel confident in saying, the direction I assume won't matter since just about any will be effective for Miss Cheyenne."

"Dadgum, when you get a burr under yur hide . . . you reckon I can bring her tomorrow?"

"I *reckon* any time you like will suffice."

"Mr Cornfield, please don't jaw so heavy with Cheyenne. Your words are like music, but if you don't know what they mean it's a bit like pissin' into a high wind."

"I'll be sure to speak slowly, but I think you underestimate Miss Cheyenne."

"It ain't the speed, Mr Cornfield, it's the weight; but that's okay, it'll be like another Christmas if she gets to meet you."

"Indeed."

CHAPTER TWENTY TWO

"So what about tenting this Friday?" Marshall asked. One of his running buddies was looking on and it tainted the proposition.

"Ah", Cyrus began. "What's he know about it?" he mumbled quickly.

"Who, Dale? Nothin'. Nobody knows anything by me."

They were outside Foster's Market, across from the feed store and domino parlor and it was the first time Marshall acknowledged his existence since their handshake. Cheyenne's comment about Marshall's friendship was on his mind, but he refused to believe his intent was just to injure him. There was something he saw in Marshall that day in the barn, real feelings from a real person or from the place he knew all too well? Still, there was an uncomfortable feeling he had about Dale eyeballing their conversation and Marshall's nonchalant irreverence about it all.

"I have to see if my Grandpas' got something goin' this weekend before I can nod all the way", Cyrus hem-hawed.

"Com' on Buckman, get on or off the horse."

He didn't like this pressure, the kind that hung a friendship on a short nail that was already in the balance between gutsy and a mamma's boy. What would Jake do? He'd knock him out with one punch—toying with the thought of tenting with Pritchett. But he was already in this predicament, so how would Jake run the course? He wouldn't think about it, he'd just answer—"Yeah okay, let's do it."

"Attaway Buckman", Marshall said, reaching out his hand. "I'll go home with you Friday after school and we'll . . ."

Cyrus interrupted, "I got chores, and I gotta think on how I play this out with my folks, first. My Gran'pa ain't the easiest . . ."

"Three!" his grandfather hollered from the feed store dock. He set off across the street, but not before he caught a glimpse of Dale's face that had the look of being lost at the fair. Although there were a number of toadies in the mix, Dale Worth was the simple version of a porch mutt; he was quiet, jumped on command and small. What Cyrus noticed about him, as he did most others, was his disposition, and that, Cyrus could smell out quicker than a bird dog a covey of quail. Dale was just like him: scared, hungry and alone, which met all the qualifying factors for Marshall's troopers.

"What were you jawin' with that Pritchett boy about?" his grandfather asked.

"You mean Marshall? He's in my school."

Correcting his grandfather was risky business, especially when he'd been at the bottle—like then, but on occasion Cyrus found it difficult not to swing at something low and inside. His interjection of Pritchett's first name was in a way showing him that his grandson wasn't the clueless loner he made him out to be. It wasn't his mission to compete with his grandfather, not at all; it was something far more salient. He wanted to be liked by him.

"I want you to listen, and listen good", his grandfather said with pointed finger. "Those Pritchett's are a passel of trouble that'll bring a world of hurt with you holdin' the gun! You hearin' me?"

"Yes sir."

Now, there was a new wrinkle in his event. It wasn't news to the world that the Pritchett name meant trouble, but it wasn't news either that his grandfather swilled sour mash from a fruit jar—did that mean Pritchett did it too? Cyrus was quickly discovering more and more about the things in this world and their packages; that what was on the inside rarely came close to its description on the cover. He knew it happened between kids, but adults? The apple not falling far from the tree thing was a crock of crap and carried no more weight than the Santa Claus paradigm. As far as he was concerned, they could have said the same thing about Jake and he could have missed a beautiful friendship—excuse me—brother-hood, if he had turned away from him on a word. No, Marshall was a risk, but—wait, a risk of what, he thought?

He sat in the truck with his hand in the wind as they sputtered down the dirt roads to home. His grandfather might say some-thing, but unless he yelled it he was usually talking to himself. Cyrus went to his own world, feeling the wind against his face and watching how his bitty hand changed the course of his whole arm by a slight bend, up or down. That's all it took and the wind did the rest. It was how he was beginning to see life—just a little bend and huge events could come, sometimes way down the road. Who was he to judge when and how these changes were to be, or who they would be for? Take Jake for instance; his coming out to that cistern to see him was not a thing in the world to Jake. It meant about as much as his moving his hand an inch or two and yet his whole arm changed the path of a nobody. Jake changed his whole life, the way he looks at it, the way he feels it. Amazing, he thought. Maybe, just maybe he could be a Jake in someone's life—maybe even Marshall's. Now he was getting way out there.

When they arrived home, Cyrus could see the back-end of a truck that also brought his grandfather's attention to a point, "What in hell's name you reckon Basil Hold would be wantin'?

I bet he's corralin' folk to crop out Thompson", his grandfather muttered.

It didn't matter to Cyrus what Mr Hold was doing there as long as his blonde-haired third grader was along. He sat to the edge of the seat with his face nearly against the windshield until he saw hair sway from the far side of the truck.

"What are you all game-rooster about?" his grandfather said through a belch. "You think he's here for you?"

"No sir, not him", Cyrus said, opening the door before the truck had come to a stop. Just as he jumped from the seat and hit the ground running, Cheyenne stepped out with her huge smile. He was running too fast and couldn't slow quick enough and flew right into her. He was face to face with her and she caught him. Not only caught him, but they stumbled back a foot or two and she held him tight, so tight his face was completely pushed into hers and for all intents, they were kissing. She was laughing so hard that his entire mouth, lips and all, were inside hers for just a second. They came to rest against the back of her Pa's truck and she was still holding him tightly. It wasn't necessary any longer, but she was holding him and it was wonderful. Everyone around knew it was an accident, but it was the greatest accident he had ever been in. Both the men were chuckling about the "young'un's". There wasn't any blaming going around, no one was in trouble and after that couple of unbelievable seconds, Cyrus pulled back from her face while she still held him gently about his waist and it hit him: this incredible reason why he liked her so much—more than Jake (which he thought impossible)—she was all the things he wasn't; she was soft, but tough, smelled incredible, even after running a mile or so, and smart about life. She so had to meet Argie!

"Hey Chey, you wanna see what I wanted to show you?"

"Is it here?"

"Yeah, just a bit into the corn."

Grandpa Cyrus and Mr Hold were talking at the front of his truck and Cyrus kept watching them from the side.

"Three, what are you and Miss Hold brewin' over there?" Grandpa Cyrus asked.

"I was gunna show her around—you know, like the barn, how clean you keep it and all."

He couldn't buck the bridle off on that, not in front of Mr Hold; the chance to show off his barn with the word to get out that the Buckman's are the spiffiest farming family in Alabama. No sirree.

"Okay, but you stay clear of that hay bin—don't want neithers of ya caught up by a rusty nail or such."

They went the long way around the barn until they were out of sight and into the corn. There were some intense emotions inside Cyrus as they fought their way through the dried stalks.

"What in the world would be back in here, Cyrus J—and your Gran'pa calls you *three?*"

"This", Cyrus pointed as they stepped into the clearing. "Three, cuz I'm the third Cyrus—get it?"

There he was in all his magnificence—Mr Cornfield. All neatly bundled in long johns with a pillow sack head and looking down at the both of them from on high. There was a period of silence that seemed forever as Cheyenne stood and gawked up at the rain-stained, straw bellowing figure that did nothing but—hang there.

"Cyrus, it's a—a scarecrow?" she finished in a question.

"Yeah, his name is Argie, Argie Cornfield."

"And . . ." she asked sheepishly.

"Well, he's more than what you see."

"So what am I seeing, besides a scarecrow?"

"Him", he said pointing and wondering.

Cyrus had no idea how to approach this gig. If he openly summoned Argie, and he was a no-show, then his goose would be cooked; if on the other hand, he decided to make an entrance with all of his educated flare, that may just as well blow Cheyenne's hair back too. In between both these thoughts left absolutely no wiggle room, so why on earth did he bring her here? To show her his prized possession, which is what you do to your best friend; but, Cheyenne was something beyond a friend and he was having a whale of a time finding a spot on his knickknack shelf for her. What was she? She was a Jake, but better.

"Cyrus, is this where you come when you wanna be by yourself?"

"Yeah", he answered relieved.

"And this is who?" she asked, nodding to Argie.

He hem-and-hawed for a second, somewhat embarrassed, "I named him Argie", he answered, waiting for Argie's needful entrance. He looked about and then to the sky—my god, he thought, what if he is really an *Imagine?* There was a pain in his chest, that old insecurity pain that was as tangible as the real one. What if he was just a crazy who was destined for little more than living in the woods, barking at squirrels and talking to *Imagines?*

"Wow, I wish I had a place like this."

"You do?"

"Course. I could get away and be with Argie", she chuckled quietly. "I bet he's an amazing friend, Three", she chuckled again.

"You ain't gunna let go of that are ya?"

"You have so many names that fit you, Cyrus J, not to mention your Christian name.

"You like 'em, do ya?"

"Yes. But not as much as I like you", she smiled through her sky-blue eyes.

Well, this is about where the conversation took a stumble. He was snake bit, as the term is used and didn't understand why his space-time continuum wouldn't continue. He put his hands in his pockets, looked at the ground while he pushed stubble around with his foot and didn't care anymore whether Argie showed or not.

"What is it you say to him when you come out here, or is that private like?"

"No, there ain't much about me that's private atoll. Ain't nothin' about the Buckman family that can be said of that. I daknow, I just come out here when I get kind of alone—I started comin' out after Jake left."

"It bothers you to say it, don't it?"

"Say what?"

"Died."

She was all too correct. He never said it. It was the infinity of final. The last hoorah, and to attach it to Jake was so far an impossibility. He didn't know she had moved, but suddenly she was behind him and put her arms around his waist, clasped her hands at his stomach and he wasn't alone again. This was something Argie could not do; something he couldn't even dream because he had not known it before, but it was so nice. He remembered when he woke with Jake behind him and he would be holding him, but it wasn't like this. With Jake he was safe, with Cheyenne he was with purpose and surrender, two things he barely knew apart much less together.

"He is my amazing friend", Cyrus whispered. "It probably sounds like I got into some sour hay, but I do feel better when I talk to him." He thought intently about his next comment because he didn't feel that sure-footed.

"Would you think me crazier than a barn rat if I was to tell you he talks back?"

"Not at all. Why would you talk to anything that wouldn't answer ya?" she answered so matter-of-factly.

"Really?"

"Really."

"Cyrus !" his grandfather yelled from the barn. "You and the Missy get back up here. I didn't say you could get out there in that patch."

"Great", he muttered. "Just like the storm after the calm."

They edged back through the dried tundra and made it to the paddock fence only to see both men still jawing next to Mr Hold's truck. His grandma was on the porch front in her ubiquitous apron, looking on as might a mamma cow eyeing her young. When they got within ear shot, Grandma Mattie hollered at them and more so to Cheyenne, who she had a thing about and loved it so that she and Cyrus had become runnin' buddies. She gained a "thing" for just about anyone who brought Cyrus out of his world, but Jake and Cheyenne way over shot the bow of her boat.

"Oh, you are sooo beautiful this mornin' Miss Cheyenne. Com' here and let me see you up close."

"Gran'ma", Cyrus whinnied like an annoyed fold. Cheyenne laughed and squeezed Cyrus' chub around his middle and he loved it; her catting with him made him smile broadly without reproach and for that split second he was free.

"Not so fast there, Cyrus", his grandfather murmured. "We're runnin' to the Thompson's for a chat about work, somethin' you ain't much akin to."

"But what about Cheyenne?"

"She'll be here when we get back. She ain't leavin' without me", Mr Hold laughed with a condescending smile.

"Miss Cheyenne, Cyrus has taken an awful shinin' to you and I am so glad", Grandma said.

"Well, he's about as special a friend any girl—or guy, could have." She paused a moment as they went into the house and helped Grandma put dishes in the cupboard. "Cyrus is special, Ms Buckman, way more special than he knows for sure, but more special than others know too. It's kind of funny", she said, pausing again. "Cyrus sees things that others either see and don't care for, or just don't plain see."

"Child, he is special, you are right about that, and I so wish with all my might that he and his Gran'pa would see eye to eye someday. They both feel the other don't like him, and they work so darn hard to hide that they do. It's the craziest thing I've ever seen of folk, especially kin under the same roof."

"Do you know Argie?" Cheyenne asked.

"Who?"

"Oh nothin', I was just wondering about something Cyrus said. Would you mind if I went out behind the barn and looked at the goats?"

"Don't mind in the least—maybe you could get Cyrus a bit more interested in them." Grandma paused a moment, "Child—who's Argie?"

Cheyenne set out to the barn and took a fast gander at the kids and their mamma, then proceeded out to the corn. She chuckled a time or two thinking about what she was doing, but it was more her curiosity about Cyrus than what was drawing her out here—wanting to talk to Argie.

She entered the dimly lit arena of downed stalks and cool mildew. The sun shown across the top of him, down to his waist and across one side where his long john could be seen stretched over the four by four that was an arm. His pillow sack head bowed towards her as if he were looking right at her and wondering what she was going to say.

"Hi, Argie", she paused. "Cyrus introduced us, but I think you were a-might afraid to say anything. He sure is proud having you as a friend, just a smidgen sheepish about lettin' folks know, I imagine. Guess I would be too, having a scarecrow for a friend would be something the entire county would clamber to see, or at least . . ." She scooted a pile of stubble up with her foot and sat comfortably at the base and stared up at the pillow sack that eerily smiled back. You know Mr Cornfield, you reckon a lot towards Mr Buckman—a lot. That's' kind of funny; you bein' Cyrus' friend and all. I guess his friendship with you is real private and all, ain't it? You don't have to answer, Mr Cornfield, I know you're a private—not sure what you would be, but Cyrus sure pays attention and you have been a great friend to him since Jake's passin'.

That thing with Jake just about killed Cyrus. There were a lot of folks thought he wouldn't come back from it, but he did, and about the only way I figured he did was cuz of you. I figure you and he have a special relationship, and there are lots of folk who would give an eye-tooth to have something like that—a relationship with someone like you." At that moment a strong wind hit the patch with such force it blew her ribbon from her hair and literally picked her up off the stubble and dropped right up against the scarecrow. She had to brace it to stop her head from bouncing against it.

"Oh my! Must have been a dust devil! Never seen one in these parts, but they sure run wild in Oklahoma." She leaned back on her two hands and stared upwards again, now about having to lay back to see his face.

"Whatdaya think of that Mr Cornfield? Or may I call you, Argie? I don't wanna come across pushy, seein' you're Cyrus' friend and I really don't have permission to take liberty—but, he did introduce us, in a fashion. May I speak plain, Argie? I'll take that as a, yes." She laid back against the stubble, put her arms behind her head and pondered a moment while she stared up at the giant.

"Argie, since you and Cyrus became friends how well have you come to know him—sorry, I imagine you've come to know each other pretty well, since Cyrus has changed so much. You should've seen him stand up to Pritchett and his gang; he didn't flinch or nothin'. He just stood ground and was willin' to shed his britches, with me there an' all. It stopped Pritchett dead in his tracks. You should-a seen the look on his face—Cyrus didn't stutter nor shake, or nothin', he just started unbuckling his britches. I knew right then that there somethin' inside Cyrus that wasn't there before, at least not a minute before." She sat up for a moment a thought.

"That's the way it is, ain't it? You belong to Cyrus and no one else; or, can you? Okay, I'll try it."

There was a long silence as Cheyenne gazed about her surroundings, her arms about her knees. There was something so conducive about this place—the quiet, the dim light and the calmness of the air that seemed like the womb to a soul who might remember.

"Cyrus thinks he's the only one who's alone, Argie. He has this place he goes. This place to that he won't let anyone, well, some folk can come in—I guess he has let me in a little, and Jake! Boy, he had a friend in Jake. This thing about girls and guys is soooo, so dadgum confusing! I'd give anything to have with one of my friends what Jake and Cyrus had, but the girls all center themselves in the kitchen or around dolls and such and I just don't cotton to doin' that kind of stuff. I love the outside, farmin' and fishin' and following my Pa about. I like boy stuff—yet have a strong turn understandin' 'em. Just like I don't quite understand why I feel different about Cyrus—sometimes I hanker to shake the tar out of him, and others I want to kiss him—and neither has place! But you! You get to be what I wanna be: friends. You get to listen to him and tell him where to go, what to do—we're all afraid Mr Cornfield. That's what I come to see in my eleven years here—everyone of us is plum afraid, and most of the time it's of stuff we've just made up in our head. My Ma one time, one time when I was real little and we lived in Oklahoma, there was a big storm that came upon us one night. Storms in Oklahoma ain't like storms down here; they topple barns and such. This storm was real big and we had to get to the cellar. We couldn't find my dog and my Ma wouldn't let me look, she just dragged me down inside while the storm brewed—I couldn't stop cryin' because I just knew Pots was gunna be sucked up. My Ma took me by the face and said, 'You got no idea what is gunna happen out there, just like you ain't givin' any credit to how smart Pots is—child, when fear knocks on the door of your heart, answer it and no one will be there.' I remember that every time I fear. It seems Mr Cornfield that you have taught that to Cyrus."

She stood and knocked the stubble from her overalls, "Well, I bes' be getting back before Ms Buckman begins missin' me. It was real nice talkin' with you Mr Cornfield, and I hope I didn't bother you none."

"Miss Cheyenne", Argie whispered, as she was leaving.

"Oh my—yes sir."

"You're not surprised?"

"No sir; well, a bit. I thought—I believed you were real because of Cyrus, but wasn't sure you'd talk to me."

"You thought I was real because you believed Cyrus, or you believed in him?"

"What's the difference?"

"A lot; to believe on an object is based on *fact*, to believe in someone is based on *faith*; creatures who find meld with the wind but hold true to who they are rare finds. Facts change but the root of a person stays. I know Cyrus J to be the real deal. Jus' spitballin'."

"I believe *in* him."

"I know you do—He has chosen a fine friend."

"I'm not sure who chose you, Mr Cornfield, I only know I feel good when I'm with him. Who are you?"

"Not rightly sure, I'm just here. Back to you and Cyrus; you say he makes you feel good, how is that?"

She paused a while: "Not rightly sure either. I guess because he's *real*. What Cyrus does and says is exactly what he believes. There's no mincing words or long ways 'round the barn with him. The sad thing about him is how little he thinks of himself; he puts so much in what he looks like than what he is. A lot of folks do though, so you can't really fault him there. He's real tied up 'bout bein' friends with someone I think—well, the whole town thinks—is bad news, but Cyrus sees somethin' in him no one else sees."

"Do you believe things are always as they appear?"

"Well sir, I believe I don't always see what's there—not like Cyrus, anyways. He seems to see right through ya, right to the guts—you really don't know who you are?"

"I have vague memories, but they aren't anything I can put a full picture to; it's like looking through a glass dimly. And you, who do you think I am?

"You're a scarecrow, at least that's what I see, and a talkin' one to boot."

"Yes. Yes I am."

"You're an amazing friend, Mr Cornfield. Cyrus is lucky."

"I'm yours too Miss Cheyenne, and between friends, I'd like to ask a favor and keep this little talk between ourselves for the time. Cyrus is busy ironing some things out and word of this might be a bit much."

"You think? Whatever you say."

CHAPTER TWENTY THREE

It was Friday, and he lay in bed staring at his pecan wondering what he was thinking when he agreed to this thing with Marshall. Yeah, he wanted to be friends and he tried desperately to see him in the same as light Jake, but it wasn't close. There were so many differences that they couldn't be counted. In between these mental swords fights he was playing with Marshall, Cheyenne would materialize with her genuine smile, glowing hair and soft smell and derail the entire train. Life was now more confusing than his make believe one and he longed for the thing that would never come—his brother's advice.

Cyrus spent more time in his head than he did on the ground, running scenes from beginning to end before they happened. It was exhausting, futile and ruined what could be, but was the only direction he had learned that kept him from harm. It was the direction Jake labored so hard to divert; the place where he'd go when life became the unfamiliar. This place Jake was so able to navigate like a sixth sense. Carrying this memory was a dead man strapped to his back that he couldn't shed. When he was in this gray haze it was difficult to breathe, much less put one foot in front of the other. He plodded through chores after breakfast, blocked out his grandparent's grumblings with shrugs and nods until he found himself in the barn hidden in a corner and crying. What! He thought. Why is this so bad? Everything he reached into his haversack for came out sad news—death and dying; being *pants'd*; Argie's lessons . . . that was it, he thought. His magic, real or imagined, didn't matter at this point because Argie always had an answer; even if it wasn't absolutely right he made him feel a part of something, this thing that was bigger than him. He had renewed strength and sense of purpose now and it brought him back; the only thing was there wasn't time for a trip to the patch.

Strange how, he found Cheyenne waiting for him at every turn. When he got to school that morning she was out front by the drain pipe, waving him in like a flagman at a horse track. She was flanked by a couple of grade school starlets she'd hang with before and after school, hammering out nonsensical nothings about others, but now she seemed totally focused on Cyrus, and it was pretty okay with him. Still strange, but okay.

"About time you got here", she said excitedly.

"Why, is somethin' going on—you look like yur about to pee yur britches."

"Silly, have you talked to Argie?"

That was an odd question. Cyrus may have looked like someone who fell off the turnip wagon just pulling into town, but the one thing about his design that was near perfect was his ability to detect the shadow behind the image; the question under the question. What saved him most of his youthful life was his honed intuition to read between the lines. He'd become so good that he could actually, on occasion, would know the script before it was uttered, just by a person's expression.

"Argie? What in the world brought him up?"

"I don't know", she said sheepishly, combing the ground with her brogan. "Just was wonderin' about him."

"I actually thought about him this morning, but didn't have time to say, hey", he answered nonchalantly. "Funny you'd ask about him."

"Why?"

"I daknow, I figured you'd think I was loonier than a tree full of owls for introducing you to a scarecrow. I mean, being nothin' more than a pair of hay-stuffed long handles stuck on a stick."

"Oh Cyrus", she frowned. "He's tons more than that—you ought be kicked."

"What's wrong with you?" he asked pointedly.

At that moment, Cyrus noticed Cheyenne's cheering squad eavesdropping and it opened up a can of worms in his head. If these ya-ho's were the least bit sharper than a butter knife, they would put together that he and Cheyenne weren't speaking about a fellow townsmen. If something like that happened, he couldn't leave town fast enough. Cyrus nodded for Cheyenne to come away from them.

"What's with you about Argie, I was just showin' you where I went for a quiet place?"

"Not a thing, Cyrus J; I don't know what's got you all flustered up. I was just askin' about him because I think it the berries you have someone like that—real or imagined."

"*Imagine*! Where'd you get that?" Cyrus blustered.

"I didn't say *imagine*; I said i-ma-gined—past tense,"

"You have been talkin' to him! Only Argie corrects like that!"

"Cyrus, quit!"

He kept working to pull her farther from the entourage but she was bigger, and if the truth be known, Cheyenne wasn't much for instruction, especially when it concerned social schoolyard etiquette. The German in her was pronounced on that point, and although a bit disconcerting to Cyrus, it was also a character element he admired, just as he had in Jake.

"Just tell me one thing, Cheyenne, did you talk to him?" he whispered tensely.

She thought hard about how to answer because she remembered the promise she extended, but she also had an allegiance to Cyrus, "Yes I did, because I wanted to see what it was like."

"And what was it like?" Cyrus asked.

"I felt good afterwards. I could say to him what I couldn't say to anyone."

"That's all? Nothin' more?"

"Nope."

There. She covered her bases on both sides fairly, even though she fudged a might about "nothin' more", which she saw as a necessary fudge. If Cyrus knew their conversation had been both ways it could have made a riff between both of them—she and Argie. The true point here was that Cheyenne believed in Cyrus to a depth she had not ever known and it had little to do with Argie. The magic between them was the same magic he and Jake shared: it didn't come from man or anywhere on this earth.

They went through their day as usual with a few exceptions: every time Cyrus saw Cheyenne she was staring at him with a cat-like grin, but with an oddity he couldn't put a finger to. This whole affair was becoming richer than one of Grandma Mattie's pecan pies and he disliked the complexity; but, it was definitely something Jake would love to bask in, so he forced himself not to think on it.

He worked the balance of the day at avoiding Marshall by acting an ostrich, that if he didn't see something it wasn't there. The only problem was that Marshall had to be acting the same way for the ostrich effect to work, and he wasn't.

"Buckman, I'll be walkin' home with you and we can plan out our weekend in the fort", Marshall hollered out openly with a couple of his toadies behind him. Just his boldness was intrusive enough without having to show the world he was commander of every affair, even the ones he hadn't been made a part. This was the most annoying element of his character; that part of every human being that should have been left in the scrap yard; that piece of foreign lint on god's finger that inadvertently got glued on. He was not comfortable with this day from the beginning and the weekend was looking even darker.

Cyrus nodded and smiled uncomfortably as they passed each other. He saw Marshall extend his hand but pretended he didn't see it. How strange, he thought, all this time seeing Marshall as a formidable friend when truly all he had been trying for was one less enemy.

"So you and Marshall gunna be pals this weekend, huh?" Cheyenne asked. "You gunna show him Argie?"

"No!" he answered angrily. "I wish you wouldn't talk 'bout him like he was a person!"

"But he—is, in away."

"No—to say it again. I should have never taken you in to that patch."

"Why Cyrus J, I'm glad you did", she answered firmly. "I think having a friend like Argie is something from God—a real gift."

He looked at her square in the face with beaded eyes of circumspection to where they nearly touched noses, "Cheyenne Hold, you have to keep this Argie stuff between us or I'll be run outta town on a rail. Yur letting this thing run loose like a Pritchett river dog, and I hate to tell you what happens to them on a full moon."

"Pritchett river dog?"

"Yep, they tarry up on traps and . . . well, they ain't around long."

"You make no sense."

"I make nothin' *but* if you knew how to tent—never you no mind."

Her expression changed and she looked to the ground and mumbled something Cyrus couldn't hear.

"Buckman! You ready to set out?" Marshall blurted from behind.

"I gotta get it okayed with my folks."

"You ain't done that yet?"

"No—hadn't found the right place. You?"

"I told ya, fool, it don't matter at my house."

"Okay then, I'll ask if I can stay at your place."

"Are you not hearin' me? We ain't stayin' at my place."

"I know that, but I ain't allowed to tent—so that leaves me snake bit."

Cheyenne stood there as though she weren't, which was so her in that regard; she had vested interest in Cyrus and if it came to it would probably "throw down" with Marshall if she felt Cyrus was in harm's way. Cyrus glanced to her with a puzzled expression, and somewhat embarrassed if the truth be known, but the moment was there with remnants of Jake fluttering about.

"Look Pritchett . . ." Cyrus began.

"It's Marshall", he interrupted. "We agreed, recall?"

"Not really, I asked and you said nothing—but anyway; Marshall, I have to make sure my bases are covered or my Gran'pa, as much a pain as he is, don't mind in the least puttin' a back cinch to my hide if the wind ain't right. How things run at your place ain't my dally", Cyrus finished.

When the smoke cleared there were a handful of bystanders gawking at each other as though Mr Burnside had just completed first bell instruction.

"Alright Buckman, so Whatdaya want from me?" Marshall asked.

"Just let me handle my stuff and I'll meet you at my barn after chores."

"And how will I know that?"

"Just come over a couple hours before sundown and wait in the barn, I'll find you."

They all disbursed slowly like the fat lady at the fair had gone back to her dressing room for a chicken pot pie and everyone was whispering, panning their hands through the air making measurements and expressions and such. Cheyenne put her hands to her mouth and beamed at Cyrus with her blue eyes that looked as if they were tearing.

"What?" Cyrus asked with authority.

"Wow! Cyrus J Buckman!"

"It's Cyrus W., and what?"

"No thing", she whispered with a smile.

Cyrus smiled wide as he could and let out a chuckle, "Jakie used to say that all the time when he was put out with me—no thing."

"Well I ain't at all put out with ya."

CHAPTER TWENTY FOUR

C yrus had been home an hour and in the barn and up to his elbows in chores since his preoccupation that morning, when his Grandma hollered at him from the porch: "Cyrus J, some youngin' is comin' up the road a-foot!" He looked out the barn door and saw Marshall coming from the main road, toting his possibles over his shoulder like he was planning a move-in. What was he thinking, or did he? He told him emphatically that he was in a precarious position here as it was, especially when considering what happened the last time. This wasn't going to work, but how was he going to get out of it? Here's the second time he's offered the chance to be brought into the world of friendship with real people and he didn't know what to do.

"Cyrus, who is that young feller? Is that a Pritchett boy?" his Grandmother hollered. She stood on the porch in her apron, complete with her wrenching napkin and looking as though she were expecting a package from a long lost kin.

He looked around the barn frantically for a spot to hide until he could gather his thoughts on how to negotiate this fiasco, when the patch came to mind. That would leave Marshall with his grandmother and could be his inevitable finish. Well, looks like another face the music thing. He set his rake to the wall of the barn and materialized before God, Marshall and his grandmother.

"Hey!" he hollered.

Marshall waved, coming up to the paddock gate and a distance from the porch. Although Cyrus knew his grandmother was hard of hearing, especially from that distance, he knew she wasn't, if you catch the drift; she could hear flies in a conversation if she had a mind to. Cyrus nonchalantly put his finger to his lips to head off any unsolicited discussion.

"What?" Marshall yelled.

"Nothing", Cyrus muttered. "What are you doin', Marshall? I asked you not to come 'til I got through with chores."

"How was I 'spose to know when you was to be through? Anyway, I can help you."

Cyrus chuckled to himself when he recognized his hopeless state. It was same thing he did with Jake. Had he not learned from the past?

Even though it was the same, it was different; this time he didn't want to go. He did and didn't. It was confusing, and then it wasn't. Okay, he thought: what is the same, what is different and why is he anxious? He wants to be popular and liked by as many folks as he can—that's always been the same. He wants to be friends with Marshall because he doesn't care to be *pants'd*—that's a given. He doesn't *ever* want to be strapped by his grandfather like he had been when Jake got hurt—that's it! He's anxious about lying to his grandparents, especially Grandpa Cyrus.

"Where are you, Buckman?" Marshall asked, setting his knap-sack to the ground. "You look like yur in China or someplace."

"Kinda wish I was. Marshall, I ain't sure I'll be able to tent—not tonight or any night."

"Cuz of me?'

"No, cuz of Jake."

"Whatdaya mean?"

"That's how the whole thing with Jake started—how he got sick and all. We were . . ."

At that moment Grandpa Cyrus came in the back of the barn with Dud and saw the boys chatting at the front paddock gate. Cyrus could see what demeanor his grandfather was in and it was a righteous one, his was liquored up. Cyrus looked quickly at Marshall and he knew instantly not to say a word, unless directly addressed, of course. It wasn't difficult to see Marshall was a professional too.

"Mr Pritchett", Grandpa addressed.

"Mr Buckman."

"How's yur Pa doin'? Hog business still boomin'?"

"Well sir, it has its days."

Grandpa paused from dragging tack off Dud and stood there staring at the boys, "Your Pa gunna be around tonight?" he asked.

"I reckon—not rightly sure, but he should be."

He only once saw his Grandpa incapacitated, and the rest of the times he was always in physical control; he never stumbled and rarely slurred his word, but it was his emotional self that was impossible to predict. You could receive accolades for burning down a neighbor's house, and just as summarily be knocked across a room for spilling a drink at the table. Parity between crime and punishment was never in balance. The only equity was his grandmother, and that would at times place her in danger.

"Cyrus, finish up Dud—tell yur Gran'ma I won't be to supper."

"Gran'pa, Marshall and I are gunna tent out."

"Okay by me, pass it with yur Gran'ma", he said on his way through the paddock gate.

Cyrus looked at Marshall, who had an expressionless, clueless look that said exactly that and shrugged, "What?"

"Unbelievable", Cyrus muttered. Cyrus saw the moment and lunged. If you were preoccupied and not paying attention for the exact moment, you'd miss the crack; the tiny, hair-line fissure in Grandpa's armor so small and insignificant that it couldn't be seen by the naked eye. You had to be vigilant. That split second he was distracted by whatever; that moment his mind wandered to another place that did not include Cyrus or his grandmother was his Achilles Heal. His grandfather wouldn't have recollection of what he okayed, only that Marshall was his witness.

"Does that mean we're good?" Marshall mumbled.

"I reckon so. I—we gotta finish up in here and then we can go."

Like with Jake, in a distant manner, Cyrus pointed here and there with instruction of what to do but Marshall seemed in a foreign land. He stood in the middle of the barn gawking about like a kid's first day at the fair.

"My God! You could eat in here", he muttered to himself.

"Yeah I know; we gotta get everything done if we're gunna get to the fort for dark."

"Why is it so—so like this—so clean? It's like a hospital."

"It's Cyrus Walton Buckman the first, that's what it is—com' on."

Cyrus was pulling the yoke off Dud when he saw Marshall over at the hay bin, "Pritchett!" he yelled. "What are you doin' over there? You need to grain Dud's stall."

Marshall was acting like a pet coon, completely immersed in everything but what Cyrus instructed.

"Jus' lookin' around, Buckman; no need to get yur panties all wadded up."

"Look, would you fill the fire box in the kitchen and I'll finish in here?"

Marshall left the barn and when he was out of the paddock Cyrus double-timed so he could run to the patch and see Argie before anyone knew he was missing. He had to have a pressure release and Argie seemed always able to fill that bill.

There was a good two hours of daylight left but it was to be a cool night, and the closer he came to Argie he felt better. It wasn't just the coolness of the corn, the containment of the surroundings and the sense of being that made him feel right with this world, but the exhilaration that Argie was going to impart something that brought the two ends of the string together; the blending of his experience and intuition into a cake he could taste, and unlike anyone he knew, could see and smell.

The sun far to the west horizon left a dream-like dimness about the scarecrow; the sun now against nothing but his torso to one side and in a way that made him look as though he were smiling broadly.

"What?" Cyrus said, looking up at the bowing head. "What you smilin' about, you ol' bag-a-hay?"

There was only silence and a sinking feeling that knotted his stomach; that dissonance that was intolerably a part of his soul and hurt more than any form of death he could envision—being alone.

"Master Cyrus", Argie whispered. "Why are you angst?"

He breathed the longest sigh of relief if ever in his existence while his apprehension faded into a slight amalgamation of pissed off.

"You did that on purpose!" Cyrus bellowed. "And what the hell is *Angst*, or whatever you said?"

"Cyrus, you remember what we agreed about cursing?"

"I ain't—I'm not real agreeable right now, Mr Cornfield. I don't like it when you act like yur not here and I see you are there!"

"I'm sorry, I was playing with you and I see that you are not in the paying mood, which is what I meant by *angst*."

"Well I'm in kind of a mood, yeah; Marshall and I are tenting out and I really don't want to—I do, but I don't. Is that what *angst* means?"

"Correct—you seem anxious."

"Yeah."

"So what are you anxious about?"

"I daknow, that's why I'm here."

"I'm afraid you'll have to put forth a bit more effort than that, Cyrus."

CHAPTER TWENTY FIVE

They made it to the creek with half an hour of light left and Cyrus began to feel uneasy the closer they came to that washout hidden by the fallen oak. It had been a stretch of time since the last tent-out and the difference now was next to him, dressed in tattered hand-me-downs held together by more paint than thread, with over-sized brogans so worn and dried that the toes curled enough to make an elf grimace. He sported a ruddy complexion better pressed for a thirty-something coal miner, and teeth that accompanied the breath with broken a smile; yet, despite his physical appearance Marshall had a glint of character only Cyrus could see. It's the finest moment; that second a soul is fixed in thought about nothing, nothing at all; from a solemn sea of tranquility where there are no facades, where the heart is transparent and smiles without reproach for any spirit with the gift to know. It was what set Cyrus apart from the many and exactly what drew them together.

"Hey Buckman, what are you runnin' for? Geez, we got plenty of time."

"Sorry, was thinkin' of gettin' there I guess."

When they reached the bank on the far side from the fort, there was a slight ridge to climb before it could be seen. The roots of the giant oak that bridged the two sides could be seen and it was about this time that the apprehension of the summit began to disappear for Cyrus. They topped the ridge and Cyrus sat down on the tree's base for a rest.

"See it there", Cyrus pointed. "We usually build us a fire right there, outside the front door, well kind of a door."

The top of the tree covered the entrance in such a way that you would have to be in the creek to see the entrance and you would have to be looking for it. This was a great place, not to mention the plush amenities like candles and perfect indentations in the limestone to cradle a ten year-old's butt where it didn't go to sleep.

Cyrus didn't flinch at his next thought; in fact, he was three-quarters the way across the rotted carcass before he realized and Marshall was yelling, "You outta yur tree, Buckman? The bark's fallen off it's so rotten—you'll break yur ass!" Marshall laughed as he scaled down the creek wall to the other side.

Cyrus was there first, of course, and the sudden familiarity brought back a floodgate of memories; even the smell triggered a pang. He sat for a moment in the solace of the half-light, staring around at the knickknacks carefully placed in what seemed years ago. Each one had a story for its existence and it made him smile.

"Pudger, what the hell did you bring this for?" Jake asked, holding Grandma Mattie's kitchen spatula. "What are we gunna cook?"

"I daknow, thought we might catch somethin'."

"Jew bring a pan?"

"No."

Marshall finally made it up the embankment, panting and gripping about the climb and that he should have taken the tree like Cyrus had. Wow, Cyrus thought. It was the first time he saw life's turnabout, or at best recognized it: now he was Jake and Marshall was him and he was in a position to be the teacher, in a manner of speaking. There wasn't a lot to teach, but the point was that all this was new to Marshall and old school to him, as banal and insignificant as it might have seemed. Tonight he was 'the guy'.

"Wow", Marshall muttered. "This place is really somethin'; I see why we couldn't find it."

"Who couldn't?" Cyrus asked.

Marshall paled with a strange expression and looked out the entrance away from Cyrus.

"You looked for it didn't you; you and Hackworth?" Cyrus chuckled. "I don't care; kind of figured you would. I would've."

Marshall looked back at him with another strange expression but behind a smile, something very unusual for this boy. Most everything from him came in the venue of cloak and dagger because that's the way everything came to him. What Cyrus was discovering was that the way people treated him was not necessarily because of him, it was from what Marshall learned by the way he had been treated; kind of a reaction. At that very second, when Marshall smiled at him, he discovered a very important thing: no one wants to be thought different than their fellow. As much as we strive to be different, we want to be seen the same.

They split the remedial chores and this time he straightened and Marshall gathered the firewood.

"Marshall, pitch me yur ditty sack and I'll put down yur bed."

"That's okay, I'll catch it when I get back."

Marshall grabbed his things and toted them outside.

Cyrus started the fire that suddenly became too big and Marshall kept pitching more wood on to where the entire creek bed was lit up like an Indian pow wow.

"Marshall! No more wood, fella, it's already burnin' the branches overhead."

"Ah, yur just bein' a pantywaist Buckman", Marshall laughed, pitching on another piece. "That's part of the fun."

He was acting a fool and completely different than thirty minutes ago.

"Stop!" Cyrus snapped, grabbing the last stick and pitching it into the creek. "If the tree catches we'll be trapped in here; what's got in you?"

The evening's ambiance was dampened somewhat by Marshall's Jekyll and Hyde thing and Cyrus was beginning to see yet another side of him that was a puzzle piece to the Pritchett family mystique. Marshall leaned back against the limestone shale that surrounded their den like a castle's parapet and smiled at Cyrus with a dazed grin that smelled of Grandpa Cyrus, yet was without purpose or reason and told a story behind it that was all too familiar.

"Did you bring hooch?" Cyrus inquired.

"And if I did", he chuckled again.

It was happening all over again. Cyrus sat back and gazed into the fire. He did something for the first time; he reached out to Argie in his thought: "Argie, you around?" he asked to his thought. "I'm in a deal here and it's comin' bad like last time. I need you Argie."

"What Buckman? You never tried it?" Pritchett equivocated.

"Yeah, but just don't like the way it makes me feel—afterwards."

"Afterwards? It's right now that's the best—here, take a snort", Marshall added as he stumbled forward into the dark just outside the fort. He returned with the ubiquitous fruit jar in hand. Was his grandmother the only one in the state who mistook a fruit jar to hold preserves?

Cyrus laughed at himself.

"What's so funny—the way I'm walkin?" Pritchett asked.

"No, jus' what I was thinkin'."

"Here Buckman, take a draw off this."

Cyrus looked at it and thought for a second. What would be the wrong to just go along? It took so much more energy to go the other way. He began to reach for the jar when he heard it: "Hey, hey Cyrus J."

"What?" he mumbled to himself.

"Here Buckman!" Pritchett hollered. "Take it, it ain't gunna bite—then maybe it will."

Cyrus took the jar and held it between his legs while he sat wondering of what he thought he heard.

"Is that you, Argie?" he whispered.

"Well it's not Miss Cheyenne", the voice answered.

"It is you!"

"Who you talkin' to?" Pritchett asked.

"Myself!"

He sat patiently for another *sign* or something and there wasn't anything. He was just sitting there holding Pritchett's whiskey. Maybe it was nothing but his hope.

"Buckman! It'll be daylight here in a short!"

Cyrus unscrewed the top and took a whiff of the noxious liquid. A part of him said it was inviting; it did bring back more memories of his 'good ol' days' that truly weren't that good, but Jake was there. What would Jake do, he thought? He knew what Jake would do—polish the whole jar in two gulps, grimace like wildcat and enjoy the ride. He just couldn't bear the thought of being sick after the feeling was gone.

"Buckman!" Pritchett snapped again.

"Ain't no call to buck the bridle off, we ain't goin' no where."

Just as he put the jar to his lips a thought came: "Cyrus, nothin' says you have to do this. It's your decision at this second—it's not for tomorrow or three days ago, and it's not from a dream—it's right now; it's real."

"You know what, Marsh'", Cyrus said slightly under his breath and screwing back the lid. "I think I'm gunna pass—I just don't cotton to throwin' up all night and bein' dizzy."

Marshall sat there dumbfounded, blinking his eyes and staring at Cyrus like his nose fell off.

"You are a strange squirrel, Buckman", Pritchett said slowly. "You won't take just a one sip with me?"

"It ain't got a thing to do with you, Marshall. It's that I don't want to. Just plain don't care to be sick—I don't understand why you care to neither."

"It ain't about bein' sick, Buckman; it's about not bein'."

"Not bein' what?"

"Exactly", Pritchett said, taking the jar from Cyrus and jamming down a swallow.

There was a long stretch of silence as they sat and watched the fire. There was something about it that lulled the soul into submission; when there was no pull, there was no push and you were able to just be. Cyrus thought for only a moment of joining his new companion in his festivities, but the realization that he had finally stood ground for nothing more than to covet that one little piece of earth he occupied, was a milestone in his identity. The bit of angst he felt was that age old worry what the world might say or think about his walking the other way, but for the first time it felt exceedingly good to not only be different but to be in his own skin.

"Cyrus, what's it like at your house—I mean, not havin' any brothers or sisters or even a dog?"

Cyrus cringed when he heard that because it immediately brought to mind Miller's Pass and that little unknown between him and Jake not so long ago.

"Why you ask?"

"I daknow, jus' wonderin'."

"How's it at yours?"

"I got first dibs", Marshall quipped, taking another swig.

"Don't that burn goin' down like that?" Cyrus asked.

"This is lots better than my Pa's stuff—ain't as rank."

"Yur Pa's stuff", Cyrus inquired with a chuckle. "Whose is that?" he asked, pointing to the fruit jar.

Marshall burst a loud with a quick laugh while Cyrus sat there amused and bewildered at the same thing, "What's so funny?"

"It's Buckman hooch."

"Buckman hooch? Whatdaya meanin'?"

"I found it in the hay bin at the barn—it must be yur Gran'pa's."

Cyrus stood up and couldn't believe what he had heard. This was tantamount to a burial at sea, except there wouldn't be any taps, any color guards or any ocean for that fact, just hard rock bottom.

"Are you outta yur mind, Pritchett! He measures that bottle with a jack knife—notches it every time. He will KILL me! You idiot! He hates me!"

"Hates you, yur his kin?"

"You don't understand! Ever since my Pa died he's had it for me."

"That don't make a lick a sense, Buckman. Kin don't hate kin; they might get irritated at 'em a might, but they don't hate 'em."

"Well, you ain't part of the Buckman house—", Cyrus said, pacing back and forth with his hands in his pockets. "We gotta fill it back up, Marshall; one way or another, we gotta make sure that bottle's right."

Marshall stood and grabbed Cyrus by the shoulders and put his face to his, "Okay, whatever makes it right for ya, but I know yur Gran'pa don't hate ya. I'll take the hidin' for ya and make sure they know that it was me and you knew nothing—alright?"

Cyrus settled down a bit and he sat down next to the fire. Marshall sat next to him and past the jar over. Cyrus held it and stared at it, put it to his lips, then stopped. What was it, he thought? Why did he feel so badly all the time and would this make it any different? It would for a while because he remembered him and Jake, but then there was after and everything reappeared, or did it ever leave?

"You think this will help?" Cyrus asked, taking a sniff.

"Won't hurt. Take one and we'll sneak over to the barn and fix everything."

"He's probably made count already—won't make much difference ifin' he has", he answered, putting the lid back. It was tricky, this stuff; he could feel the warmth surround his sides and his head where the tension eased just as if he had taken a belt, but he hadn't.

"You know, I've been afraid all my life of everything—sometimes even my own shadow. I'm sick to the bone of bein' scared of my Gran'pa; I just can't figure why he hates me. I been a problem once in a spell, but I always done what I'm told—might tarry on occasion, but I get 'er done."

"Buckman, ain't no house like mine—six brothers and two sisters and a Pa who stays away as much as he can—and when he's there, ain't no fear like that. Ain't no skinnin' like one from Haskell Pritchett. Once I had it with an ax handle and couldn't n'er stand nor walk for a week."

Cyrus looked at him stunned and shook his head, "Axe handle?"

"That's the least, Buckman. It ain't so bad now, is it? And yur Gran'pa don't hate ya cuz yur kin; it's a rule that can't be broke. You might pain him a stretch, but he don't hate you. Go ahead—take you a bump."

"Naw", Cyrus said quietly as he handed Marshall the jar.

"Whoa, I done near half a fruit jar of this stuff—it ain't like the rot my Pa sucks on; you talkin' about sick."

"Is this it, Marshall? Is this what it's about?"

"Don't reckon I'm hearin' ya right; is what, it?"

"This—you and me tryin' to figure out on our own—sittin' in front of a fire, suckin' on a fruit jar to feel nothin', hoping we ain't found out. If this is it, I don't want it."

"I don't think it is, Cyrus."

Marshall put his arm around Cyrus and pulled himself close, then put his hands around the jar.

"I ain't nobody like you Cyrus."

"Like me? What's that mean?"

"You don't know?"

"I ain't got the foggiest, Marshall—you mean the town no-account?"

"Yur kiddin' right?"

"No", Cyrus answered with a childish laugh.

"When you first came to school no one knew who you were, what kinda kid and all; you just kept to yourself so everyone figured you to be a hoddy-toddy, a too-good or something."

"Me! You got the right fella?"

"Yeah, I reckon I do—everyone punched about ya at dinner, tryin' to figure you and Jake was the one who set it straight."

"Jake?" Cyrus said.

"Yep. He said you was sent here from another place to try this world out; that you were special and everyone who treated you bad like was gunna get it back ten times what was dished out."

Cyrus laughed out loud, but was absolutely taken in by what Marshall was saying, "Yur greenin' me!" Cyrus mused.

"No I ain't none neither—he was as serious as a hungry bear and everyone was intent on listenin' too."

"Then how's it you kept rankin' me out every chance you had?" Cyrus asked.

"Well, cuz I'm a Pritchett and we always go the other way; everyone expects it. But that's before I got to know you, Buckman. I kinda knew you was special before and really wanted to be yur buddy and all, but I knew Jake would never have it, so I never tried."

"I'd of been yur buddy anytime, Marshall."

They both sat staring at the fire in a comfortable silence, which rarely came that way, the silence that is; every move was like that of a chess board in their world, where they were on constant guard, each an opponent. Actually it was never meant to be that way, not in Cyrus' thoughts, not after these moments with Pritchett, which was disproving the general consensus with every passing minute; that he was a rogue being to be set apart from, like the rest of the Pritchett's. Cheyenne, Jake, his grandparents, even the townsfolk were wrong about him.

"Buckman", Marshall began. "We better take to the barn to put somethin' back if we're gunna do it, lessin' you wanna take the chance."

Cyrus stood and Marshall next to him, but with an unsteady lean and Cyrus grabbed hold of him before he went into the fire, "You okay?"

"Yeah, just got up too fast."

They ambled out of the fort and stood in the creek bed for their eyes to adjust. It was a lot colder than before as Cyrus faced the full moon and blew warm puffs of breath into the evening sky like he was smoking.

"Ever smoked anything before, Marshall?"

"Smoked a mess of possum last fall", Marshall answered, then chuckled.

"No, I mean . . ."

"I know—of course. Tell me that's another thing you ain't done."

Cyrus shrugged and put his hands in his pockets. It didn't take long to get to the edge of the farmhouse, close enough they could see Grandma Mattie at the kitchen sink drying the rest of the supper ware. The barn was shut up tight with the only light came from the moon that shown eerily against the ground fog, lifeless and frozen like a photograph.

"Dang!" Cyrus whispered loudly. "What are we gunna put in the bottle?"

"We won't need much", Marshall muttered and then began to giggle. "I say we dip a bit from Dud's bucket."

Cyrus smiled broadly while Marshall kept laughing with his hand over his mouth; it was pretty funny, but the moment was jaded by the purpose and difficult for Cyrus to enjoy like his counterpart. As bad as Marshall thought his own father's retribution, Cyrus knew he had him beat hands down.

They snuck into the barn by the creep feeder that was just big enough to crawl through on their bellies. The barn door weighed as much as a truck and its Gothic hinges would squawk like a yellow-tailed hawk that could be heard all the way to town. When they were inside, Cyrus pushed his way in front as he knew where most everything laid. The moon was the only light that came from the hay loft door; it yawned and stretched from the edges of the neatly stacked bales in a staggered mosaic of blue-green beams and acted a light show for the intermittent appearance of moths and dragonflies who seemed content in their late night bug burlesque. Stone silence surrounded everything as if God had commanded it, so quiet Cyrus could hear his heart. Then came the all too familiar click. He grabbed Marshall's arm and pulled him down to a squat.

"What?" Marshall painfully whispered. Cyrus covered Marshall's mouth and with his other hand behind his head, mashed his lips into his palm as if to say, *feel my expression you can't see.* The click came again and this time with a flare that shattered the darkness. It dimmed then swelled, then dimmed and swelled again until it exhausted. Both sat crouched and wedged together like coons after a shotgun blast of rock salt. Another click came with a flare, but this time the barn lit up from floor to ceiling with the shadow of Jack's beanstalk giant as it swayed and parried towards them with a lantern—then it stopped.

"Three", the voice bellowed from one side of its mouth, as the other was occupied by the drawing end of a pipe. "Zat you? Don't make me hunt."

Marshall motioned to surrender by trying to stand, but Cyrus pulled him down and held him tightly. Grandpa Cyrus held the lantern outwards like a wayfarer on an inland point signaling a

distant ship, but Cyrus didn't budge. Cyrus' thought at that immediate moment was that a beating either way was eminent regardless, so what was the point in surrender? After all, it could very
well interrupt a divine intervention, which in this case, almost did.
At that moment, those gargantuan barn doors that seemed better
suited hinged to a castle began to squawk.

"Gran'pa, what in blazes are you doin' out here in the pitch of
night?" Grandma Mattie questioned.

"Well I was out here seein' if there were coons piddlin' about or
my grandson and his henchman makin' all the racket."

Everyone in that private tavern, even Pritchett, knew what he
was doing in that barn at the pitch of night but he outweighed
everyone there glued together, so to mention the truth as it were
known, would be something like a black man interrupting the
Emancipation Proclamation for a question: it would have accom-
plished little more than stun the audience and draw a beating.
The fact he was holding the very bottle in his hand was pretty
much the tell-all anyway.

"Since I now knows who was doin' the racket, I also want to
know which one of you has been at this?"

After all his hoorah about making his stand outright, Marshall
stood frozen as if he was homesteading on that spot. Cyrus nudged
him with his hand but nothing came forth.

"Well!"

"Gran'pa, how is it you know either of them had a thing to do
with yur bottle when yur drawin' on it all day long?" Grandma
Mattie blurted.

"Hush up Mattie; I knows 'exactly what's in this bottle at every
days end cuz my notch is right there", he said pointing to the tattered label.

His grandfather eased forward towards them and both boys
eased back as one might from a hot flame.

"Nothin' to be scared of, jus' wanna show you my notch and where the juice lay—I'm figurin' about four or five fingers in a fruit jar."

Dadgum he was good! How in the world he knew what he knew and about the fruit jar to boot, both were thinking. His grandfather looked at them with his seductive smile that Cyrus knew all too well, but Marshall was clueless. A mountain of man up close, he had bear-like paws that were bent and knurled by years of hard farming, his hand the width of a fence post that had been broken more times than not but could still hurl a fifty pound hay bale twenty feet or better.

As he came up to them within arm's length, he put the bottle to the other hand and crouched a bit to show them the label. It was here Cyrus' timing came as honed as a panther's lunge; when he saw the expression change at his mouth. His smile disappeared as his teeth bit down against his pipe and Cyrus dropped to the ground at the split second his grandfather let loose with a backhand. Meant for Cyrus, he missed him completely and smacked Marshall as square as hitting a pig's rump with a two-by-four that sent him in the air like a paper cup. He could hear his grandmother screaming in the background, tack racks falling over with riggings and gear hitting the ground all around him. Cyrus scurried faster than a coon to the way he came in which would stop his grandfather in his tracks. It would take him the better part of ten minutes to get to the patch, let alone catch up to where he was headed. It was now or never for his friendship to be put to the test. Argie was either real, or he was nothing but straw-stuffed long johns and Cyrus was as good as dead.

CHAPTER TWENTY SIX

Again he found himself running in the middle of the corn patch in the dead of night and for the same reason as always: his grandfather. At least he was the common denominator. Only vaguely could hear the commotion behind him a distance back, but that wasn't what lingered in his skull at the moment. With every breath he mustered he was exhausting it with one name at the end—ARGIE! His hands were getting torn to pieces by the sharp edges of the dried corn shucks as he fought through the dense tundra, hoping he wouldn't run smack into Argie like the last time. He stopped for a second to think on his position and bearings. The only sound he could hear was his breathing, so he held it a second to listen behind—nothing. Maybe they had surrendered? Maybe they had to see about Marshall? He began to chuckle a little from the last thing he saw: Marshall's expression as he watched him come off the barn floor like Peter Pan in a cartwheel fashion he'd seen a buckaroo do once in a traveling circus in South Dakota. Now whose old man should he fear, he thought?

He walked several steps to the left remembering that Argie was the other way from where he started at the barn. Now he began to hear stalks falling behind him under foot, so someone was coming towards him but still a ways back. There it was; he penetrated the clearing and there Argie stood as he had for the summer. He was completely out of breath and Argie brought the sense of safety, in spite of the exhaustion in his legs. He fell down before Argie and looked up at his head:

"Argie, you gotta help me—you gotta take me some place—any place, just get me outta here."

There was only silence.

"Argie! I swear to god you had better not be an *Imagine*. I believe in you! Please be real!"

"Calm yourself, Master Cyrus; what are you so done up about this time?"

"Oh thank god! Argie, you gotta use all your power and get me outta here now!"

"Get you outta here?" Argie questioned. "You just got here."

"No Argie, it's my Gran'pa, he thinks I got into his whiskey with Marshall, and it wasn't me it was Marshall—and Gran'pa whacked him instead of me, and . . .!"

"Cyrus! Calm yourself, I'm not following you", Argie interrupted.

Cyrus jumped to his feet and ran to the base of the scarecrow and grabbed him about the ankles.

"If you really love me and care about me like you say you do, you'll get me out of here NOW! He's comin' and he's liquored up. I swear to you Argie, he will kill me. Please fly me from here."

"Three!" his grandfather yelled from the edge of the corn. "If I have to come in there to fetch you again I promise it will be the last time!"

"Cyrus", Argie began. "Listen to me very carefully. Lie down in front of me, spread your arms, close your eyes and don't open them for any reason—do you understand?"

"Yes sir."

Cyrus did as he was told as he whimpered. He grandfather kept yelling into the corn and his fear was the greatest he could remember. If he was found, there would be nothing anyone could do, not even Argie. What was he doing just lying there in dead corn? This was all a joke—Argie, him, his life and everyone in it. Just a stupid, fat lonely kid who had nothing at all but a make believe world and who sat in a patch talking to grass stuffed in an old pair of underwear. He began to surrender.

"Cyrus, listen to me and concentrate on what I say, and keep repeating it without stopping—I am not about fear, fear is not in me. I am not about fear, fear is not in me. Believe it, Cyrus, believe it with everything you have."

Cyrus began saying what Argie told him, but his grandfather's voice seemed to come closer and closer and his fear became stronger and stronger.

"If you want this Cyrus, you will have to believe it—the fear will keep you here."

He kept repeating it louder and louder and the fear seemed to get smaller and smaller. It was a miracle, because the more he said it the more he wasn't afraid. After a moment he wasn't hearing his grandfather; he wasn't even thinking about him. He was thinking how on earth this was working. Just then he began to feel as light as air. In fact, he was beginning to feel cool underneath him like he was leaving the ground.

"Do NOT open your eyes Cyrus for any reason. Keep repeating it, my child, I will be with you."

Now it was getting stranger and stranger. The fear wasn't a factor any longer.

"Argie", he whimpered, his eyes pressed shut tightly. "What's happening? I can't feel the ground and there's wind all about me."

"Master Cyrus, I don't hear your chant."

"My what?"

"What I told you to keep repeating."

"It's gone, I ain't afraid no more. I am a bit jammed up about where I am though."

Argie chuckled and told Cyrus how much he loved him and that he was going somewhere no one like him had ever seen before; that it was a place forbidden but he wasn't worried, both because he had him as a friend, and he wanted him to feel safe—forever.

"Argie, when can I open my eyes? If I'm going someplace forbidden is everyone there blind or something? I won't tell. I'll act like I'm the same way."

Argie laughed aloud again and told Cyrus to roll over onto his tummy, but to keep his eyes closed.

"What? I'm lying down Argie—or at least I thought I was", he whispered.

Cyrus began slowly to turn over onto his stomach, which was the strangest turnover he ever attempted—there wasn't any ground under him. He kept feeling about himself, but there wasn't a thing under him.

"Argie!"

"Okay my son, open your eyes, but know that you asked for this."

Cyrus opened his eyes slowly and he was right, there wasn't a thing under him but air and clouds—and some trees, but only the tops. He was flying!

"Oh my Argie! Why didn't you do this a long time ago? Can I bring Cheyenne?"

"What did I say, Mr Buckman?"

"That it was forbidden for me to be here. If it's forbidden will you get a hidin' for it?"

"No, I don't think so."

"Will you get into some kind of trouble?"

"I guess we will soon see."

It was sure enough amazing alright; the night was spectacular because the moon was so bright. It nearly seemed like day time.

"This can't be Alabama, it's way too pretty. Look over there Argie, is that the ocean?"

"No. It's water for sure, but much too small for an ocean."

"It's huge. What's the ocean look like?"

"Nothing but water for miles."

"Can I go around it—I mean, turn around and see it again?"

"Sure."

"How?"

"Just turn like you would *imagine* turning."

With his arms outstretched like a hawk, he bent his body to the left and started to turn until he was moving back towards the lake he'd passed. He then began experimenting with other maneuvers like dipping and going up; he even spun like a drill bit. When he put his arms to his sides and pointed downward he got to going so fast that his eyes began to water and he could feel the tears dribble back in little streams towards his ears.

In a second or two, he came up on a flock of ducks that had just taken flight and it was mighty strange next to them, so it he made it stranger: "Quack, quack", Cyrus mimicked with a great laughter, and they looked at him with confusion. "Look Argie, they don't know if they're in park or drive."

"Okay Cyrus J, let's get back to flying straight. You're going to have to find a landing spot because I'm beginning to tire."

"Tire? I'm the one flying."

"I'm sorry, what on earth was I thinking?"

Cyrus was so consumed with flying that the thought of how he was there didn't register any more than why.

"Look Argie, is that the sun or the moon?"

"I believe the sun."

"Wow. A new day beginning."

"Seems so."

"Argie, the ground is comin' up pretty fast."

"Well I guess you had better think about putting your legs under you."

"I'm just gunna hit the ground runnin'?"

"If you don't you're going to hit it with your face."

Now that his position was coming clearer, as well as how and why he was there, the once serene surroundings that were more storybook than real—became very real and were coming quickly.

"Whoa, I ain't sure I can run that fast", he squelched. "Look! A truck right in front of me—I'll just put 'er down in back."

"Oh no you won't, Mr Buckman; a kid plopping into somebody's truck out of thin air, uninvited. Wouldn't be prudent."

"Wait—I'm turning off the road, Argie. I'm goin' towards the corn! Please, not in the corn Argie. I just came from the corn!"

"Feet!" Argie commanded. "Feet! better get the feet down or you'll be eating raw corn."

Cyrus gritted his teeth and held his breath as he began to skim the tops of the corn. He pulled his legs underneath him and was really hitting the corn when suddenly something snagged the toe of his brogan and he did a header, end over end. He put his hands over his face as he kept tumbling in air like a snowball down a mountain. He was waiting for pain because all the cracking and popping the stalks were making sounded like bone. When he came to rest he was back in the quiet of his old home place, but different. Even the smell wasn't the same. It was corn though. Corn is corn, he thought, wherever it is, but this was all different.

A distance from him where he thought the road was there was a sound of cracking stalks again as if they were under foot. Ah geez, he thought.

"Argie", he whispered. "Argie, you here?"

This was too much: Flying through the air, over lakes, above the trees—and talking to ducks. Nobody was going to believe this, not even if Argie, in all his barnyard regalia danced a jig while he explained it. Apart from his goose seeming to be cooked in a foreign land, he couldn't put his finger on where his benefactor was at that moment and it appeared that someone was rummaging through the corn towards him. All of this combined with the image that he was alone was hard to handle. Maybe whoever was driving the truck down that dirt road, he thought, was who was in the corn. Apart from why he was there it was truly astonishing he was as calm as he was, but there was a reason for that; he just got through falling out of the air from a height ten year-old's never get to, not in that day; not to even think about the ducks, or that his navigator was a straw-stuffed pair of under britches. Are you seeing it? There was already enough crazy in his life that what had just occurred could pretty much pass for normal. He sat dumbfounded and yet relieved because he was on ground, but where was the question.

"Hello!" a voice came from several yards away. "Is someone in here?"

He sat patiently for a second, gathering his thoughts on whether he should answer, and if he did, what he should answer with? "Hi sir, I was flying by when my scarecrow ran outta gas and I just plopped into this here corn patch."

He smiled a bit at his wit and humor.

"Well hello there, young man" a gentleman said as he appeared as Cyrus had—from nowhere. Cyrus stood, knocking the dirt and corn kernels from his pant legs and looking up to the man with absolutely nothing to say.

"I thought I saw you—or somebody bobbing up and down in the corn, so to speak, and then disappearing, but wasn't sure I was seeing what I thought I was", the man said.

Cyrus was fixed in a stare at the gentleman because he knew him, or he felt he did but couldn't place him. A nice looking man who looked very business-like, with square, brawn shoulders, a flat stomach that gave him the appearance of authority or someone who definitely wasn't afraid of work, and a face that said he was well liked and respected—wow! He looked just like his grandpa might thirty years back. Yeah. His eyes, his nose, even his ears looked just like his grandmother. Cyrus began to smile broadly.

"Not used to having little boys fall out of the sky here."

"Where's here?"

"The corn patch."

"Where's it?"

"Right here."

"I have a feelin' this ain't Alabama", Cyrus muttered.

"Alabama? No, I don't reckon. Would you care to come with me?"

"Where to?"

"I was on my way fishin' until I saw you", the man said as he turned about the way he came and Cyrus followed. "We can ask around for Alabama."

"Fishin'! My Gran'pa has told me since I was knee high to a piss ant that he'd take me but never has. Are you serious?"

"Not at all, I go all the time."

"No sir, about Alabama."

When they stepped from the corn and into the bar ditch just outside the patch the man turned and put his hand on Cyrus' shoulder, "You must be some-where's round ten or eleven and you've never been fishin'?"

"No sir, and I'm almost eleven; are you sure you ain't heard of Alabama?"

"Well by-golly, today's your lucky day; seein' you don't appear to be in any kind of a rush, let's pick up where you came in. I guess first we should see about your Grandpa on Alabama, if I can find it. Been gone long enough for him to worry?"

"Oh I imagine he's missin' me about now but I don't reckon it'll be from worry—You gunna fish in your Sunday-go-to-meetin' dress?"

The man laughed out loud and it sent a chill up Cyrus' spine; it sounded so much like his grandpa if he had closed his eyes there would have been no mistaking it.

"By the way, I was so taken by your entrance that I have totally forgotten my manners", the man said, extending his hand. "Walt is my name."

Cyrus answered in stutter-stepped hesitation, "—are you sure sir, that you want me to call you by your Christian name? They whomp you for that in Alabama."

"If I want you to use it, yes, and I do respect your position but you're not in Alabama right now—whomp, huh?"

"Yeeeesss sir, and they call me Cyrus."

"Hmm", the man sounded. "Cyrus", he whispered to himself.

They walked to the truck and he couldn't get over the serenity this place showered over him. He wasn't afraid either. He wasn't fearing of anything and here he was miles from nowhere in nowhere. In fact, he was in the greatest calm he had known—and where in the blue blazes was Argie?

They started back down the dirt road in Walt's truck, which by the way, was near as clean as the Buckman barn and made him a smidgen uneasy when he thought on it, but then the thought disappeared just as quickly—he wasn't in Alabama now! A phrase he couldn't dwell on enough, but where exactly was he?

"Sir", Cyrus began, when he saw Walt's disapproving look. "I mean Walt; just where might I be?"

"That's a might difficult to say, Cyrus. I think we can agree it's not where you're supposed to be even though you're welcome here", Walt said with an affirming smile. "You're safe in **Timbuktu**."

Okay, Cyrus thought, but that wasn't an answer he would be allowed to get away with, not by Argie or his grandfather. Walt's vagueness wasn't that unsettling since it was Argie who brought him here, one; and two, Argie did say it was forbidden; but where the heck was **Timbuktu?**

They sputtered down the road for several miles until it went from straight and boring with crops all around like Alabama, into curves and mountains that were brimming with tall evergreens, cypresses and pines which seemed to hold the clouds in their places. It was absolutely serene beyond description, and the smell; it for sure wasn't Alabama.

As they topped a hill just past a curve, a quaint and unusually beautiful town appeared. It was like something from a painting. The entire village was set between two mountains at their base as though it was there before the mountain and everything around it had been hand placed by god. It was all amazingly still; smoke rose from the chimneys so straight it looked like strings from the heavens suspending the world below. Cyrus set his chin on his arm outside the passenger window as they approached so he could feel and smell all he was seeing.

"Cyrus, I have to run in the drugstore for an item and won't be more than a minute or two, would you like to come in?"

"If it's okay I'll just stay here and watch. I ain't ever seen anything like this, not that wasn't in a frame on a wall anyway."

Walt disappeared into the store while Cyrus became mesmerized by the town folk who ambled over the boardwalk, in and out of shops and across the streets; there were even some on horseback, which he hadn't seen since his younger days in South Dakota. His thoughts went back there for a split second until the moment he saw him. He was staring right at Cyrus, about a hundred yards from the truck in between two buildings.

"What the . . . !" Cyrus muttered. He jumped from the truck and darted into the street nearly being smacked by a milk truck that laid on its horn but didn't trick his attention a lick. The boy was only there a second after he started across the street and vanished between the buildings. "It can't be, it can't be", Cyrus kept murmuring. Cyrus was crossing between two buildings off from the boardwalk just before he approached the alley where he'd seen him, when a dog appeared from nowhere and was just as quickly between Cyrus' legs. The dog yelped as Cyrus took a header off a set of steps and went crashing into a stack of empty milk cans. It sounded like the entire building fell, people dodging and dipping trying to miss either a milk can, Cyrus or a yelping dog. When it all ended, Cyrus was on his hands and knees looking desperately for a glimpse down that alley but he knew the boy had to be long gone. An elderly woman was helping him up when he noticed the dog. It was, like the boy, staring right at him and only feet from him, "Oh my god—Bear?" He quit panting the moment Cyrus called that name, turned and trotted off down the alley where the boy had been standing. He worked to follow but the elderly woman who had hold wouldn't let loose, "Now you have skint your hands all up and they need a scrubbing, child", she said.

"I'm okay, mam."

"You children need to watch where you're going and stop that rush, rush, rush all the darn time."

"Yes mam, I thought I saw my brother and . . . I'm sorry for makin' a mess here. Did you happen to see the boy who was standing right here a few minutes ago?" Cyrus pointed.

"No child, I don't recall any boy."

At that moment Walt came up behind them, "Cyrus, what the world happened?"

Cyrus smiled broadly and explained what he thought had occurred because everything up to that point didn't fit his puzzle all that well; which was to say, Argie was nowhere to be found, he was in a very strange place, and Jake just appeared and disappeared— or so he thought—oh, and a dog whose head he had week's ago witnessed blown off, made him crash into a stack of milk cans. Was anything left out? So how was this to be explained when he didn't know and it all happened to him?

"Mr Walt, sir, I have no idea how to explain anything, just nothin' at all because I ain't sure you'd believe it in the first place, up to getting' how I got to **Timbuktu**, or however you say it", Cyrus summed in exasperation.

"Let's take us a deep breath and load back up in the truck", Walt said, setting a can upright and smiling at several of the passersby.

What a great guy he was and the townsfolk seemed to look at him as some kind of an authority, which was perfectly fine with Cyrus. Being in a strange place it seems fitting enough to be with the guy everyone looks to for answers.

They got back to the truck and no one else seemed concerned with what just occurred except Cyrus. For a fleeting moment there was a blackness that came over his soul and it made him ill. It was the all too familiar pain that had plagued him all his life; that emptiness. His seeing him, whether he was there or not, brought back his memory that he felt sure wouldn't bother him anymore, but it did. Jake left an indelible print on his life that he just then realized would never be removed.

"What's on your mind there little man?"

"Don't rightly know, Mr Walt. One minute I'm not caring what's goin' on and the next minute I get so flustered that I feel I'm just plum crazy."

Cyrus wanted to explain everything he couldn't understand, but he didn't want to sell the farm just yet, in a manner of speaking: in a huge way he did feel he was crazy. And worse, he was feeling this way alone.

"I think I can vouch that you are about the least crazy person I have ever met; you feel crazy at times, but it doesn't mean that you are", Walt said with his usual confidence.

"Mr Walt, there are some things you don't know about me that might just about push your wagon over the bluff ifin' I told you."

"Really? Well let's first see if my wagon is even close enough to the bluff."

"You might want to pull over, Mr Walt, cuz what I got to say is gunna make it difficult to peddle at the same time I reckon."

"Let's say that I've heard about everything there is to tell."

So Cyrus began to tell him everything, beginning with Argie, how he got there and what happened in town. He had to tell him about Jake, of course, the gun, the whiskey and Bear for him to make any kind of sense out of what happened that morning.

"You see Mr Walt, when I felt it was Jake across the way, but couldn't be for sure, I ran to see when this dog came from nowhere and got twixt my legs and caused the wreck—and that's when I seen it was Bear, clear as day, no farther than from me to you."

By now they reached the pond where they were to fish and he had parked under a huge pecan tree to finish hearing the saga. Cyrus sat uncomfortably fidgeting with his trousers and waiting for some hint that he wasn't a nut. Walt took a long breath and looked out over the water, pondering everything Cyrus had said.

"So, you were flying overhead with your friend the scarecrow, who was gettin' you out of another whiskey pickle with your Gran'pa, and he got tired, the scarecrow did, and you plopped down into one of our corn patches outside of town—saw your dead friend in town and a dog your friend had shot some time back—and you say you came from this Alabama place?"

"Bag a worms, ain't it?" Cyrus muttered.

"No, no Cyrus not at all. In fact I commend you on telling it exactly as it came to you, as most your age would have nipped and tucked a story a bit more palatable—easier to swallow, but you stayed the course. What say we worm up a pole and take to that spot right there so we can free our minds to figure a little more, not on how you got here but why?"

"I'm ready as a game rooster, Mr Walt, but know I'm greener than a raw Granny Smith on this fishin' gig", Cyrus said.

Cyrus watched with baited breath every move and gesture Walt showed him, even the things that Walt didn't say to watch, Cyrus made note. There was something about Walt that was magic to him and it was easy to see why the townsfolk thought well of him. His hands were large yet nimble as they worked to tie the fishing line like he'd imagine a doctor would handle a patient. He had pearly white teeth he noticed when Walt bit the line, but they were carefully hidden by his long black mustache that was neatly groomed and waxed to the ends that curled slightly upwards. Apart from all that Cyrus saw, he was caring and that was what he could feel.

They chatted some about the boyish things in life and even some about Cheyenne, who Walt said he was lucky to have as a friend. All this and other stories brought them up to the moment Cyrus and Marshall were in the barn to replenish the whiskey Marshall had stolen.

"Sounds a bit like you were working yourself up to a drinkin' problem at a young age."

"Weren't me Mr Walt, it seemed everyone I ran with had a taste for it. I really didn't care much for the stuff since it made me ill."

"So then your buddy, the scarecrow, took you up in the air and brought you to me."

"That's about the twist of it."

Right then Cyrus had a hit on his line and it was a big one. It near dragged the pole out his hands when Walt grabbed him and the pole.

"Hang on, Cyrus! He's a big-un. He may break the line if we don't give him room. Release it!"

"Release what!"

"The line!"

Cyrus let go of the entire rod and Walt stumbled about five feet *onto* the water, catching himself, the pole and coming back on shore. He let the line out and the fish took off towards the middle, then Walt careful pulled him back to shore. He did this two or three times, letting it go out then pulling it back in.

"You see there Cyrus, when they are this big you have to let them wear down or all their fight at the front will snap your line," Walt explained. As he reeled the fish close to the bank he told Cyrus to get the hand net and scoop him up. Cyrus did and just as Walt had walked out in the water he made about two steps and went under like a rock from a roof top. He came up sputtering and gagging trying to catch his breath as he climbed on shore.

"Whoa! I swore there was ground there. You walked way out to there and barely got your shoes wet."

Walt stood there laughing to beat the band while Cyrus stood there dripping and wondering why.

Walt took in the fish and kept chuckling, "Cyrus my boy, I'll bet this baby weighs in at seven pounds. Pretty dadgum good for a first go."

He stood shivering not truly looking at the fish. "Dang, I was sure there was ground there—you walked way out there, Mr Walt."

"Ah Cyrus, this day has been rough on you and you're missing the part that should be making you smile."

"I can't figure most of it Mr Walt, and can't stop thinking about why I'm here or where, or even *where* I am. My friend ain't anywhere to be found and for all I know I'll be in **Timbuktu** forever."

Walt took Cyrus away from the bank and sat him in the passenger seat of the truck. He pulled a towel from the tack basket, gave it to him and knelt in front of him.

"Why do you really think you're here, Cyrus?"

"I don't know, except that I asked Argie to take me away."

"Why?"

"I was afraid. I was afraid of what was about to happen."

"And what was that?"

"I didn't know."

"Exactly. Hasn't that been your approach to most everything in life?"

He thought for a while even though he didn't have to because he knew his response immediately. His hesitation was because he hadn't a clue why; why he was afraid of so much before he actually had cause to be afraid. And how did Walt know this?

"Do you feel safe here?" Walt asked.

"Yes sir, but how do you know all this 'bout me?"

Walt shrugged, looked to the side and shook his head, a bit like the answer was so commonplace it didn't deserve attention: "Then do not fret."

"What's wrong with me Mr Walt?

"What makes you think something's wrong?"

"I'm afraid of everything that happens—the worst of it is I'm afraid before anything gets there to be afraid of", Cyrus answered. "It's like being afraid of being afraid; that, and I ain't like anybody else."

"Nobody, huh? How's it you know more about the rest of the world than yourself?"

"What's that?"

"Well, my guess is you're seeing something in folk you don't believe you have, which begs me to ask how you know you don't have it to be able to tell its missing?"

"I ain't—what was that?"

"Seems to me you're all frustrated about things you don't feel you have that you really don't know you don't have—any time you mirror yourself after another, Cy, you will always find something they have you don't and that brings you to discount what you do."

"Boy, you can get me as tangled as Argie."

"Not a thing wrong with admiring attributes in others, and to a point, liking them enough to want them for yourself—but just as much, why's it difficult to believe they aren't thinking the same about you? If you gave the same effort to seeing the beautiful strengths in your own person you'd be a giant; maybe good for all that you don't know", Walt laughed.

"A giant, huh?" You never knew Jake and you barely know me. There was plenty Jake had he didn't even care about but everybody wanted."

"Jake. You really think he was more important than you? With all the beautiful gifts no one else in this world has but you, and you still keep looking over the fence."

"How do *you* know what gifts I have, Mr Walt?"

Cyrus sat thinking about what Walt said when he looked down at him and directly into his eyes.

"You're him, ain't ya—him?"

CHAPTER TWENTY SEVEN

His vision was blurred and the voices that echoed in his ears seemed to be coming from the bottom of a well. The image before him was vague and the words garbled but the tone was familiar and kept saying, "Cyrus, open your eyes." When he heard Mattie's whimper his memory crept backwards; the pain about his head and shoulders came as suddenly as the truth that his life was a lie. It was all too good to be real and he should have known it. How many times would his gullibility have to be shown him, etched in stone?

"My grandbaby, you're just gunna have to quit bangin' that head of yours up like this", Grandma said as she sat next to him on the bed.

"Cyrus, I'm sorry for my spell", his Grandfather sheepishly mumbled, as he held hat in hand, twisting and twirling it about. "I'm gunna be working on some things 'round here, so you get better and we'll do some fishin' like I been saying."

"I caught a big one—near seven pounder", Cyrus said as the room looked around at each other. Doc Wash stood some ways back from the bed and kept staring at Grandpa, then at Cyrus. "He's probably going to show some amnesia here once in a while", Doc said.

"Son, you popped yourself nicely when you dove for that creep feeder—steel and concrete don't usually give before a skull does", Doc Wash mused.

"I hit my head?" Cyrus asked. "What about Marshall?"

"Who?" Doc Wash shrugged.

"The other boy who was with Cyrus", Grandma Mattie added. "He's fine, honey, you just get some rest."

"No Gran'ma, what happened to him?"

"Your Gran'pa took him home", she answered. Grandpa Cyrus and Doc Wash were mumbling to each other as they were leaving and Cyrus yelled to them: "Wait! Ouch", he grabbed his head that was bandaged tightly, tighter than before and throbbed even harder. "What happened, exactly?" he asked his Grandmother. "You don't know the story; you're gunna think you do, but I bet you don't", Cyrus added.

Grandpa Cyrus stopped and came to the foot of the bed. His demeanor changed; Cyrus could always tell by the eyes what mood he was in. They were the rudder to this large ship and its path was known when they were open.

"Pritchett told us everything that happened; he told me he snuck the whiskey out and you knew nothin' about it."

"Does his Pa know?"

"I reckon."

"Did you hurt him?"

The room came deathly quiet as his Grandfather looked to the floor for a second and then to his Grandmother, who looked away towards Cyrus' ever present pecan tree.

"He's okay", his Grandfather said,

"We are all okay", Grandma concluded. "I want you to rest and not worry", she added, patting his arm.

Grandpa and the Doc were just about out when his Grandma stood from the bed to leave and Cyrus grabbed her arm: "Gran'ma, please tell me what happened—all I recall was—well, all I recall *here* was Gran'pa whackin' Marshall and me running out of the barn through the creep feeder."

"Here?" she asked in a whisper.

Cyrus stared at her blankly for a second laboring whether he should mention anything about what he *truly* remembered. There wasn't any lag at all in his recollection between the moment he saw Marshall flying through the air and his run into the corn patch. If he had hit his head it was without his knowing, but something sure happened with his head throbbing like it was.

"Uhm", Cyrus mumbled, his thought fluttering between confusion and truth. "Gran'ma, I don't recollect hitting my head at all. I do *recollect* something, but it'll sound farther out than Miller's Pass from the porch front."

"Does this have somethin' to do with *Imagines* and such?"

"Gran'ma, I'm not sure anymore what is an *Imagine* and what ain't—isn't. There's been so many things happenin' that it's come hard to tell one from the other, or even if there is the *other*."

"Child, you know you hit your head because of this", she said pointing to his bandage. "Now it would be real easy to see why you don't recollect what came after since you were out cold as a catfish."

"Boy, there's so much to say and all of it so wacky. Maybe you're right. I mean, you were in the barn."

"And thank the Almighty for that! You just rest and don't study on nothin' else for a spell", she said as she started out again.

"Gran'ma, who's the Almighty?" he asked abruptly.

"God, or course."

"You ever seen him?"

"Well, not as a person I don't reckon, but I wouldn't put it past Him to come as someone on at a time, why?" she mused slightly.

"Oh, nothin' particular; you reckon he could show as a scarecrow or something like that?

"A scarecrow? Why child, I think he could come as anything he had a mind to since he's the Lord, but why a scarecrow?"

"I daknow, why not?"

She smiled broadly at her grandson and shrugged her shoulders: "You absolutely beat all, Cyrus J. Is this somethin' to do with you and Cheyenne?"

"Cheyenne?"

"When she and her Pa were here a spell back, you all went over to the Thompson farm and she stayed here with me. She asked me about someone I heard you mention before—some fella's name that was a bit strange soundin'."

"Argie?"

"Yes—I believe that was it. Who is that fella, or is it a fella?"

"What'd she say 'bout him?"

"She didn't. She asked if I ever heard of him and then she wanted to see the goats. Who is he?"

Cyrus chuckled uncomfortably, "A scarecrow—one of Gran'pa's scarecrows I named Argie."

"And you think the Lord is out in our patch as a scarecrow?"

"I daknow Gran'ma. Everything has been crazy since movin' here. The only thing normal is I keep ending up in bed tied in poultice sacks, mending from either a beatin' or head bangin' and no one but me recollecting somethin' that can't be."

"Child you ain't makin' much sense atoll, but that seems the way to a mend."

There was a pause as Cyrus thought on what to say, what to mention of his trip—it was all so dadgum real, but what words could he find to explain even the most unearthly.

"What is in that mind of yours, Cy?"

"I think I saw Pa, Gran'ma. I truly do; I mean, I did."

Mattie sat down again and took Cyrus' hand in both of hers almost as a child sitting next to kin about to tell a Christmas story.

"What?" she whispered.

"Gran'ma, I don't recall anything of hitting my head—in my recollection I just ran into the patch trying to find Argie after I got away from the barn and Gran'pa."

He went on to tell her about Argie, this new found friend of magic and wisdom who had become his confidante since Jake. He explained that when everything happened with Marshall in the barn he went to Argie to beg his protection. He briefly mentioned the thing about the ducks but it was difficult to go into detail since flying with them didn't occur that often, not at his school. He also felt it important to brush quickly through the tricky stuff like Argie's tiring, his falling from the sky into another corn patch, catching his brogan on a corn shuck and doing a header, all the way up to meeting Walt; this is where he slowed in his telling—cuz, you know, it was a bit of a story.

" . . . So Walt was driving by in his truck when he saw me plop out of the clouds and land in his patch—well, not sure it was actually his patch, but he came in to get me."

"Uh huh", Mattie nodded with her hand to her mouth.

"Are you stayin' with me, Gran'ma?"

"Yep, you tripped over the corn tops and landed on your head . . . this Walt feller gotcha outta the patch, which might-a been his patch, but you ain't quite sure on that . . . yeah, I believe I'm followin'."

"An' the part with the ducks and fallin' from the sky?" He asked her with a bit more confidence. "I just breezed through those parts so's not to get you all jammed up—but I did do it, just don't get hung up there!"

"Oh no, I heard it alright and I'm not getting jammed at all, just lettin' it soak in slow like."

When Cyrus came to the part about seeing Jake and Bear it was a little too much to bring into the story, since it was the large piece of history they conveniently left out of the original one that fateful night.

"So you see, Argie is not just a scarecrow, he's a bit more."

"Yes, I certainly see that. And this Walt fella, you and he went fishin' did ya?"

"Yes mam, but that wasn't the main part—maybe when he walked out on the water was kinda strange; the strange thing was that he looked at me like he knew me, Gran'ma—like he knew me more than *knew* me, if that ain't too crazy."

"Oh Cy, it makes sense that it makes sense to you sweetheart, but there's a lot a puddin' between the cake here that takes more than one bite to chew and swaller."

Cyrus laughed aloud and shook his head: "Mr Walt was funny too, Gran'ma; hadn't a clue where Alabama was and claimed I was in some place called Timbuktu, of course I knew he was joshin' me and . . . what Gran'ma?"

She stared at him with such a strange look of dismay all stirred with amazement that he thought maybe he'd run a wheel off his own wagon: "What Gran'ma; what'd I say?"

"What did Mr Walt look like—tell me all you recollect."

"Well", Cyrus began deliberately. "He was tall and clean-cut with a long black mustache that curled a bit at the ends, but ne'er a whisker outta place—strong lookin' too, with . . . what?"

"Go on", she whispered, holding to his bed post as she turned and sat at his feet, her hand to her mouth with her thoughts far away. Cyrus sat up and put his hands in his lap and watched her mouth: "Timbuktu", she whispered as he mouthed with her. She winked at him as though they were sharing a memory that only one of them had experienced.

"Who am I talkin' about, Grams? Who?"

"Child, I just had a rush come over me like I was fifteen again, sittin' on our back porch, barefoot in knickers and pullin' cockle-burs from my hair I took up runnin' through my Aunt Lottie's grape vineyard; Papa bustin' up a rick at the end of the porch while the neighbors sat watchin' and listenin' to his stories of Teddy Roosevelt and the big war. He was somethin', Cyrus. Even my brothers' friends would find reason to meet at the house instead of the creek or the town garage, or wherever they'd gather as long as Papa was home—is that not the strangest thing? Young'uns lookin' to be around an old fella, but he had this magic that drew everyone 'ceptin his own boys."

"You thinkin' it was him who was with me?"

"Oh Cy, I haven't an idea who was in yur head; he's been gone near fifty years and it's hard for me to recollect him, but when you said 'Timbuctoo' it was like I was seein' him right there—he would say that all the time when he didn't want to answer you directly 'bout somethin'—Timbuktu in Kalamazoo."

"Why'd your brothers not take to him?" Cyrus asked.

"Don't reckon it was so much that they didn't take to him, as it was that he weren't like the other fathers—Papa grew up real hard, Cy; he didn't trust many, kept his cards close to his chest and joked out loud a lot which brought the other boys to be comfortable with him. I reckon it was your Gran'pa he had the biggest wrestle with and all concernin' me—I was fifteen and he was ne'er twenty and the cock-of-the-walk", she laughed aloud. "Oh heavens! They could not sit still about each other for a second."

"So who would he be like, that I know?"

"Heaven sake's child, ain't no one alive you'd know to *imagine* with; I got milk older than you, sweetie—but I can sure tell you about a cookie-cutter likeness you would know *of*: your Pa. Lord have mercy was your Pa the spittin' image of his Gran'pa, Walton Jessup; sweeter than buttermilk and straighter than blue steel, which is why he was so respected and loved."

"My Pa, or Pa Walton—hey! Mr Walt, Gran'ma? I'll bet you a dollar to a bucket-a beans that Mr Walt was Gran'pa Walton Jessup", Cyrus yelled.

Grandma Mattie let out a boisterous laugh and patted her over-zealous, battle-scared grandbaby gently atop his white tunic, a bit to his chagrin, but painfully acknowledged when he replied gruffly, "Gran'ma, I know you think I'm crazy when I say this kinda stuff, but Argie is real, as real as you or me; just cuz he's hemmed up in a pair of long-handles full-a straw and nailed to some sticks; even Cheyenne has talked to him, and she believes . . ."

"My sweet Cyrus, I do believe that you believe, I most certainly do; but, you are here in bed and not but a few hours back you were as limp as a rain-soaked tow sack faced down under a creep feeder—you weren't with as much a meadowlark than some ducks over an ocean . . ."

"Lake", Cyrus quipped.

"A pond, for that matter; I'm with you, baby, in every adventure, but twixt you and your Gran'pa I'm fadin' fast. I just can't muster the strength any longer to keep you two apart, ne'er pull you together either. Just do not have it in me anymore."

"It ain't no adventure, Grams", he muttered, but she was already down the stairs.

He lay in the soft light of his room that covered his walls with quiet silhouettes of dancing leaves that came as a gift from the wind and moon, and for once, thought of nothing at all.

CHAPTER TWENTY EIGHT

Doc Wash, who had been on Cyrus' side ever since the Jake debacle, watched him as a physician might someone with small pox or the plague: with paternal protection. Although no one blamed him for losing Jake, he bore a deep wound he could not shed of himself and there were many times he toyed with the surrender of his license to become a mountain man. You see, Jake wasn't just any patient, he was Doc's nephew; his only blood-kin from his only sibling as he had no children of his own. From this it had been easy for him to see the love his nephew and Cyrus shared, a love so strong that it was palpable and when he tended to Cyrus it was as though he tended to his own. One of the many things Cyrus did not know.

"Mr Buckman, I want you to homestead this bed like a gold rusher does a claim until that knot there on your head is back flush with your scalp", Doc said. "Which means in layman terms, I will personally hide-strap you to a barn door and finish the job that feeder slipped up on."

"Doc, there ain't but a month 'fore Christmas and I done missed enough school this year to keep me back in third grade for another, and I just as soon be hide-strapped than ride that pony another go", Cyrus screamed from his quilt top.

His stay in bed for the weekend was discontenting, of course, but more so was Cheyenne's absence. Not seeing her brought a melancholy. She was the last person he trusted. This was another confusing part about him: why he had such difficulty being comfortable in his skin. It was this part of Jake he wanted to emulate so badly and couldn't see it. The most genuine thing about Jacob: he was real, true to himself. No one person lorded a thing over him and he could care less if anyone tried. That was it.

His first attempt at the new Cyrus was to get back to school like nothing had happened. As far as he knew, no one outside of Marshall was privy to the incident which was probably the reason why Cheyenne hadn't been to see him.

Even though there was a good chance of getting into trouble if he disobeyed Doc by taking off for school, he was fairly comfortable with the notion that his days of being "hided" for a while were on hold. Yet, he also knew that the bottle could change things as quickly as the weather.

He was down to getting his brogans on when he heard his grandparents grumbling in the kitchen. He could usually hear their conversation if they were close to the stove because the kitchen ceiling was his bedroom floor and the stove pipe was right by his bed. His grandmother said something about Argie, a name not easily displaced, even in a whisper, but he couldn't quite get what was said. His grandfather would grunt a word or two that sounded more like a bear rumbling through a trash can, and then both would stand hushed. Whatever the situation, Argie appeared in the middle and that did not set well with Cyrus. There wasn't a reason in the world for his grandmother to have made mention of him, except for the fact that Cyrus had acknowledged Argie's existence to Cheyenne. He was deeply skeptical about acknowledging him to anybody in the first place, especially to his grandparents, but the fact that Cheyenne had mentioned Argie to his grand-mother was enough to admit that the "cat was out of the bag".

He snuck down the stairs by the kitchen where his grandpar-ents were still embroiled in their no-nothing whispers, then out onto the porch front. He was a quarter way to Burle Barn when he heard the front porch screen door slam; it couldn't be missed because it sounded like small arms fire. If either had known of his missing they would be screaming his name. His feelings were now all in a fluster: he had just openly defied the Doc, his grandpar-ents and presumably Argie; but, he hadn't done anything directly to Argie at this point, he only felt that he would disappoint him. He chuckled about the possibility of Argie being upset with him— a dadgum pair of hay-stuffed long johns in the middle of a corn patch?

He'd run for a spell thinking that it would make better time, but school wouldn't be up for an hour or so, and besides, running made his head hurt. He stopped to listen. The morning was crisp and clean and the wind, which came in gusts, like the ones his grandma would blow in his face when he was small. The clouds were thick and laid low and made everything seem close like fam-ily should be. He began thinking of Mr Walt and why he only got to be with him for a short time. This was his great-grandfather who walked on water, literally. Geez, what was all this about?

When he got to school there were a few milling about who looked at him with a side glance like he had done something wrong. He just needed to see Cheyenne; he wanted to know she still liked him. He was so alone. Everybody is this way once in a while, he thought.

"Hey you", a voice came from behind. It was her. Cheyenne. He ran to her like a lion to game and grabbed her and hugged her. It was beyond description to hold her, and everything he could not put into words became so in her arms. For a split second she was enthralled, and then she put her arms around him and squeezed tighter than he did. In all his expressions he had ever known this one because it was home.

"Are you okay, Cyrus J?" she asked as she pulled her head back and looked into his face. She took her thumbs and wiped the tears back on his cheeks and then held him again because she knew.

"It's so good to see you, Chey", he said. He kept his head down because he felt naked and ashamed.

"It's good to see you, Cyrus. And will you quit!" she said sternly, putting her hand under his chin and forcing him to look at her. "No one gives a flip. They want to be like this, just don't know how."

"I know", he said, causally looking about. "I don't wanna let go." He wiped his nose with a cuff and began to smile uncontrollably. "Will you quit--yourself?" he asked playfully.

"What am I doing standing here?" she asked.

"You know."

"No, I don't."

"You're lookin' at me and smilin' and stuff", he said.

"Can I help lookin' at someone I'm crazy about and who won't stop hugging me", she said and he loosened his grip.

"No! I didn't say I wanted you to stop!"

"Oh", he smiled. "I thought because everyone was lookin' and all."

"I don't give a flip who's lookin!"

Love was such an incredible thing that had only a name and no face. It smiled a lot, of course, but no dadgum face. Love was awkward, like a three-legged gazelle or a ballerina with brogans; it looked sleek and well-formed but absolutely no grace. This was the first time it had come out of its cage in public and Cyrus was as captivated and stupefied as a scientist who had just proven the world round. There was just nothing like it and he could not stop smiling: she liked him and told him and there was no taking it back.

They stood for a time, then walked, then stood again, all the while touching each other's finger tips and smiling at the sky. Others around them began looking at the sky too, wondering what the world they were laboring to see. Mr Burnside was on the front steps with both hands cupped over his forehead and looking something fierce for whatever there was to be seen.

"How's your head, Cyrus J?" she asked with enthusiasm, putting her hand to his head then cupping his face in her hands. "Doc Wash told you specifically not to get out of bed unless he said you could", she scolded.

He smiled again like cat to a bird, "It's just fine, Chey, and Doc said it would be fine if I went to school."

"Fine, huh? I know you well enough Cyrus Buckman that you do as you please unless it comes from Argie. What?" she just as suddenly asked.

It seemed as though a fine spring day had turned to a damp, drizzly winter and just at the drop of that celestial name. Cyrus hemmed back and forth with his hands behind his back, looked at Cheyenne, then at the ground. If a storm was brewing then she was there before the clouds could circle. Deep down she knew it was her mistake for bringing Argie into the conversation and only because there was this vague but ever present jealousy thing between them. Yeah, believe it or not, jealousy, and Cheyenne knew it—oh, not between she and Cyrus but Argie. She had honored Argie's request since their conversation in the patch that afternoon; her pledge not to mention that she and Argie had a full two-sided conversation, and when Argie had politely asked her "to keep this little conversation between them". She honored it not because it came from a pair of stuffed long john's on high, but because she felt the love Argie held for Cyrus. That was the jealousy.

"Argie?" Cyrus bellowed quietly.

"Yes, Argie", she answered, her hands on her hips. "What about him?"

"I was just sayin'—Argie!. And so now he's a him?" He hollered.

"Yeah, he's always been a him, Cyrus. He might be in hay-stuffed long-handles, but he's a Him."

Cyrus tried to assert himself as the dominant one but it wasn't going to happen, not this day or any day with Cheyenne. There was something about her that would take the wind plum out of his sails. It didn't matter a lick how fast he was clipping along, he would stop as quick as a bug against a windshield when she bowed up. Wasn't mean. Wasn't discourteous. Just Cheyenne and a lot of German.

"Can I ask something without you gettin' all banged up?" He asked.

"Yes."

"You believe in him, don't ya? I mean, believe he's real?"

"Yes, I do", she answered deliberately. "Now answer a question for me: Why has your attitude changed all of a sudden? Why does it always change when Argie is brought up? One minute I'm so likin' being with you and the next I'm ready to stove-in your head with a river log; which, by the way, the log would most likely lose out."

Cyrus sighed perturbed, "I didn't know I did."

"Are you kiddin', Cinderella's horse and buggy ain't got nothin' on you. You are the PUMPKIN!"

The mood and atmosphere had changed so abruptly there were skid marks in between them. It was the most uncanny thing he'd ever been party to; one minute touching finger tips, making goo-goo eyes and nonsensical wishes upon a star to all of a sudden landing belly first in a foxhole against mortar fire.

"Sorry . . . just sorry for whatever I did, or Argie did. I don't understand it", he said with hands in his pockets.

"Argie? What could Argie have done?" she asked. "He may just be a scarecrow, but he's the grandest, most beautiful per—spirit I ever met and he thinks more of you than—well, I don't know, maybe God", she stuttered excitedly.

Cyrus listened intently because there was little else to do that wouldn't stir the pot, he felt; then, he recognized something from all the dust she'd kicked up, something that had been there all along that he wouldn't or couldn't see.

"Wait a minute Cheyenne", he began with deliberate thought. "That day you and your Pa came to the house, and we went over to the Thompson's and you stayed with Gran'ma, that was the day you said you talked to Argie, right?"

"Hmm", she gestured looking away.

"You didn't just talk *to* him; you talked *with* him."

"What's the difference, Cyrus?"

"A lot, Chey. You told me you believed in him because I did."

"That's what I said cuz that's what it was, Cyrus. If I hadn't believed in you, I wouldn't have believed in what you said—which means I wouldn't have believed in Argie. I got to meet Argie because I first believed in you."

"I asked if you talked to him and you said you hadn't, that it was just you who did the talkin'."

Cheyenne looked to the ground and put her hands in her overalls. Cyrus could see her tears and she sniffled a time or two.

"Cyrus, I really didn't think I was fibbin' by not tellin' you everything, I was so happy to be included. Argie—he said I shouldn't say anything, that he wanted to tell you."

Cyrus was stunned and baffled. Why, he thought? Why would Argie make him odd-man-out? Argie was the one who picked him up when he fell down; told him what a wonderful person he was; taught him everything about life that Jake forgot, or didn't have time to. He was the one who saved him from his Grandfather's rage; who showed him how to fly with ducks and gave him a safe landing. . .

"Are you mad at me, Cyrus?" she asked.

"I can't be mad at you for somethin' you didn't do. I don't reckon you lied; you were doin' what you figured right. He did talk to you, right? I mean, you ain't greenin' me?"

"No."

"What did he say?"

"Not much. I was so takin' aback that he spoke that I missed most of it. He said that you—he mostly said how much he thought of you, that we were really lucky to have each other that—oh, he said he wished he could have what we have."

"What?"

"Not sure, but it felt like he wanted to say—he sounded real alone, Cyrus. It was kinda like he wished he was Jake, or that he wished he had a friendship like you and Jake."

Cyrus' mind was caught in a loop the rest of the day. Even when he knew he'd be facing a storm when he got back home, the only thing swirling in his head was Argie and his purpose for not mentioning this conversation with another human being; a conversation with the most important human being in his world. He near came to tears a time or two; the thought that Argie had excluded him intentionally. It hurt more than he could bear. Alone wasn't as much a word anymore because it was him; he was the definition.

Without notice, he found himself sitting at the water cistern and staring down the dirt road to Burle barn. He was sitting in the very spot when Jake found him, when he rescued him. A shiver came over him as quick as the wind; his blood ran ice cold for a second and it made him spit up. He had to cry and tried to hold it but it came too sudden. It stuck in his chest and took his breath. He rolled over to his hands and knees and pushed his face into the earth, his mouth full of grass, he pushed until it came out and it sounded of a rabbit in the jaws of a coyote. It felt too good when it broke and he could breathe. Then he lay on his side, away from the school in thought and body, and in its place dreamed of going home. When would he be able to go home? When would it be his turn?

He lay out there for a long while until he heard folks leaving. Cheyenne yelled for him but Cyrus ran ahead pretending he didn't hear her. It wasn't that he wanted to hurt her, but the human condition as he was in was strange enough that his reaction was exactly that. He hurt and the only remedy was to move, but whether it was to be away had always been the question?

When he came to the turn row at the front of the farm, about a hundred yards or so from the paddock fence, he stopped and looked behind. There was a part of him that wished she were in view, because if she was, he would wait for her so he could explain; explain that he wasn't mad at her, that he was upset at Argie for his shell game and for his "white" lie.

He climbed his way through the dried stalks that cracked and popped with every step. His grandfather had let the corn stay past harvest and probably due to all the things that had been happening outside the farming realm. As he marched through the patch, he wasn't sure to be mad or complacent with his mentor. Sometimes complacent was much better than mad because the receiver wouldn't know how to take it. Mad was a commonplace emotion that had its own signature; but, complacency was vague and would leave them rightly confused. You could argue with complacency, though, which is what Argie loved to do.

"Wake up, Cornfield!" he yelled, choosing angry.

"I'm not sleeping, Buckman."

"Why did you not tell me about you and Cheyenne?"

"Oh. I knew that a matter of time, but didn't *not* tell you to upset you, even though after some thought, I felt you would take it like that. I made a mistake, albeit a small one."

"All—what? I can't believe you, Argie. YOU are MY friend, in my corn and you make friends with somebody and don't say anything! Especially with Cheyenne!"

"You know, Cyrus, I can understand your anger, and then I don't. Which is a luxury I have as a Scarecrow--would it be fair to say that my conversation with anyone, including Cheyenne, would be my MY business, especially since it really had nothing to do with you?"

"Are you saying you didn't talk about me?"

"Your name did come up, but nothing was truly discussed about *you*, only concerning you, since this is *your* corn."

He wanted to be mad but it was impossible. Being mad, genuinely mad, at Argie was hard even when he felt it deserved. There was no mistaking that something was out-of-whack in his young life and Argie was good medicine. Argie's tone told him that he knew something was awry in his world but what drove Cyrus up a wall was that Argie wouldn't just come out with the answer; instead, he made him discover it solo by a long, arduous journey that was more like a tooth pull than a life lesson.

"So you went to school today, did ya?" Argie asked.

"You know I did", he said, pulling up a pile of stalks and laying back. He stared up at the pillow sack head with the charcoal smile bent to one side, two poorly drawn and faded eyes that drooped like they had been placed by a well-oiled alcoholic, and three or four stands of hair that went nowhere. "You'll be leaving soon, won't ya?" Cyrus mumbled.

"I may not be before you but I will never leave you."

"You recall the ducks and Mr Walt?"

"Yes."

"No one believes it. I tried it on Gran'ma and she bucked the bridle off, which means no one will believe it."

"Is that so important?"

Cyrus smiled, "I reckon not."

"What's in your heart, Cyrus?"

"I think you know."

"Yes, but will you move to understand it?"

"I will try."

"Spread your arms and clear your mind. Think only of your goodness, your value to others and how you will give it away."

"Will you remember me?" Cyrus asked.

"You can't see it, but I'm smiling", Argie answered.

CHAPTER TWENTY NINE

He was sitting on a wooden stoop with his head between his knees when he heard chatter. He was so comfortable that he didn't have the gumption to disturb his own slumber until a familiar woman's voice called out to him.

"Excuse me young man but you're sleeping in the middle of the stairs."

"I'm sorry", Cyrus answered, standing up. "I was just . . . I don't know." He looked over his shoulder and realized he was in front of the very hardware store he and Mr Walt had stopped at when they came into town. "Hey, I been here", he whispered.

"Oh my, you're . . ." she said pointing with her hand bobbing like he was in a line up. ". . . that little boy who was trying to find his friend with the puppy dog."

"Yes mam, that was me, it rightly was", he answered with a giggle and coming alive like a two dollar pistol on Founder's Day. "You haven't seen that boy as of late have ya?"

"Oh heaven's child, that was a time back."

"A time back? I reckon maybe a week."

She looked at Cyrus like he'd rung his out sock in her soup, scrunched her face up like a persimmon and then shook her finger towards him again, "A week, plus a year perhaps. Just because I'm old doesn't mean my calendar's off. I have an impeccable memory child, so pointed I believe I can recall your name if given a second—now just a minute."

He shook his head, "I don't think I ever gave you my name . . ."

"Cyrus! That surely is it. Cyrus . . ." she bolstered again, waving her hand about like a carny who just pinched a nickel on a fortune tell.

"Wow! I had no idea—I didn't recollect givin' my name to a soul, but you got it alright."

She smiled and headed into the store.

"Mam, excuse me again, but do you recollect seein' that boy with his dog since the last go?"

She put her hand to her chin, looked off distantly and then looked back to Cyrus.

"That's okay . . ." Cyrus said.

"Just one small moment there Master Cyrus, you certainly do throw in the towel quickly—your friend is the special one, isn't he; yes, he is."

"The special one?" Cyrus replied. "How'd you know about Master . . ."

She interrupted: "He stays up there in the hills", she said pointing. "You see the muscle shell off the end of that mesa—if you look just above the church steeple, you'll see a hollow spot. I think you'll find him there with a female panther; he and that dog, I believe."

"A panther?" he muttered. "Alright, is there a way I can find Mr Walt?"

"Mr Walt?" she smiled. "Sweetie, this town is filled with Walt's, Walter's, even a Wilbur, who I could direct you to with the point of a finger, but for just a *Walt* would be like looking for a needle in a stack of needles."

"He has a black mustache that curls tight on the ends, big guy, real neat dresser, has a truck . . . can't recall the color."

"There are a few Walt's who match that bill", she laughed aloud. "A Walt that matches that Bill. You don't find that funny?"

Then like a storm out of nowhere she blurted, "What are you doing here? I mean, I've seen youngun's there and about but not like you, worried up in a fret like you seem? Oh my word! You know who you're the spittin' image of . . .?"

"Lyda!" a man barked from inside the store. "You are just a second away from losing them slippers you wanted to Ida Frohm, with pink-striped stocking's and all."

"Thank you Vern. So good to see you again, Master Cyrus", she finished.

"Miss Lyda, who am I the image of?" He followed her but when he reached the threshold she was gone—outta sight, vanished, poof! He thought a moment how strange it was but then remembered where he was—flying with ducks, landing in corn patches, folks walking on water.

He moved to the middle of the square where there was a gazebo he could use as a focal point and hopefully catch a glimpse of Walt or Jake. The last time he was here the town was of an indescribable beauty that emanated from the inside out; now that beauty was dull and faded, folks seemed slower, less lively and the air was thick and hard to breathe. As foolish as the thought came, the town seemed to be dying.

He looked up the mountainside and squinted, shading his eyes to see the spot Miss Lyda pointed out to him. It didn't seem too far, but up in a mountain? With a panther? It was sure strange where he was, but then so was his travel to wherever—Timbuctoo—in search of a dead friend corralling a dead dog all guided by a scarecrow? He would not allow the strangeness of it all dissuade him from the *reason* he believed he had been brought there. There was a feeling he could not escape, either; a feeling he was being watched, watched by everyone; but, no one seemed to be looking his way or care one iota he was even there.

"Son", a voice behind him called. "Are you looking for someone, or some place?"

It was another Samaritan who popped up, popped in, came from behind—just materialized when he wasn't looking.

"Well sir, I ain't from here but . . . yes sir, I'm kinda doin' both. A part of me sez I should just wait here because I'm s'posed to; another part says to move my butt and neither thought fits, which is a smidgen like bein' here. Pretty stupid ain't it?"

The man smiled. Whatever lay in front of Cyrus didn't have any more importance than what was behind him and he never approached life that way. For the first time he could recollect, he was living in the present, but just where the question was. This thing that someone was working so hard to teach him was indescribable, untouchable, without substance or form yet was all over him like the water he was born from.

"What?" Cyrus asked. "What is it I'm supposed to do? I'm just tryin' to find my brother and folk keep lookin' at me like there's a joke bein' played."

"No joke, son. It's something you have no other soul does and it is beautiful to be near."

"What?"

"You're looking for your friend; the one with the dog?"

"Yes sir."

"Then look", the man said, nodding his head towards the mountain.

Cyrus started towards the cave. He had no idea how far it was or exactly where it was, just that it was 'above the steeple' and what would he do if there was a panther with him? It mattered about as much as it made sense.

He had to scale a fence and traverse a gully before he actually began up the mountain, which was much steeper than it looked from the square when Miss Lyda pointed it to him. He stopped for a moment to catch his wind and looked back to see the town, but it wasn't there! The entire town was gone. Now he was beginning to come scared. He turned back towards his climb to the cave and he was already there—right in front of him was the cave and he was on flat ground now. He didn't move; he stood there waiting for a panther to jump him. There was a large boulder he cautiously walked over to and sat down.

"Jake—you 'round?" he called. He called a couple more times and then remembered he was to wait. *Something* kept needling his insides to not be anxious that what was to happen was to happen in its time—so he waited.

There wasn't any sun to speak of; light from the source he had been used to all his life wasn't there, that fire ball in the sky that emanated light so bright it was painful to look at. Whether it was covered by a cloud or behind a mountain didn't matter, you knew it was there. But here, it was just light that came from nowhere. While in this ethereal gaze he heard a twig snap and it brought him back. He looked to the cave entrance and wanted to go inside but his instincts again told him different.

"Bruiser", he called. Whether it was for the lack of sun or a dimming in the cosmos, it was definitely getting darker. Being there, with no town below any longer, next to a hole on the side of a mountain that didn't seem to be a mountain any more, it was hard to hold on to optimism that he was there for a *reason*. Being alive had never been at the top of his list, but being alive in this nomad's land with no clue towards a purpose and all alone near dark made it difficult to think rationally.

"Bruiser, please be here", he whispered.

"Hey Pudgie", a voice behind him whispered.

He jumped off the rock and spun around, "Jake!" he hollered, but nothing was there. He looked side to side and then ran towards the cave entrance. "Jake!" he hollered into the giant hole, his voice bouncing about like a rubber ball until it died deep in the dark.

"It's just a game", Cyrus whispered to himself. "Why do I keep . . ."

"No it ain't", Jake answered, behind him. Cyrus turned slowly and there he was—same Jake, not one hair different, not one freckle out of place and his smile; the smile that made the world light up. Cyrus was cautious. He reached out his hand, and then the other and held them out making sure he wasn't seeing a mirage. He walked forward a foot or so and stopped, not once taking his eyes from Jake.

"Say somethin', Bruiser. Anything, just say somethin' so's I can see your mouth."

"Shut up, Cyrus; you talk too much."

He shot towards Jake like a bat from a burning stump and when he was about three or four feet from him he took to the air, crashing into his chest and landing into him taking both of them to the ground.

"That hurt, Cyrus. Now would you mind getting off?"

He climbed off Jake and helped him up, then grabbed him again and wouldn't let go. He kept hugging him and Jake tried to push away but he wouldn't have it.

"Cyrus! getta-holt of yourself. You act like I came from the dead."

Cyrus backed off and again found no humor in what Jake thought hilarious. Commonplace midst their friendship, though; neither saw humor in the other's antics or expressions nor probably ever would, but it's what held them together: diverse in every sense yet indistinguishably synonymous. A coin.

"Looky over there", Jake said, pointing to the rear of the boulder. Cyrus looked close but didn't see anything.

"What?" he muttered.

"Right there."

It stepped out from behind a bush. It held its head down and tip-pawed forward, occasionally looking up with the big brown eyes that hinted a stain had been left on someone's carpet.

"Remember?" Jake asked.

"Yeah; how could I forget? Hey there, Bear", Cyrus whispered, holding out his hand.

"We found each other at the same time and became friends."

Cyrus looked up at Jake and they stood staring at each other. There were questions he knew well enough would not be answered, but did not care as long as they were together in the *end*.

Dark came in the sky without a sun. It seemed he was coming to understand some of the things that were his mystery: pain, love and what life might be like without them.

"Are you really living in there with a panther?"

Jake looked into the blackness and shook his head, "A panther? Who told you that?"

"Miss Lyda."

"Lyda? You listened to Lyda?"

"I found ya didn't I?" Cyrus answered.

"Well, yes and no."

Jake put his arm over Cyrus' shoulder and they started walking. He explained some things, the obvious ones, and left the complicated ones alone. He told him the cave was a place he'd stay to remember the nights in their fort, but that the place he mostly stayed was one he could not explain because there were no words for him to understand. But there was one thing he did tell him that made him smile, and that was that he went back to the fort on occasion when he really wanted to remember; when missing him became too much.

"So is Cheyenne still crazy about you, or have you managed to wreck that?"

"Why can't I stay here with you, Jake?"

"Cyrus, you have no idea what there is for you to do where you are."

"Oh, and you had nothing to do—there was nothing someone like you had to do?"

"Yes there was", Jake responded. Cyrus bowed up but Jake blocked him, "Stop Cyrus! I'll talk but you gotta take what I can muster and expect no more—you have NO idea what kinda favor you've been given to bein' here."

"I don't even know where *here* is Jake! Timbuctoo? Wherever it is, I'm told I can't stay; and I don't care about the *why*, I'll take my chances."

"You don't see it, Cyrus, this is all for you."

"What's all for me, dreams and shadows; a voice from straw-stuffed underwear?"

"I've been given this chance to be with you, to show you what no one has ever seen before and gone back."

"Then where are we?"

"No questions, remember? That's the deal."

"Jake, I don't really care about anything but you. I never cared about anything but you and our friendship. You were the greatest thing that ever happened to me and then you left. My Ma and Pa left. Everyone and everything that was supposed to mean normal in my life, that was s'posed to be grass root was taken from me. I'm odder than a five-tit cow, or a cat that barks. You were the first real friend I ever had, Jake. Ain't that strange? Near eleven years-old and there's maybe one friend I had more than a month who didn't pants me, cut me down or ditch me. I don't belong in Alabama, or Nebraska, or anywhere where there's folk because I ain't right."

"What is right, Cyrus? Me? Is that what you think is right? You beat all with your looks routine; that if you don't look like Clark Gable you ain't *right*. Looks ain't got nothin' to do with bein' *right*, as a matter of fact, the sweeter lookin' folk are pretty much the ones whose cheese ain't on their cracker. You wanna know how special you are, Pudger? How special you are to the world—it was proved to ya and you let it run right past you because it didn't quite fit your puzzle; there weren't enough lights or hand-clappin' to make a stage bow that set well enough with ya."

"What are you talkin' about?"

"And you still don't know! So full of yourself on how poor off you are that you missed the most important thing any third-grader has ever done."

"Try me, and I'll bet it ain't ne'er the thing you're makin' it neither."

"Pritchett."

"What about him? You gunna say that he's a *better man* cuz of me, or . . ."

"No."

"What, then?"

"You recollect the afternoon when you ran into him at Burle Barn?"

"You mean with Cheyenne?"

"No! you see, you don't even recall the time the most important thing of your life happened."

"I don't know what the . . . oh, the afternoon I was stonin' crows?"

"Yeah."

"That was the most important thing of my *life*? If that was so important . . ."

"Shut up Cyrus!" Jake interrupted. "And yes, smart-ass, it was. Why'd you go into the barn?"

"I heard commotion."

"Really? Commotion? Have you ever gone into something like the Burle Barn, the scariest place in Alabama, by yourself? And better yet, for no reason at all 'cept hullabaloo?"

"I don't reckon, but I wasn't thinkin'."

"Nothin' ever crossed your mind that Marshall could be in there?"

"Why the world would that cross my mind? And I just told you I wasn't thinkin'!"

"And I thought you were sharp. The commotion you heard was Marshall climbing up on a tack rack and throwin' a riggin' girt over a roof joist."

"What the world for?"

"He was going to tie it off about his neck."

Cyrus' swallow stuck in the middle of his throat; it just stopped like a log turned sideways in a stream.

"How—how'd you know?" he asked.

"I just do, Cyrus. It's one of the *amazing* things you been given."

"Why me, Jake? Why am I anything special?"

"Everyone is special, Cyrus. Every person has gifts and talents. It ain't just you, but believe it or not, everybody thinks like that. Folks all believe that they don't matter, or they just matter a little, or they only matter when the corn needs plowin', or the cow needs milkin' and that ain't what it's about."

"I think I matter more than that."

"Not much! You have no idea what Pritchett thinks about you, not-a smidgen more than a guess, and that's wrong too. Ain't it funny? You just gotta laugh!"

"So what's Marshall think of me?"

"You know how *you* think of me?"

"No—you're my best friend ever."

"Add a bit more."

"That's impossible—you're my brother! You're like nobody else . . ."

Cyrus began to smile with Jake; he was about to pitch this puzzle piece he'd been holding for years, this piece he resolved had no place in his life. It was coming clear and how was the funny part.

"Wow, so I helped him?" Cyrus asked.

"You think? You beat all, Pudger. You can't dance alone on this one though, I did the same thing—when somethin' bad happened I pretty much chalked it to bein' worthless myself. I thought for years my Ma passed cuz I was a no good kid. I didn't let it show much, 'ceptin when I was by myself. You think the same of your Gran'pa—you believe he hates you and he don't. You are set that he spites you on account of your Pa's accident and all."

"Bruiser, there are a lotta things you know about me and what you don't you ain't scary on and there ain't no bark on that tree; but, what you think you know 'bout me and my Gran'pa ain't even close to your ditty bag. I don't reckon even God knows 'bout it."

"There won't be any swayin' you on that cause just by words, Cyrus, because it's too close to home. It'll have to be showed ya— and it will be."

"Whatdaya mean?"

"I mean it will be made light to you, and there won't be no mistakin' neither."

"You greenin' me?"

Jake laughed: "You're *here* with *me* in this place and you can ask that?"

Cyrus sat down on the great boulder and Bear came over to him. When he reached out to pet him, Bear bowed his head in a sheepish way, inched himself forward on his behind until he was just up to him and then laid his head on Cyrus' knee. His eyes where big and brown and would only stare Cyrus in the face when he wasn't, batting them open and shut and looking off when Cyrus would look at him. He laughed and wondered what Bear was thinking about.

"You think he remembers, Bruiser? Remembers that night?"

"Don't know, Pudgie, but only you would ask. You only see things in others and can't see a single, beautiful thing in yourself."

"Now whatdaya talkin'?" Cyrus said perturbed.

"Don't get yur panties all balled up—that's exactly what you do, Pudge, you close your mind to anything that concerns you, but are more than bit-chompin' to chat about others."

"You told me that things *ain't* always the way they seem—and Argie says things *are* always the way they seem."

"The way you see others, Cyrus! You're turned around. You've never cared for yourself like you care for others; you see yourself on the outside with nothin' to add and that has to change!"

"Okay Bruiser, now whose panties are ballin' up?"

Jake whistled quietly and both Cyrus and Bear looked over to him. "What?" Cyrus muttered. Bear walked over to Jake and sat down and Cyrus asked him again, but Jake just whistled and then made a kissing sound like he was wanting something fetched. About that moment Bear's ears came pointed and his eyes sharp. He stood, sat down and stood again wagging his tail. Cyrus smiled at him and then Jake, shrugging cluelessly with a grin: "What?"

As quickly as he asked, immediately beside him was the biggest kitty he'd ever laid eyes on. Kitty in the academic sense: it had lots or fur, huge paws with the dead giveaway; it purred—loud. Cyrus wet his pants—just a little—because he caught himself quick.

"Oh my God!" he whispered from a frozen posture. "Jake! It's a lion!"

"Tiger, Cyrus—it's a big tiger. Lions ain't got stripes. That's Moo Moo, she's been here longer than me and keeps me warm when the winds come."

Bear ran over to Moo Moo and they both jumped into attack mode, but playfully; both had their rear ends in the air and their front feet down with their heads between them. Bear pounced on Moo Moo which was something of a sight; Moo Moo held up its huge paw and Bear hit it like a fly to a windshield. When Bear fell backwards Moo Moo held him down with the same paw and then bent over and licked Bear. Her tongue was about the size of Bear who now resembled a large, brown lollipop. Every time he struggled to escape she'd lick him, and liked him and licked him. After several passes he was soaked.

"So you don't live with a panther, but a tiger?"

"I live with a lot of things, Cy", Jake laughed.

Cyrus reached out slowly to touch her all the while looking at Jake, who was smiling big and watching with his arms crossed. Bear was preening trying to get all the tiger spit off.

"She won't eat me, will she?"

"I daknow; if she's a hankerin'. Who knows about tigers these days."

She looked at Cyrus and for a second he felt a bit like a steak, or a bologna sandwich. He swallowed hard. Moo Moo grinned to show her teeth, so Cyrus thought, but Jake laughed and explained that she was just smiling.

"Pet her you possum. That's what she's asking you to do."

So he did. Her head was as big as Cyrus—all of him, and she pushed it into him with her ears against his face. He could feel her purr that was more like a truck idle. Her paws were as big as the column bases that held up the foyer of the Kansas Capitol building. He ran his hand over and over her head, holding each ear with his little fist so he could see down inside and imagined falling in.

"What does she eat?" Cyrus questioned.

"Not sure, never seen her do it."

"Come to think of it, what do you eat?" Cyrus asked.

Jake sat motionless in thought for a moment: "You know, I don't know if I do", he chuckled. "She's gunna lick you."

"Please ask her not to, Jake."

"You."

"Jake!"

"Moo Moo, go on now." And see did.

As everything began to slow, Cyrus sat staring at Jake and Bear and suddenly realized he was soon to leave. His entire life was about leaving and now he was going to leave the only person who ever meant anything to him in the world. But he wasn't in the world anymore—neither of them was.

"Jake, why is this?" he asked.

Jake left Bear and came over to Cyrus and sat down next to him. He put his arm over his shoulder and Cyrus began to cry.

"It's so hard for me, Jake. For everybody else, they have their war and they fair, but for me, sometimes it's hard to breathe."

"As much as you believe you're alone, you ain't. I wish I could tell you the why for the how, but there ain't no words. I know you can't see for the smoke, Cy, but there is a picture more beautiful than anyone can know and you are part of it—a huge part. What you're livin' right now is nothin' compared to the story. Everything happenin' is to bring you ready for the count. You see Cyrus, it would be impossible to for you to recognize beauty if you ain't seen ugly: How would you know light if you ain't been in dark, or thin if you ain't never seen thick?"

"Jake, I don't care about anything but staying with you. Everything is nothin' without my brother."

"Then will you believe me?"

"Yes", Cyrus answered reluctant.

"Then it's so."

The light began to fade quickly and Jake knelt at Cyrus' feet while Bear rested his head on his knee. Jake cupped Cyrus' hands with his and smiled.

"There's a storm comin', lil' brother. Don't be scared none."

"I promise."

CHAPTER THIRTY

R ain drops landed against his face while he lay in the corn
rich with the smell of fall and mildewed shuck. Again he
was staring at Argie doing what he did best and so naturally—wondering: wondering where he'd been and why exactly he wasn't
allowed to stay. Even if he told his closest living soul where he
had been she wouldn't believe him—well, she might because she
believed in Argie, but to tell her that he just came from a sit down
with his dead friend, a dog and a very, very big kitty might just
push her too far into a corner. Cheyenne was just a hair away from
meaning as much as Jake, but was an expression he was not able to
extend to her like he could Jake and it confused him consistently.
For whatever reason, it was so easy to tell Jake how he felt and so
difficult to Cheyenne. Even when the feeling was there and the
actual gumption to follow through with it, he'd choke on his words
the second he looked into her face. Those blue eyes stolen from an
angel would take his breath away and leave his mind in a foreign
land. This was the easy part: thinking about her and relishing the
feeling that came with it alone.

"Three!" his grandfather yelled from behind him.

The raindrops were getting larger and the pelting around him more vigorous as he began to sit up, but his grandfather was already there. He was carrying a kerosene can in one hand and an axe in the other. It was all happening so fast that his thought was a handful of seconds behind his action.

"What in hell's name . . . ?" his grandfather lashed out. "You and this damn scarecrow have come to the gate!"

"Gran'pa I was just layin' here. I weren't botherin' no one!"

"What is it with you? All your strangeness; never any friends about 'ceptin' ones who believe in *ghosts* and *Imagines* like you. I've had it plum to here", he said, motioning with the axe overhead.

"Gran'pa, what are you gunna do?"

"I'm riddin' myself of your buddy", he said, moving to Argie. He dropped the axe at the base of the scarecrow and began to slosh kerosene over him.

"No! No Gran'pa, you don't know who he is!"

"He's nothin' but straw-stuffed under britches on a stick! If he's anything else, I guess he'd get down off there in quick fashion, wouldn't he?"

Cyrus rushed to Argie but his Grandfather looked at him with a sudden glance of malice that chilled him. Everything came from the eyes and Cyrus knew his Grandfather had been at the bottle. It wasn't out of the ordinary at all: his Grandfather's morning sickness to his afternoon meaningless tirades. From sun up to sun down, nothing made sense of his Grandfather's character or disposition, and worse yet, they had nothing to do with Cyrus.

His Grandfather began sloshing again and Cyrus was compelled to stop him, but what a wayward thought; David trying to stop Goliath—with his bare hands? His Grandfather saw Cyrus' approach and swatted him back like a gnat. He hit him in the chest with such force that it knocked the wind out of him and took him off his feet. His Grandfather then grabbed the axe and

Cyrus ran out of the patch. When he looked over his shoulder his Grandfather was lighting a match but the rain was now coming down hard, hardest he'd seen in a time. He stood at the edge of the inner circle, this place that was his prayer room of sorts, a place he communed with his benefactor, and with this he now knew it was over. His Grandfather was fit-to-be-tied and it brought a smile.

He ran through the patch as the rain came down harder and harder. Thoughts were racing through his mind of what was next, where was he to go? He could run to his Grandmother but she could help only so far and his Grandfather was way past that point, he felt. Cheyenne came to mind but her parents, especially Mr Hold, would only place him back into harm's way the second he discovered him. Anything that came to mind ultimately became short run and that was where Cyrus' magic came into course: he played situations in his mind out to the very end, methodical in the construction of every cause and effect scenario to its end. It had kept his pants on him many times, but just as often, estranged him from some beautiful would-be friendships.

The fort! Oh my God, that was it! He broke out with an ululation that could have been heard for miles if not been for the rain. Jake had told him that a storm was coming and to be ready; well, it had and he was. The more excited he became the faster he ran. Maybe this was *the* rendezvous with Jake, what he was to be patient for. After all, Jake hinted that he occasioned the fort when he was really hankerin' to be there. How more obvious could this be, he thought?

By the time he reached the creek's edge it was pouring down fiercely. It was coming down so hard that it was difficult to see farther than a handful of feet, and when he looked straight up the rain literally took away his breath. He had to stop ever so often to get his bearings, going now by landmarks he could recognize when he was close. There it was! The base of the old oak that lay across to the fort. This time the creek bed for passage was a definite no-go. It was running water that would come well over his head and even Jake would have approved the tree this time.

When he got to the top of the embankment he rested on the huge roots. As quickly as he came covered in mud from falling he was just as soon washed clean. It made him laugh out loud, to nearly a scream, as he looked straight up at the sky and held out his hands to the heavens: "Thank you Argie! Thank you God! Thank you for bringing me here! Thank you for the chance to believe!"

He set out over the top of the treacherous tree. It was more difficult this time because the rain had made it slick. He could feel the difference with each step towards the middle. It was softer and bouncier and came mushier to the center; the consideration it would not stay the weight of a short and pudgy third grader didn't stay in his mind for long.

Now across the tree, he edged his way through the branching that covered the well hidden entrance and into the cavernous hole. Inside he was consumed by the silence that cocooned him from the raging world he'd come and it brought a deep comfort. He was home. He sat down on the ledge where Jake set the candles, setting upright the two that remained while he looked about. There was just a smidgen of light because the rain clouds were dousing what was left of the day and that tiny bit was finding it tough to get inside. He remembered where there were matches so he lit the candles. There was some kindling about and remnants from an old fire so he made one. He was beginning to shiver from the wet closes so he stripped down to his socks. It brought him to remember the time when he woke to find Jake sitting out on a chunk of limestone in nothing but:

"What are you doing?" Cyrus asked perplexed.

"Nothing much. Just watchin' a Yellow-tail hawk", Jake muttered. "You know that's the kinda feather a new brave gets; he's gotta do somethin' real brave though."

"Really—learn somethin' every day. Ain't you freezin' your raisins off in nothin' but skivvies?"

"Naw, it's chilly a might but that's the way they done back in them days."

"What days?"

Jake smiled broad, put one knee up and his arms behind him, "You're talkin' to me again. I guess I'm back in the family way, huh?"

"What you did weren't right, not right at all, but I guess there wasn't much else you coulda done. But you made such light of it."

"Said I was sorry."

"Yeah—I remember."

It was a struggle making amends at this age. The part of adolescence that was so tricky; you either bluffed your stand or stood toe to toe and Cyrus didn't have the sand for either.

"Whatdaya really think of me Jake? I mean, am I really a brother or is it you feel pity?"

"You beat all, Cy. If you don't know by now then will you ever? Look, did Indian's sit around all day ponderin' who liked 'em and who didn't? No! They went out and did stuff like kill cowboys, whack a buffalo for supper and then watch the sunset—maybe smoke the peace pipe or somethin' after, but the point is they didn't set mullin' over who liked 'em."

"Why is it you reckon I do that so much wonderin' who has a feelin' for me?"

"I don't know, Pudge, maybe cuz your Ma and Pa got took when you didn't get to know 'em. I believe there are things that are supposed to happen natural and when they don't there's some kinda order that's messed up. Think your Gran'pa wonders the same? I bet he wonders why he's been given you to raise after he done raised one boy. It's gotta weigh heavy, seein' your kid die off before you."

"You'd figure he'd have the same feelin', at least some of it, for his grandson. I am his blood", Cyrus mumbled.

"How do you know he don't? How do you know that he ain't feelin' for you the best way he can right now? Just cuz it ain't the way you wanna it see don't mean he doesn't feel for you. With you Cyrus it's all or nothing when it comes to other folks and what they think, and it can't be that way atoll. You have no idea what some-one else is thinkin' about you—and in a lotta ways it ain't none of your business!"

"Ne'er thought of it that way, Bruiser."

"You ne'er think of any way 'ceptin' your own, Cyrus Buckman—Here's the prettiest example I can conjure: Cheyenne Hold. Prettiest pullet in the entire school all the way to six grade and she picked you. But you, you on the other hand, can't see it for the life of me."

"She's all over you Jake Thompson! She's only seein' me as a way to get to you."

"If that ain't the dumbest damn lame excuse I have ever heard! It ain't even worth me fendin'. You can't see her expression when she's lookin' at you? Nope—this is what it boils down to—you're plum afraid for anyone to like you cuz that'll mean a risk."

Cyrus stared blankly at his buddy because he knew that to be the truth and Jake was too close to it.

"I don't see anything but her eyes—and her hair, I kinda get lost thinkin' about how nice it smells. You know . . ."

"Stop there", Jake interrupted. "You're just as smitten and you won't let on a bit—that's the Buckman in you, Buckman. Who else do you know like that? I'm curious?"

Cyrus smiled broad and somewhat embarrassed. Jake was always able to handle Cyrus when he didn't know he was being handled and really the only one smart enough to do it. It was the love they had for each other they truly didn't know the depth of. Both of them.

As the fire grew and he came warmer, he dressed his wet clothes about the branch that covered the entrance and over the fire. What hadn't been burnt by Pritchett's bonfire served well as a clothes line and that too made him laugh; another strange occurrence in life he recognized as a puzzle piece he would have ordinarily thrown away, but saved because of Jake: "You never know, Pudger, where something fits until the time gets there. Your problem is nothin' ever gets there cuz you pitch it before it has a chance!"

It was now well into dark and he was fairly certain his Grandfather had informed his Grandmother of their go-between in the patch and his Grandmother was now pacing the kitchen floor like Napoleon at Elba. He was distraught over the grief he might have caused her, but she was strong, stronger than any blood Buckman and Cyrus saw it in the eyes of his great-Grandfather. At least the man thought to have been him—Mr Walt.

The rains would relent for a minute or two then begin again. He thought for a spell on his Grandfather and whether he would roust a search party, but he hadn't been gone long enough to raise a brow much less get his Grandfather worried.

The warmth of the fire brought kindred memories and the dance of the flame a sober breath of slumber. He could hear echoes of children playing with laughter and the low tone of couples talking. He remembered the window box he slept with Jake, the time that he ever felt a part of anything. His hand moved against his own leg but he felt Jake's. It wasn't much more than the knowledge that someone was there who wanted to be. That to Cyrus was the epitome of the human condition, to be with someone who wanted to be with you and not who needed to be.

He woke as suddenly as he'd fallen to sleep and the waters sounded higher. He stumbled to the fort entrance that was canvassed in utter darkness; the fire had burned out and he was trying to see what was happening in the creek. He was sheltered and warm, but hungry was beginning to work against him. A chunk of johnnycake and a glass of milk would be the turn, but it was all between a raging creek and a pissed off old man. He scrounged up a pile of kindling for another fire. He was covered in dark and wasn't afraid. How funny he thought by this fact alone: he was in this darkness and wasn't in fear and it told him he had changed. Jake had told him several times: "Pudger, sometimes the change in a folk is so slow that they don't even know it but the world does."

He started the fire and sat back. It was a big one this time; a Pritchett fire where there were no survivors. It lit the entire fort, crannies and all, which brought him to stumble onto a can of crème soda and stale crackers. He also found one of Jake's multi-colored quilts that covered more firewood, a couple of candles, a comic book and a fruit jar with two fingers of sour mash. Hmm. The whiskey brought a lot to mind. He set it to the ledge with the candles and ate a cracker.

"Jake", he called out with a whisper. "I could sure use you right now. I'd call on Argie but I think Gran'pa chopped him down and burned him up."

Nothing came but the crackling of the fire and the ominous shadows that reflected on the walls of the cavernous fort. Vaguely from the entrance could he hear the current. Distantly, a flash shown through the branches of the giant oak with the rumble of the thunder to follow in a second or two and it made him calm, which too was also unusual of his character. He began to think of his Grandfather and why on earth he found such disdain in him—or did he truly?

"I am changing", he said. "I have changed. There's a lot of me that has changed. I mean, look at me right this minute: I'm sitting here all by my lonesome in a dark fort with floodwater's at the door and I ain't ne'er scary one iota. Now if that ain't change I don't know what is. If I can change why can't Gran'pa? That ain't the question right now. The question here is why does he hate me so much—or does he really? Okay, let's measure this thing all the way out."

He held his hand out and began to enumerate the pros and cons, the good things and the bad things, which brought him to run through a set of fingers quickly but these were the obvious ones on both sides. So he then began to consider things which weren't so readily noticeable, the incidences of both good and bad he had typically dismissed as either an accident or because his Grandma made them happen. He began with what he considered the easiest and the shortest: the good list.

"He's meant to take me fishin', which is kinda good since he's been meanin' to do it—at least a hundred times. I'll give him a finger for it anyway. There's the time he told me I was smart for untying' Dud from the hitch rail when the storm came in Oklahoma, even though he didn't know I had left him untied by accident in the first place, but it should still count for one."

He went through his list and came up with seven times his Grandfather had done something good to him or for him and he felt the list to be genuine. Before he began the *bad* list an unsuspected thought occurred that brought him immediately to look around the fort, "Argie, is that you?" There was nothing but the fire and its crackle. The thought was there and powerful: his father. His coming to mind was so strange because he was the farthest thing from it; in fact, he rarely thought of him. Well, he had at the moments when he rummaged the attic for photographs but those times were far and fleeting.

"What?" he said quietly. Just at that moment a gust bolted through the entrance with such force that it blew ash, sparks and pieces of fire over the den. He frantically knocked off the flaming chunks that stuck to the quilt with some about his face and hair. The fresh air brought a massive rise from the fire as though a god had just entered his dwelling and demanded presence. The branches and dead leaves that guarded the entrance burst into flames like gunpowder; the entire cave was now brighter than any Alabama summer noon, while he craw-fished backwards over rocks, lit candles and kindling. He came to rest against the back of the fort wall, working to catch his breath and gazing about for whatever else might be ablaze. This was the first that came to mind: was he able to get out? As suddenly as the blast of wind had come it was gone. Some small flames flickered on the tree branches as the remnants burned and disappeared. His blood slowed and his breath resumed its normal pace while he relaxed and pondered what just happened.

"Is someone mad at me?" he asked to the cave. "Is that you Argie?"

He moved back to his spot at the fire, shook out his quilt and made his bed. Though he was hungry, he was more tired than the pang's growl and his eyes became heavy. He lay down to watch the flames dance their finale and his thoughts drifted between Argie, his father, Mr Walt and Moo Moo; only once did his Grandfather appear and just as quickly vanish. It was difficult not to think on what his Grandfather was doing and how his Grandmother might be weathering his missing.

"Cyrus! we have to round folk up an' look for him. I am not goin' to set idle while we wait for him to come hungry and just show up! Cyrus!" Grandma Mattie screamed from the stove, waving her spatula. Grandpa sat at the table, his pipe in hand and a two-finger shooter next to the other, clacking his teeth against the ivory mouth piece and grunting after each puff.

"He don't have the sand to stay out in this, he jus' don't."

"I don't give one hoot on what you *think* now! You went way too far takin' to that scarecrow with petrol and an axe and with him there to boot", she finished with her voice cracking.

The front screen door slammed and brought Sterling Thompson to the kitchen threshold.

"I apologize for the boots Miss Mattie", he said.

"Oh don't you bother none, Sterling Thompson, I can't begin to sing your praise loud enough—I'm so far from wits end I don't know what-fer."

"Sterling", Grandpa Cyrus muttered with a nod. "Care for a might?" he asked with a gesture at his bottle.

"No Cyrus", he said, glancing to Mattie with a vague smile. "I understand we have a boy about in the weather."

"How'd we hear that?" Grandpa Cyrus asked.

"I told S.T. when he came for the hobbles this evenin'", Grandma blurted.

Grandpa snorted like a ruttin' buck, banged his pipe on the table's edge and onto the kitchen floor and giving Grandma a stern stare in the process.

"I reckon he'll climb back in here just as soon as his belly begins growlin' and his . . ."

"Sterling!" Grandma interrupted. "I jus' do not want to wait 'til that *might* happen; would you take me to lookin' where he an' Jake used to frolic—anywhere you might know?"

"Mattie Fay! You will do nothin' of the sort cuz I will", Grandpa Cyrus bellowed as he stood from the table, downing the last of his whiskey. "Sterling, I don't know where those boys did their gamin', but I'm willin' to look."

The rain eased to a slight drizzle as they got into Mr Thompson's truck, but not before it had turned the caliche roads into a mud pie. It was somewhat like walking on a frozen lake, every step had to be flat-footed with a stout, steady object close for grabbing.

"I recall Jake talkin' it up with S.T. a spell back, sayin' something about a place he'd found down in that creek he called a fort", Mr Thompson said as they slide down the road towards Burle Barn.

"I never allowed Cyrus time in that thing for this very reason—that boy is a magnet for trouble and can never fend his way from any hot spot", Grandpa Cyrus growled.

"Hmm", Mr Thompson began. "As Jake told it, he was the most sought after spirits midst the boys and gals—said he could handle just 'bout anything pitched his way."

"Cyrus? My Cyrus? You must've tangled that boy up with someone else—my Cyrus; short, fat, little Cyrus who is not only scared of his own shadow, he could wreck an iron anvil with a rubber mallet."

They drove the road that shared their property line until it came to the backside of the Buckman place. It was here where the creek split the properties and ran along the back of the Buckman farm and where the fort made for a decent lookout into Grandma Mattie's kitchen window. Mr Thompson stopped where the road split and the lights from the truck shone out another twenty five yards or so.

"I ain't real steady in thought on goin' out much farther, not in this anyways.", Mr Thompson suggested. We could walk her a stretch by the truck lights."

"I just don't 'magine atoll that boy bein' out in this, not my Cyrus."

"At least you claim him", Mr Thompson mumbled inaudibly.

"Whatdaya sayin', Sterling?"

"Aah Cyrus, I ain't ne'er been a life to reflect on another's, on what he has, what he don't or how he runs it; if it ain't somethin' I can put a yard stick to I don't concern myself with it, but ever since I lost my Jake I come to see things in a different light, or maybe just the brightness. He was surely special and a lot a folk knew it, but for me it was hard. He reminded of his mamma every time I looked him in the face and it plum tore me up—not once in a while, every stinkin' time! I began to resent him. I began to resent my own blood for somethin' he had nothin' to do with and I couldn't explain it."

"What might this lend to me?" Grandpa asked somberly.

"When I first saw Cyrus and Jake together I thought, 'now this is gunna be an interesting wreck', yet the more I watched 'em the more I realized what a gift you were given in your boy. Ain't that the shiner; I saw in Cyrus what you saw in Jake."

"Now that is plum out of the saddle because that is exactly what I saw—I saw Jake as the picture perfect boy that would be any man's desire for a son. By god that is the most flip-flop, bass-akward thing I have ever see'd in my absolutely worthless life! You wanted Cyrus and I wished for Jake and now where are we!"

They sat in silence with everything said and nothing left. Jake was gone and Cyrus was missing. In the dimness of the blue moon it wasn't difficult to tell what glistened from their cheeks. They sat for a long, long while.

"I'm gunna start walkin' the creek", Grandpa said finally.

"I gotta a couple a hand flares; you take the creek from here and I'll take it from Pritchett's and we'll meet when we meet."

EPILOGUE

Cyrus lay on the dirt floor covered in darkness and a quilt. It had stopped raining for the while and unbeknownst to him, his Grandpa and Mr Thompson were still walking the creek and hollering his name. Even if they were at the fort entrance they wouldn't have been heard, the creek's rage would have drowned out gun fire.

It was late and he rarely woke without cause. When he opened his eyes he wasn't sure where he was until the smell of burnt wood swilled him. The ember's glow pulsed with each bit of wind and the light from the moon silhouetted the leaves that guarded him. Alone, and he was safe. He was thinking what was to come when he was startled by a sound inside the cave; a sound just feet from him. He turned over his shoulder to see the shadowy figure.

"Argie", he whispered. "Zat you?"

There was a candle on the ledge behind him and enough ember in the fire that he could blow on for a flame, so he lit it. If it were a shadow it would have disappeared. It was a man. A man he had never seen before but seemed to know.

"How'd you get in here?" he asked the man. "How'd you know where this was?"

"I'm not sure", he answered.

He was another stately man, one of importance or at least in ambiance. He had the same mustache as Mr Walt, so neatly groomed he could have been mistaken for a statue. He wore a suit and he sat with his back erect as any gent of his time might, but what was his time?

"Who are you, sir?"

"That too eludes me for the moment. If I may ask of you, where am I?"

"You're in my fort—it ain't got no name."

"Hum, *ain't* got *no* name?" the man repeated with a sardonic grin.

"Oh, you're from Argie" Cyrus muttered.

"Pardon me?"

"The scarecrow fella?"

"Don't know any scarecrows."

"Argie didn't send you?"

"I'm sorry, I don't know an Argie either. Mind if I stand a moment; I'm a bit cramped?"

"You won't stand too tall in here, but you might stretch your legs a bit."

When the man stretched forward Cyrus immediately pinned him to a memory.

"Oh my God! You . . .you're my. Your name is Cyrus isn't it?"

"Strange—that is familiar."

"You are Cyrus Walton Buckman the second!" Cyrus said deliberately.

"More like Buckman, junior that I can recall. So strange though. And being here in this place is even stranger. I was talking to my wife—I think—and then I'm here."

"My Ma!"

"Your Ma?" he said sitting back.

"Of course, your wife—the one you was talkin' to."

The man stared blankly at Cyrus like he was assimilating life. It was his father to him. Right in front of him was the wish of wishes, dreams to beat dreams, but just as suddenly he was filled with angst.

"You ain't real, are ya?"

"I was thinking the exact same", the man said.

"I've dreamed about you, ifin' you are who I think you are. When I met Argie I thought you was him", Cyrus said as he sat to the ledge with candle in hand. "Have you ever dreamed of me?"

"Although *dreamed* is acceptable, *dreamt* is more appropriate—not exactly sure if I have. I seem to feel you more than I know you."

Cyrus smiled, "You're from Argie." The man smiled and Cyrus inched towards him.

"You reckon it would be okay if I was to touch you? I won't ifin it ain't allowed; I was hankerin' to see if you was just a dream."

"It's fine with me. Better yet, why don't you come up here", he said, patting his knee. Cyrus jumped into his arms.

"When you gunna leave?" Cyrus asked.

"To be candid, not sure that I have."

"Candid. What you're meanin' is *candor,* that means you're tellin' me you're gunna be honest in what you're 'bout to say, or you are honest—still kinda stump broke on that idea, why anyone would have to tell somebody that. Do you know, Pa? Argie gave me an answer but it seemed more an excuse."

"Pa", the man whispered. "Wow, music to my ears."

"Music, huh", young Cyrus answered.

"Look Cyrus, I'm going to say some things that will—well, that I'm not supposed to. It's really difficult to articulate—to make sense of, but I'm *gunna* break some rules here."

"Gran'pa misses you somethin' terrible."

"He has you."

"You kiddin! You been gone awhile; I'm the last thing he wants."

His father cupped his face with his hand and pulled it to his. He kissed him on the forehead and his cheeks and held him like a banker might gold. He was lost for word and young Cyrus did not care if another was uttered. He was home. He was in the place his entire life had been in search—his Papa's arms.

"I gots so much to tell you, Papa—Argie is this scarecrow, well he's this friend who—"

"Cyrus, I don't have much time", his father interrupted. "I so wanted to touch you that I begged to come and it was granted, but only if I held to certain rules and I've broken them."

"So you are real! You are my Papa and Argie is real and when I saw Jake was real!"

"Cyrus, real isn't what you think—it's what is. It is so difficult to explain."

"You're gunna go again, ain't ya?" Cyrus screamed.

"Yes—in the way you know, but not in the way I do", his father said.

"Then what's *real* Papa!"

His father knelt at his feet and clasps his hands, "Do you recall when you were with Marshall in Burle Barn?"

"Yes sir."

"Then you recall real."

"You ain't—aren't going to leave me here alone are ya, Pa?"

"You *ain't* ever been alone, son. There are so many watching."

"Watchin', me? I ain't no more than a wet sack-a sow meal."

"I have to go, Pudger. You know you're my boy?"

His father laid him to his quilt and he fell to sleep whispering.

The morning came none too soon. When he woke the sun was edging its way to his face and the immediate thought came—there's nothing for breakfast. It was "spot rainin'", he'd heard Grandpa say a thousand times—"There ain't no more a worthless day for a farmer than spot rainin' days!" To Cyrus they melded into every day, but on mornings like this his Grandma cooked a great breakfast—all the leftovers of beans and fatback, corn, hotcakes in molasses and every meat imaginable.

His bones creaked for the first time of his young years but he was warm. Suddenly he remembered his father and turned over his shoulder—nothing. Everything a dream like always.

"Pa! Papa!"

The creek was running but not like it had been. It was a cool rush and the waters weren't spanking the banks. He eased his way to the entrance to see that so much had been washed away. The giant oak that bridged the gap was sagging deep and looked like it was trying not to break in two. There was a smell from the farmhouse that was a honing for a hungry boy. The scent came like the ones he'd catch of Cheyenne when she passed him and the breeze was right. He crawled from the broken rubble to see if there were any about, any who might be in search for him. He moved out to edge of the tree.

It was different; its weight beyond the burden of its years and so much so that he glanced to the creek as the way across. It was huge; mammoth like his tree, but commanded more majesty.

Hot cakes and ham were in his mind with only a thought for the condition of his surrender once to the other side: what will happen when he walks into the kitchen? Maybe they will be so elated to his safe arrival that nothing will be said? Maybe. He crawled out onto the burgeoning trunk, through the roots that reached over the top of him like a spider's talon and into the open. It was tempting to wait for assistance but that would be a fat chance.

At this moment he heard a distant siren. It had come before and meant nothing then. He concentrated on the task at hand—getting to the other side. The wind was up; the creek flowing fierce and the treachery of the tree definitely there, but this wasn't it. This wasn't what was gnawing at him.

It was this: the presence of all these people the last days who took his fear away, but was it really *them*? The question answered itself; a hurdle he had never considered. This was *it*—today, this day, this minute. Anything in front of this was without consequence because it hadn't become. It wasn't *real* because it hadn't happened. What *was* to happen was in a greater hand and he didn't have to think about it anymore!

He started out onto the tree with this peculiar smile. What a thing, he was thinking. The wind picked up again in gusts that swayed the tree. His weight brought it to sag deeper and the slippery bark drew him further to the center. He threw his hands in the air to balance himself and a knot caught his foot. He fell forward and near into the creek when he grabbed the very knot that felled him. He was sideways but held on. He worked himself up to one leg on the tree when it dropped another measure nearly taking both to the creek. He was back to hanging on for the creek below and it made him laugh. He laughed at the clouds and at the water that came against his face. It was a laugh of joy because it was all making sense to him. He couldn't explain it because there was no one to hear. He just laughed.

He looked up to the roar and there was a wall of water coming at him higher than the creek's shelf. It was so high that the trees tumbling in it looked like twigs. It hit him with a force he never knew and pulled him into a blackness he'd never forget. He worked to breathe. He peddled to get air but it was chaos and it held him. He broke the top of the stream for a split second, enough for a breath and then under again. So many things hitting him. So much black.

In everything it became as calm as sudden as it was there. He remembered. He was seeing faces from the past—his Papa, his Mama, his brother. Everything became as quiet as the dawn and there was peace that covered him like the water. He relaxed and did not fight anymore—that was it, he thought. Everything that he struggled against was meant to be—everything! Jake, Marshall, his parents being taken, everything. It was all on purpose and there was someone who had control. It just would not make any sense to think otherwise.

Now a breath was necessary and there wasn't one to be found. He was fading and the thought of surrender was upon him as he tumbled. He could be with Jake and his family, he thought. He was going home. That's what all this was about. It was a coming home thing.

To Cyrus, all was done.

He came out the water with a rush. He gasped for the air that teased him as water passed over his eyes and his weight was in space—it was his Grandpa! Grandpa Cyrus had pulled him from the waters. He was so clueless. His Grandfather wiped his face and he could see him. He held Cyrus' head with his hand and kissed him on his forehead and his cheeks and told him how much he loved him, and that he never wanted him to leave and that he was going to change. Although Cyrus heard him his attention was across the raging creek at a young boy standing on a piece of limestone. He was dressed in nothing but a deerskin loin cloth and a leather band about his head that donned a single yellow-tail hawk feather—he was a brave now. Behind him were so many, many people. This was the puzzle piece.

And they smiled, because they knew.

Made in the USA
Coppell, TX
05 August 2024